PENGUIN BOOKS
TROUBLESHOOTER 2

Sir John Harvey-Jones, MBE, was Chairman of ICI from 1982 to 1987. He is, among other things, a non-executive Director of Grand Metropolitan plc and Chairman of the *Economist*. He has written two autobiographical books, *Making It Happen* and *Getting It Together*, both of which became bestsellers. *Troubleshooter*, written with Anthea Masey, was also very successful, appealing both to the general reader and to the student of business. Sir John lives near Ross-on-Wye in Herefordshire.

JOHN HARVEY-JONES

TROUBLESHOOTER 2

PENGUIN BOOKS

PENGUIN BOOKS

Published by the Penguin Group
Penguin Books Ltd, 27 Wrights Lane, London W8 5TZ, England
Penguin Books USA Inc., 375 Hudson Street, New York, New York 10014, USA
Penguin Books Australia Ltd, Ringwood, Victoria, Australia
Penguin Books Canada Ltd, 10 Alcorn Avenue, Toronto, Ontario, Canada M4V 3B2
Penguin Books (NZ) Ltd, 182–190 Wairau Road, Auckland 10, New Zealand

Penguin Books Ltd, Registered Offices: Harmondsworth, Middlesex, England

First published by BBC Books, a division of BBC Enterprises Ltd, 1992
Published with new postscripts in Penguin Books 1993
5 7 9 10 8 6

Printed in England by Clays Ltd, St Ives plc

Contents

Author's Acknowledgments

I would like to thank all those people, both inside and outside the organizations which are the subject of this book, for their help and patience in its preparation. I would also like to acknowledge the tremendous contribution of my BBC producers, Judi Rose, Michael Mosely and, especially, Robert Thirkell.

INTRODUCTION

One of my problems as a businessman, and as an individual, is that I find it difficult to anticipate the results of success. I am always careful to examine the consequences of failure, both personally and professionally, for businesses with which I am involved, but I have an almost superstitious fear of taking success for granted. I have seen so many dream castles built on quicksand that I prefer to think only of laying the foundation stones. As a result I did not think through the pressures which would be unleashed by the success of the first *Troubleshooter* series, and so I was taken by surprise. It may seem naive, but it was only at a lunch with Richard Reisz, the executive producer, just before the first series was launched, that I realized that my relative obscurity as a businessman could be threatened. For some time I had been used to being in the public eye, both as the chairman of ICI, and subsequently as an author, but it really had not occurred to me that taking part in a television series, devoted to a single subject about which I care passionately, was any different in terms of public recognition from the few appearances I had made on shows like *Question Time*. I now find that almost everybody I meet wants to talk about their business.

I had not allowed, either, for the effect on my mailbag. No day goes by without quantities of people either writing, or telephoning, to ask for my help on some business problem or other. Before the series I had not fully realized how lonely the life of someone running a small business can be. Of course every businessman has relationships with his customers, his suppliers, his bank manager, and so on. He also knows a number of his competitors. But remarkably few people running small businesses have any friend or confidant on whom they can test their ideas, or with whom they can talk openly about their business, its opportunities and its threats, and their feelings about the business. It seems to me that business people badly need a business equivalent of that excellent organization, The Samaritans. In many cases just talking about the way a business is running brings a feeling of support and a strengthening of conviction, which is badly needed when you feel alone and threatened by immense external forces.

The first *Troubleshooter* series evoked interest and requests for assistance from the most unlikely organizations. Schools, churches, the National Health Service; almost every sort of organization under pressure to change. They all hoped that our independent, unbiased view of their circumstances would help them. One of the original intentions of the series was to alert a wider public to the problems and opportunities of business, and the vital importance of business success for the well being of the UK. Without question the first *Troubleshooter* series had a major impact on my alleged retirement – which is beginning to look more and more like a third or even a fourth career, rather than the pipe and slippers idyll which my wife and I had fondly imagined for ourselves. At the same time it has opened up a whole new realm of interest and collection of friendships, for which I consider myself incredibly fortunate. The series, and my subsequent experiences, gave birth to a seminar at The Royal Society for the encouragement of Arts, Manufactures & Commerce, on small businesses, and some continuing initiatives in that area. I believe it has led me to understand more clearly some of the underlying economic problems and opportunities in the UK, and it has certainly given me an even greater admiration for the small business people of this country. Their businesses may be small, but as people they stand tall. They exhibit all the human qualities which I admire, although their determination has been sorely tested over the last few years.

The first series sparked a latent field of interest which far exceeded my expectations, and one of the things which pleased me most was the considerable interest shown in the series by women, many of whom were not directly involved in business. There has always been an implicit assumption in the UK that it is only men who are concerned and interested in the business world. In my view the reception of the first series has challenged that belief, and I have been delighted at the numbers of women, of all backgrounds, who felt that they had gained some understanding of what business involved, and of its excitements, by watching the first series.

I was not the only person who was unprepared for the interest that the first series aroused. The decision to sell packs of videos as an aid to training was a last-minute decision when it became clear that there would be a demand from schools, colleges and firms both for the book and for the videos. Indeed my mailbag is still full of queries from anguished students who are trying to read into my comments or actions much deeper meanings than I had ever intended. The initial viewing figures far exceeded my expectations and the figures increased during the series. The amount of press comment, and the subsequent reaction, showed that there is a considerable interest in the practices of business and management in the UK, more than I had ever thought.

Not least of the consequences of the first series was the effect on the companies themselves. With the sole exception of the programme about Tri-ang, which was made a year earlier than the rest of the series as a pilot, and where really our intervention was too late, all the companies or families have prospered. Perhaps the free publicity which the programmes themselves provided had a small effect on this. I took great pleasure in the very much better results achieved by Apricot Computers and Churchill Tableware, and in the impact for change that the programmes made on the Shropshire District Health Authority and the Copella fruit juice business. The Morgan Motor Company, which remained impervious to my blandishments, has achieved a modest increase in car production. None of the participants' businesses have been harmed, and to my great pleasure I remain in touch with all of them, and continue to take a vicarious pride in their personal and business achievements.

In the summer of 1992 the *Troubleshooter* team and I returned to talk about their progress, and the changes they had made, in front of the cameras. These *Troubleshooter* revisits are the subject of Chapter 7: 'Troubleshooter Revisited'.

When the first series ended I remember turning to my producers and saying, in that pontificating manner which infuriates so many, that it was plain that we had made the last *Troubleshooter* programme, if only because I thought it unlikely that there would be any more companies prepared to discuss their problems before a very large television audience. I was also concerned that, despite the infinite variety of possible business problems and solutions, a second series might produce the spurious view that there are standard solutions to business problems. I was worried that I would begin to take the problems for granted and become more aware of the task of making the programmes, and less focused on the business activities of the companies themselves. I felt that we needed to take a year out, and my strong urge was not to attempt another series.

It was in the late summer of 1990 that the *Troubleshooter* production team suggested troubleshooting in Eastern Europe. Although I had considerable knowledge of the Soviet Union, I had little first-hand experience of operating in Poland, Hungary, Czechoslovakia or Eastern Germany. I was well aware of the constraints imposed upon business by the Communist regimes, and over a number of years I have struggled with the tasks of achieving movement in business situations in the Soviet Union. I was aware of the slow pace of decision-making, and the almost total absence of any of the stimuli to efficiency and business effectiveness which we enjoy under the Western capitalist system. In Eastern Europe, until the Communist regimes collapsed, the whole problem of business was looked upon as a production problem. The decisions about what to make, what to charge, where to make, and how to distribute were not seen as anything to do with business, and were almost invariably dictated by considerations of 'national' or 'strategic' interest. The systems of training, and all the systems of reward and punishment are upside down. Technical training throughout the whole of the Eastern bloc is excellent, but concepts of productivity and general concepts of the importance of change are almost non-existent. The punishments for failure are draconian, but the rewards for success are tiny. There is absolutely no reward for taking a risk, and no understanding that the absence of risk-taking is also dangerous.

I had no doubt whatsoever of the vital necessity of trying to help the progress and liberation of the Eastern European countries from an oppressive system which severely limited individuals and entire countries from achieving economic growth and prosperity. I have many Polish friends, and have never forgotten working with Eastern Europeans during, and after, the Second World War. It seemed to me that if I could help to promote a wider understanding of the problems that Eastern Europe was facing, so that practical help could be produced for them, then this was a challenge which I could not ignore. Therefore I agreed enthusiastically to make two one hour programmes, one in Poland and one in Hungary. Even I, however, balked at the idea of trying to troubleshoot an entire country. I have run the largest public company in the UK but that hardly fits me for the task of administering a newly pledged democracy, particularly as I have always believed that the skills of the politician and those of the businessman are, to a large extent, antipathetic: the politician is essentially interested in the preservation of his power, while the businessman is primarily motivated by the desire to achieve specific results.

We took the approach of looking at some sample businesses, and attempting to help some individual companies in both countries. It proved to be a fascinating experience – but it was also extremely time-consuming. Sadly, my knowledge of the Russian language was of little help in establishing the direct dialogue necessary in order to develop confidence when working with others, and the limitations of working through interpreters under these circumstances are obvious, excellent though the interpreters were. The programmes, which were transmitted in October 1991, left me with a deep feeling of concern about the ways in which we are helping the new Eastern European democracies and the enormity of the tasks that they face. They desperately need time, and they desperately need practical help of a fairly mundane order if they are to avoid the levels of suffering increasing to totally intolerable degrees. Indeed, the material circumstances of the majority of people in Eastern Europe have worsened dramatically, and their perceived economic security has been equally reduced. In many ways they have been thrown into the eye of the storm with little preparation and totally inadequate equipment, to cope with the ferocity of what they are experiencing. I have no doubt that they will succeed in retrieving their economic prospects. However, my own view is that their economic revival will take a terrible toll in terms of human suffering and social cohesiveness.

We turned our attention back to the UK and the continuing debate about whether it was appropriate to make a second *Troubleshooter* series. It was by no means an easy question. We were particularly concerned about two things: would we find enough businesses willing to take part in a second series, and would those businesses have problems that were sufficiently different from the problems examined in the first series to prevent the second series from becoming a repetition of the first? After a great deal of debate we decided that we would try one more *Troubleshooter* series, which would be the last in the present *Troubleshooter* format.

The BBC *Troubleshooter* production team contacted organizations and advertised in management magazines. We found a plethora of companies who wished to take part. As in the first series their motives were mixed, and in many cases did not relate solely to any immediate business problems they were facing. However the variety of companies coming forward was immense and we had no problem selecting businesses which posed a range of challenges totally different from those which we had looked at in the first series. The organizations participating in the second *Troubleshooter* series are: Double Two (clothing manufacturers), The South Yorkshire Police Force, the Tollemache and Cobbold Brewery Limited, the Bradford Hospitals Trust, the Charles Letts Group (diaries and books), and Norton Motors Limited (motorbike manufacturers and engineering conglomerate),

It is the infinite variety of business problems, challenges and opportunities which is, I suppose, the greatest single source of interest and excitement in the business world. It is a fact that nothing is ever routine. The external environment and internal problems are constantly changing, requiring new solutions and new approaches, and creating opportunities and challenges. I am confident that the business problems we have been asked to look at in the second series are different from those in the first. Perhaps one would expect them to be, since the external environment has changed so much.

The first series, apart from the Tri-ang pilot, was made in 1989 – a time when most of us were still full of optimism, when house prices were still rising, and when the future seemed to promise continued growth, prosperity and opportunity for us all. The second series was made at the end of 1991 and during 1992, a period when optimism and confidence were in notably short supply during the longest recession since the Second World War. A time when the level of bankruptcies in the sort of companies that we have been looking at are the highest in living memory, and a time when people running small businesses feel threatened and ill considered. A time when the interests and concerns of business people are much more related to survival than to growth, and a time when the skills of the bad weather sailor and the recessionary manager are more in demand than for many years.

It is worth remembering that many business managers are dealing with the first recession in their experience, and dealing with it in a situation where access to money is extraordinarily difficult. It is a time of very high real interest rates, collapse of consumer demand and, despite continual noises to the contrary, little sign of a light at the end of the tunnel. While the particular management skills required may be different, the human qualities remain the same, and the demands on the individuals are even greater than when things are going well. They include the ability to look ahead, the ability to retain focus and direction while minimizing risk, the ability to hang on to the principles by which good businesses survive, and the ability to continue to care for your people – who in these circumstances are more harassed, worried and concerned than ever. All of these things ultimately depend upon the courage, perspective and determination of the business leader. In a small business those decisions are very frequently made regardless of personal cost in terms of commitment, and the possible impact on the individual's wealth and future prospects. Business is not for the faint hearted. It really does sort the strong from the weak, and it tests and exposes beliefs and values in what may be considered a cruel way.

Much of business is about risk minimization, and I have always been concerned about businesses which are prepared to 'bet the company' without seeming to realize what they are putting at risk. Similarly businesses should undertake new initiatives with a clear aim in mind. In the introduction to the first *Troubleshooter* book I set out, as clearly as I could, my motives for making that series, and my hopes for what the series could achieve. Those motives, hopes and personal objectives still apply. To reiterate, briefly, I have always believed that the future well being of every person in the UK depends upon improvements in manufacturing performance: I see no other means by which we can pay our way in the world. I am very concerned that the brightest and the best of our young people look on business in general, and manufacturing in particular, with a distaste and disbelief which leads too many of them to turn their backs on a career in business. If the *Troubleshooter* series can show people who have never even stepped into the world of business that business is a human concern and that its dramas, excitement and fascination are similar to those that our other human activities engender, that alone will make a second series worthwhile; but if it can also help the participating businesses to greater success, so much the better. And I love factories. A visit to a well run works with modern equipment, and a well motivated workforce creating wealth before your eyes is, to me, both a thing of beauty and a source of real pleasure.

I believe that the fundamentals of business affect practically every man and woman in the country. Business is serious and important. It is not just about personal and individual promotion. It is about the creation of the wealth upon which the living standards of us all depend. Business is not the purpose of life, but it is a microcosm of life and it can reflect all the things that make life exciting and challenging. As a nation the British need a much greater appreciation of this. Moreover, they need to have a much greater appreciation of the people who make their lives in this most testing and demanding way. Just as the British people profess to admire the sailors of the past who bravely ensured that Britannia ruled the waves so, today, they need to view their business people in much the same way if the UK is to prosper and to preserve the things that we all care about.

And those business people must know how to manage. I have always been obsessively concerned with problems of management and those who manage. I have believed all my life that management is a much underrated skill and, particularly in the UK, management is often confused with administration. Administration is a necessary skill and a part of management, but true management is a much broader and more interesting and demanding art. Administration is essentially about the maintenance of the status quo and ensuring that the machine runs smoothly. Administration is not about change or about improvement. Management is about continuous change. It is about the continuous growth of people and the continuous creation of a better tomorrow out of today. Management in practically every field is about the creation of more, of better, from less. Management is about striving to reach a destination. It is about gaining the commitment of all the people in an organization to achievements which they and their customers believe to be better than before. I very much admire the Japanese for making management a fine art. They are always looking for ways to improve not only the product, but also the process by which it is made, and the way in which people work together to make it.

The first *Troubleshooter* series apparently produced an impression which I had not in any way intended. Some people seem to have felt that I thought I knew best how to run everybody else's affairs and everybody else's life. I can assure you that this is very far from the truth. I cannot emphasize often enough that, as in the rest of life, there is never a single correct solution to a business problem. It is all too easy to criticize, or to make comments which seem unhelpful. I hope that what I do is to make constructive suggestions about things which might be done differently. In business the art is in actually running the business and producing the solutions – and that can only be done by the people who have the problems and who are involved. Sometimes, by drawing on my experience from a very wide variety of business situations with which I have grappled over the years, I can come up with a new idea, or a new approach. I try to say what I would do if I were in the situation which is presented to me, but people must choose the actions they want to take and the way they deal with the problem for themselves.

The only test of business success is business success itself. There are no clear rules. There are some rather obvious pre-conditions for success: do not spend more money than you have; sell things at more than they cost you to make. But these should be self-evident. You do not need a business expert to advise on the few basic principles which apply. The paradox is that to succeed in business you have to care and to be involved, and yet if you care too much it becomes increasingly difficult to accept the inevitable logic which lies behind most decisions. It is often much easier for somebody from outside to look at business problems from a different angle, and from a less involved and more dispassionate viewpoint.

I certainly do not consider myself to be a business guru. I am what I am: an old businessman who has, by good fortune, had the opportunity to see, sample and test a very large number of businesses in totally different situations, throughout the world. I have one other advantage. I have actually done it, and I continue to do it, so I do not talk purely from theory – I talk from practical experience. Above everything I talk from a heartfelt feeling for those men and women who actually have to do things, to make things happen. I know the difficulties of achieving business success, and I would never minimize the practicalities involved in trying to change business situations.

I am not a consultant, and have never sought to be one. I feel that the businessman who believes that a consultant can resolve all his problems is making a grave mistake. The final actions have to be undertaken by the people in the business themselves – and ultimately that means all the people. The trigger for this action must come from the man or woman at the top but, in the end, businesses succeed or fail by the wishes and involvement of all the people in them. That includes everyone, from the humblest member and newest recruit to the most exalted member of the board. Business is always about teams of people working together to achieve objectives which will hopefully benefit them all. In this situation the outside visitor is privileged to have the opportunity of trying to help. But help is all that can be offered. The problems cannot be resolved by people from outside, and the credit for any good which results from a troubleshooting visit must rest entirely with the people in the company concerned.

One of the key signs of a good company is the almost tangible feeling one gets that it is going somewhere. This drive for progress towards an unknown destination can only originate from the leadership of the company. Moreover, the sense of direction will inevitably be subject to change – if only because the world outside is constantly changing. The successful company has a clear goal in mind and everything that is done is directed towards achieving that goal. Even when survival is uppermost in everyone's mind, those who are clear about their goals will act very differently from those who are merely trying to keep bankruptcy at bay.

The ambition attached to these goals is one of the most important single decisions the businessman or woman can take. It must be testing and yet achievable at the same time, and this is a very difficult mix to manage. One of the surprises to me in the first series was that companies appeared to be satisfied with levels of achievement far below what I judged their potential to be. This is partly a matter of the self-confidence of the people running the businesses, and also a feeling that to aim too high was to take an unjustifiable risk.

All too often in the UK ambition is equated with greed and, of itself, is considered to be a bad thing. And yet ambition for your company is really ambition for others. It is ambition for your people and your products. Curiously enough, nobody thinks ill of a man or woman who wants to make the best product in the world. Yet if the ambition was described as being to run the most successful and profitable company in the world there would be a very different reaction. It is very difficult for the leaders of small companies in the UK to get this judgment right. On balance I have been surprised at the very moderate expectations that British people have for their companies. Also, at a time when mega-salaries are much in the news, I have been surprised at the low levels of personal reward which people have been prepared to take out of their businesses. Most of the small businesses I have met so far really benefit from the wholehearted commitment and involvement of their top managers. It is as though their businesses are an extension of their families, indeed in some cases, the businesses seem to have taken over the families. This is another area which the *Troubleshooter* programmes revealed quite strikingly to me.

Family businesses are, almost by definition in my view, more difficult to run than publicly owned or professionally managed ones. Inevitably, for a family business to succeed, the ambitions for the business and the ambitions and interests of the family have to be congruent. From experience this seems to me to be extraordinarily difficult to achieve. Very few families sit down together and appraise where they are trying to go, and what they want from life. Even when they do they are often understandably concerned that each family member should be able to express his wishes and future ambitions, and that one or another of them should not become overbearing. When such family aims, often inadequately expressed, clash with the demands of the business it is inevitable that the running of the business becomes more difficult and less professional. It is extraordinarily difficult for family businesses to be managed as professionally as publicly owned companies. Inevitably the employees in the company eventually take the view that, since the company belongs to Mr X, Mr X's views must prevail. It is a small, but nevertheless fatal, step from there to believe that whatever Mr X thinks must automatically be carried out within the company. The owner and leader of a family business finds it more and more difficult to be told the facts honestly. And when the bad news is told, it is often disguised so that it can be ignored, or simply missed, unless the owner is particularly alert. The result is that problems develop to a considerable extent before the top management is aware of them. In this series of *Troubleshooter*, both Double Two and the Charles Letts Group experienced the personal versus the professional dilemma which so often confronts family businesses.

It is this interplay between the personal and the professional which makes the pursuit of business excellence such a fascinating one. It is like one of those Russian nesting dolls. You start by seeing a business problem, the doll, and then you open the doll, only to find within it a personality problem, another doll, or a family problem, another doll, which leads you to a different business problem, yet another doll, and so on. Businesses and companies can only work when the personal issues and the business issues are skilfully led so that they are moving in the same direction.

The other area of major challenge to the businesses which I have seen is that of change. The paradox is that small companies are able to change more quickly than large ones. It is one of their advantages, because there are not so many people to be persuaded and the channels of communication are shorter. The whole business is more sensitive to external stimuli, since there are fewer interfaces between the outside world and the business situation. But the difficulties of changing are no less, not least because most small businesses do not have the reserves of professionalism and experience to call upon. Any change or deviation from past experience seems very high risk. Sadly, in their current position, there are all too few businesses in this country which can afford to take unnecessary risks and face the financial consequences of mistakes. Therefore there is a reluctance to face up to change until it is so abundantly obvious that it is inescapable. By then it is often too late. The opportunity for taking the initiative is gone, and forced change is a very different matter from change embraced with free will.

All the businesses which I have seen during this second series of *Troubleshooter* are involved in change, and change which is being conducted at a breakneck pace. Perhaps this is why the second series is, in my view, so different from the first. In the first series, besides the overall feeling of confidence, people believed that they had time, and were able to make choices. In the second series far more people feel that they are racing towards a closing door and that they are being driven more by the situation than by their own personal volition. At times like these the demands on management skills are even higher, for one can only regain the initiative in such circumstances by making a determined jump ahead. By definition this is a risky thing to do. It is to the credit of many of the people with whom I have worked that they have been prepared to take these actions.

Despite the number of small businesses which have gone bankrupt during the past two years (a Dun & Bradstreet survey showed that 14881 British businesses collapsed during the first quarter of 1992, 4.5% more than the 14245 business collapses recorded by the same survey for the last quarter of 1991) there are still plenty of men and women today who have ideas which they believe can form the basis of a new business. They face horrendous problems, particularly in raising money. In order to get the financial backing they need, they often have to pledge almost all the collateral they own. The costs of money are crippling, for it is difficult for a business to earn at a higher rate than the current true interest rates, which are higher than they have been for years. And yet there are still people prepared to risk everything they have in this way. We should be glad that there are. Not all will succeed, but some will – and they represent the merchant adventurers on whom we rely for the future.

I remain unwavering in my admiration for the businessmen and women who have taken part in *Troubleshooter*. It takes guts to be willing to discuss your most personal business problems publicly, and it takes even more guts to accept or to reject advice because you think it may – or may not – help your business to succeed. Only professionals and people who care about the success of their business and the future of all the people in it, are likely to be willing to take the risks which participating in the *Troubleshooter* programmes requires.

CHAPTER ONE

DOUBLE TWO

TROUBLE SHOOTER

No matter how large a company is, it always begins with one person. Even when the company is a partnership there is always one person who takes the lead, one person who has had the imagination and determination to create something new.

Isaak Donner, the founder of Double Two, sought asylum in the UK in the 1930s. He ran a successful shirt-making business in Vienna, but he left when the German invasion of Austria became inevitable. It was no surprise to me that Isaak planned to set up a shirt-making business in the UK, but I was surprised to hear that an unknown hero at the Board of Trade suggested Wakefield in West Yorkshire as a good place to start, because times were not easy in Yorkshire in the 1930s. Wakefield was a fairly depressed area with a particularly large number of unemployed women, and although Yorkshire is renowned as the home of the textile industry now, in those days it was primarily famed for its production of wool material and depended upon mining for much of its prosperity.

Isaak founded Double Two in 1940. It is now part of a larger group of companies, but it remains in Wakefield to this day, and the group as a whole is still making a profit. And Isaak, at 87, is still involved with the business. He is a visionary, and an absolute stickler for detail. He combines the ability to see opportunities and to take risks on a breathtaking scale, but at the same time he never forgets that a business is only as good as every stitch, every delivery, every movement and every action which turns human endeavour into products which people want to buy. Initially in 1940, and until 1946, the bulk of Double Two's production was ladies' shirts because most of the men were away in the armed forces and the working women of the UK needed shirt-like blouses. With his understanding of the business and ability to motivate large groups of people, Isaak was soon running a fairly considerable shirt factory.

Isaak's business is now called The Wakefield Shirt Group of Companies, but to many people of my generation it will always be known as Double Two. Before the war there were virtually no collar-attached shirts. Shirts with attached soft collars were primarily used for leisure wear, but not many were worn. When we got up in the morning those of us who went to work struggled with one of two kinds of unattached collar, euphemistically described as either a soft or a hard collar. Both had studs and often resulted in broken finger nails and frayed tempers. As I recollect it the difference between a soft and a hard collar was an infinitesimal degree of starch. You could have cut bread quite easily with a hard collar, whereas with a soft collar you might have had a little difficulty getting through the crust. I endured such collars from my early days at school when, to add insult to injury, on Sundays we were incarcerated inside Eton collars which were even more starched. Eton collars were calculated to sever your head if you did not move extremely carefully. Isaak simply could not understand these curious habits for despite the formality of his country, he came from a somewhat more practical background.

In 1946 Isaak produced his first shirt with an attached soft collar. But, being Isaak, he made it even better. He provided two collars with each shirt, so that when one wore out, the other could be sewn on in its place. Hence the company name, Double Two, and the genesis of an advertising campaign which I remember to this day. The late 1940s were days of explosive change in the UK and an almost limitless demand for clothing of all sorts. During the war most of us were in uniform and until I was twenty-four, I only owned one civilian suit. Isaak's idea hit the jackpot. In those days there were companies that specialized not only in taking the tails off shirts to make new collars, but also in turning cuffs, and repairing and renovating men's shirts of every sort. It seems a very far cry from today's disposable society.

Isaak was not satisfied with his initial innovation and was constantly on the look out for new ideas and products. In the late 1950s British Nylon Spinners, a company which was set up by ICI and Courtaulds to develop the commercial use of nylon, approached him to see if he could utilize nylon in any way. Nylon was a byword for luxury during the war when women would practically sell their souls for a pair of nylon stockings. It had other claims to fame as well: countless lives were saved by nylon parachutes. Towards the end of the war ICI were asked to develop nylon, which they did: it was a product of immense chemical sophistication and complexity and when I first joined ICI it was our wonder product. There seemed no limit to what it could do.

Isaak Donner manufactured the first nylon shirt and he still owns one of the originals of this trailblazing garment, more than thirty years later. I am one of a small number of people who believe that nylon was the best material ever for shirts. It certainly required the least ironing of any fabric I have known and if you travelled around the world, as I did then, and had to be both mobile and smartly dressed, nylon shirts, which could be rinsed through and would dry overnight in any hotel room, were an absolute blessing. They were later superseded by terylene, and terylene cotton blends, but some of us still stuck with our first love, nylon.

It was Isaak's constant search for new ideas and products that led him into partnership with my old company – ICI – and which really ensured the pre-eminence of the original Double Two shirt company. It was natural, therefore, that when terylene was first produced it was Isaak who introduced it into the shirt market. Nowadays, when we are relearning the advantages of partnerships between suppliers and customers, we would do well to look back at the business practices of the 1960s when the development of these products, and their introduction into the market, was accomplished by companies the size of ICI working with small manufacturers like Isaak Donner.

Isaak's son Ricky was born in 1939, and there was never any doubt that he would join the company to take over from Isaak in the fullness of time. Isaak was determined that Ricky should learn the job at first hand, so he gave him a rigorous apprenticeship in the business, before sending him to Harvard Business School to complete his training. Both the Donners are outstandingly intelligent people and full of enthusiasm and drive. Ricky has had a more difficult start in the business than Isaak: it cannot be easy working for a father who created the whole business from a standing start, and who still knows every cuff and button in a company which is really an additional member of his family.

Over the years Double Two expanded, and in 1968 Double Two bought another family firm in the area: William Sugden and Sons Limited. The combined group – The Wakefield Shirt Group of Companies – now has six factories in Yorkshire and the north east and, unusually for a major UK clothing business, has continued to manufacture practically all its garments in the UK, despite the inevitably higher cost of British employees. The company prides itself on its care for its workers, and a trip around any of their factories instantly shows how involved they are with all their people. The Wakefield Shirt Group of Companies – even in this recession – is still turning out over 40 000 garments a week and, although Isaak can be found somewhere in the Wakefield factory most days and still keeps a fatherly eye on things, it is Ricky who drives the company now.

Ricky invited me to visit the company, to see whether I could help. Like any British businessman at the moment he is really concerned about the problems of entering the European market, and he is well aware that this can represent an opportunity or a threat. Despite the fact that they have been trying to set up in Europe in a rather desultory way, their efforts have so far been relatively unsuccessful. They are well aware that many large producers in Europe look upon the UK market as a major opportunity, and if Double Two is not secure in its home – UK – market, it cannot possibly hope to survive. The irony is that Double Two has had the almost unique experience – for a British company – of licensing a very successful Japanese programme. To my immense surprise they have not only licensed the name - which is now the most fashionable and fastest selling imported shirt in Japan - but they have also taken their production ideas into that market. The Japanese operation is a highly profitable one.

As well as the six factories there are four separate businesses in The Wakefield Shirt Group of Companies – see the organization chart on page 20.

Double Two manufactures men's shirts and is developing a ladies' wear business. There is a jeanswear business which manufactures jeans, shirts, jackets and casual trousers both on contract for high street retailers and for their own brand, Jet, under The Jet Clothing Company label. There is a workwear – or corporate clothing – business called Topflight which supplies the police, fire and ambulance services, among others, and sells under the Double Two brand name, and fourthly there is a service business called Threadneedle, which supplies corporate clothing directly to company employees: the employees discuss the various options on their corporate clothing directly with Threadneedle, thus taking all the hassle away from the employer.

The fortunes of these companies have been extremely varied, and take a bit of disentangling from the annual reports which I was sent. However, one of the major advantages that a private company has is the ability to take a longer term view of its businesses. Since they only have to satisfy the family's financial requirements – and not those of a wider public – they are not under pressure, year in and year out, to improve earnings. They can afford to take a long term view, and invest patient money – money which will not make a quick return – for an eventual payback. Generally speaking family companies also accept a much greater degree of personal responsibility for their employees. They know them all well and look upon them as an extended part of their family. They are much less willing to lay people off in bad times, and are prepared to share the pain of recessions with their workers in the conviction that they will reap the benefits when the good times return. Inevitably the financial statements are produced for external reporting purposes rather than for internal management. In a group which is quite complicated, like The Wakefield Shirt Group of Companies, it is sometimes not easy to disentangle financial movements between the various constituent companies which make up the whole. It is, however, apparent from the financial statements that William Sugden and Sons Limited and Double Two have, to some extent, changed places. Sugdens, which five or six years ago was not making

DOUBLE TWO
the original company, founded in 1940 by Isaak Donner, Chairman
now known as
THE WAKEFIELD SHIRT GROUP OF COMPANIES

|

RICKY DONNER
Group Managing Director, Joint Managing Director: William Sugden and Sons

|

WILLIAM SUGDEN AND SONS LTD
founded in 1869 bought by Double Two in 1968
David Sugden*, Joint Managing Director; John Sugden*, Production Director

Double Two	**The Jet Clothing Co.**	**Topflight**	**Threadneedle**
Men's shirts and Ladies' wear	Jeanswear division Makes jeans on contract for, eg, Next and other high street retailers Own label: JET Distribute Italian label: RIFLE	Workwear, boiler suits, overalls, and in 1980s/ 90s developed smart career clothing Supplies the Police Fire & Ambulance services (among many others)	Corporate clothing systems

Double Two and William Sugden and Sons are approved suppliers to the Ministry of Defence.

DEPUTY MANAGING DIRECTOR	**SALES DIRECTOR**	**SALES OPERATIONS DIRECTOR**	**JOINT MANAGING DIRECTOR**
Brian Curzon-Tompson (also known as Brian Tompson)	Kevin Burton	Ken Birch	David Sugden **CHIEF EXECUTIVE** Ken Birch

* John and David Sugden are brothers and are fourth generation Sugdens. William Sugden and Sons was founded by their great grandfather.

—————— existed when William Sugden and Sons was bought by Double Two
– – – – developed by William Sugden and Sons after Double Two purchase: registered on 25 July 1989

a good return, has become profitable, and is now the mainstay of the group. Double Two, which was the main driver in the past, has had a much rougher time recently.

I spent a lot of time working through the history of the two businesses in order to try to find out what went wrong. I only had four years' accounts to look at, but it was plain that in two of those four years Double Two made a loss, and in one of the four years alone more money was lost than the entire amount made in the previous four years. At the same time turnover at Sugdens has been steadily increasing, and even in the generally bad year of 1990 Sugdens' turnover only dropped by a small amount. Sugdens is now far and away the more profitable of the two outfits, and contributes massively more than its share to the group profits. The more I puzzle at the accounts, the more my mind dwells on the amounts of stock and work in progress which are held at Double Two. The figures worry me. If I add everything together they only appear to be turning over their stock twice a year and at the present time that is a recipe for disaster. Companies can achieve stock turns up to ten times a year, but in the current climate five or six stock turns would be necessary, since the high cost of money in the UK at the moment severely penalizes the cost of carrying excessive stocks.

Although the group's trading position was not as good as I would have hoped, their balance sheet has been brilliantly managed. They have hardly borrowed any money at all, and they are in an immensely strong position. Moreover, the group as a whole has not lost money for a great many years, an achievement which very few in the textile industry could claim to match. The business shows every sign of being well managed, but the accounts tell us to worry about the changes in the external environment, such as the fall in demand due to the recession, and the very high real cost of money, and I do wonder about the degree to which the company has actually responded to those changes.

Plainly they are still full of ideas, since the Threadneedle concept is a new one, and it is already making significant profits after only two years in business. The textile industry is one in which I can claim a little previous experience. In my ICI days I was a director of Carrington Viyella, and so I had first hand experience of the problems with which British textiles have been struggling over the years. I know how difficult it is to make money out of shirts. It is a great many years since I have bought a Double Two shirt, and it seemed to me that I ought to find out what the product was like today. Accompanied, as usual, by my producer and the film crew, I paid a visit to a central London stockist of Double Two shirts.

My first surprise was to find that the large retailer we went to was the only large retailer who stocked Double Two shirts in central London. In my early days Double Two was a top of the market brand, rather like Van Heusen and other famous names. I had expected to find the shirt more widely available. My second surprise was when I saw the range. Men's shirts are very much a matter of individual taste, but in order to achieve a significant overprice they must be different in some way. Double Two sell in the middle range and have failed to market their shirts upwards. Shirts must either carry a very strong brand name (and since I could remember the name of Double Two it seemed to me that they started with that advantage, although younger men would not agree since most of the difference achieved in the early years has not been repeated), or they must have significant design differences, or some other gimmick. Isaak Donner understood this brilliantly in his early years. Double Two always stood for innovation, new ideas and new products, but that advantage has long since gone. The Double Two display was not really different in any important way from a myriad of other comparable shirts. This was reflected in the pricing, which was at about the middle point of production-made shirts. I began to wonder again how, with such a small stock turnover, it was possible to sell at middle point pricing. The only answer must be through very long runs, in which large numbers of a single design are produced, thus providing economies in manufacturer's costs. I looked forward to my visit to the Double Two factory so that I could judge for myself.

Ricky was returning from the Far East the evening of the day I visited the factory, so I met Isaak first and he told me something of Double Two's history. It would be difficult not to be inspired by Isaak and his story. There is no doubt that his ideas and spirit are still very much the basis of the business; when William Sugden and Sons was bought in 1968 it was run independently from the rest of the group, and it seems to me that the businesses are still run fairly separately. I was interested to see how the group added value to its constituent parts. One of the many business theories of the early 1970s and 1980s, which has not stood the test of time, was the concept of the conglomerate. It is a concept for which I have always had a healthy cynicism. It seems to me that, unless each part of the company supports and adds value to the rest, there is little reason to have a group at all. The shareholders utilize their money better, and probably get a better return, if the businesses are split up and run as separate self-standing companies. In theory it is not difficult to see what the strengths that each part of the group could add to the other are, but to obtain this added value is very much a matter of philosophy, and organization. I was far from clear what the actual core business of the whole group was. Plainly the founding business was Double Two itself, but the figures showed that the corporate clothing businesses – Topflight and Threadneedle – had now taken the lead, and represented the major future opportunity. If this was the case I felt that facing up to the realities of the situation would be stressful for everyone involved. Again and again I have found that one of the characteristics of family businesses is (an understandable) reluctance to abandon the original business upon which the whole edifice was founded.

Isaak himself was everything I had expected: bright as a button despite his age, still fascinated with the business and very proprietorial about it. He still walks the floor and checks the quality of the work. The group employs 1000 people in its six factories: 300 in Double Two; 200 in the jeans division and 500 in Topflight, Threadneedle (the corporate clothing businesses) and the administrative offices. Many of the workers have been with the company for more than twenty-five years and there is a great family feeling about the whole thing. Their Twenty-Five Club – for employees with twenty-five or more years' service – boasts over 100 members.

After I met Isaak I went off on a tour of the factory. Although I knew Ricky Donner was not in the factory that day, his presence could be felt everywhere I went. Morgan Gustafsson – the group production director – took me round. Morgan is a splendid example of the openness of mind of the company. He is a Swede, and Swedes have a justifiable reputation in the textile industry for continuing to respond to very high cost bases by constant innovation and the introduction of new technology. Morgan has been with the company about three years. He is plainly a man who knows production technology backwards and has been responsible, with Ricky's encouragement, for the introduction of the technical innovations which have enabled Double Two to compete. The computer systems and the Eton production line – an automated assembly line – are very much his baby. He looks on himself as a production man but as I walked around with him I became a little concerned about his overall breadth of view of the business.

My worst fears were confirmed when we arrived in the cloth stockroom. There were approximately 500 000 metres of material, and throughput was about 14 000 shirts a week. The stock was enough, therefore, for six months', or more, production. And it wasn't only the quantity of stock that worried me, it was the range. They stocked every sort of material that you could think of and practically all of it was imported from the Far East. It is almost impossible to consider production in isolation from the commercial philosophy of a business, and the way in which a business is actually conducted. The cloth stockroom really worried me. The range and quantity of materials held, and Morgan's lack of knowledge about rates of turnover and what constituted dead or live stock, made me suspect that I might be on the track of Double Two's problems.

I asked how the buying was done. Ricky made an annual visit to the Far East and bought materials which he thought were likely to find a market. In addition they had a design department which created their own designs for the materials for shirts which were then made up in the Far East. I know from bitter experience that one of the problems about buying from the Far East is the very long lead-time involved in delivery. The container voyage alone takes weeks and either a massive supply is bought in one delivery and the money tied up, or regular deliveries are sent out every month or so. Obviously there was a pipeline which was delivering more material at regular intervals, which made me even more concerned about their stock levels.

Morgan then took me to the main cutting room, pausing on the way to show me their button dyeing facility. This caused me serious surprise. To describe the button dyeing process as primitive would be the understatement of the century. I suspect this is the last button dyeing bastion in the west. Double Two purchases plain mother of pearl buttons and then dyes them in a tiny vat. The button dyer only works part time and Morgan told me that it was cheaper to dye the buttons themselves than to hold stocks of all the different colours that they might need, but I had mixed feelings. I was relieved to hear that somebody had worked out the sums, but the approach seemed to me to be in stark contrast to their strategy with the cloth stock, which was costing much larger amounts of money.

The cutting and assembly room was very cramped but appeared to be laid out in a logical way. As far as I could see the work rates were well up to standards which I have seen elsewhere. However my main impression was of the very large amount and variety of work in progress, with all the attendant problems of scheduling and control. And Morgan was not as well acquainted with the costs and times involved as I had expected him to be.

When I came to the assembly rooms I felt Ricky Donner's omnipresence very strongly. Morgan explained that when they bought the Eton line in 1989, he wanted to install it the opposite way round, but Ricky insisted on the line being installed as it now is. I was surprised that Morgan allowed Ricky to overrule him, since the positioning of a piece of technology like this should be the responsibility of the production director, and – as it happens – the Eton line is a Swedish invention.

The Eton line delivers shirts in the most convenient way to the various work stations, enabling the machinists to maintain a very high rate of machining. It is a tremendous boost to productivity and Double Two bought this one secondhand, from a company which had gone bust. Despite the fact that it only takes twenty-one minutes to assemble a shirt on the Eton line, it takes over four weeks for the shirt to go through the factory from pattern cutting, to assembling, to packaging and warehousing. But the Eton line showed up some of the difficulties of control in the Double Two factory, and as a result they had sharpened up many of their procedures. It took some time for the new technology to be accepted, but with so many long serving employees that is not altogether surprising. I encountered a number of different views about the line, but those who had accepted it said that things were very much better with the line than without, and they were pleased that it enabled them to earn more consistently.

My overall impression in the assembly rooms was of a pretty modern operation, but one that lacked tautness and tightness of control. I could not make out whether this was because of the organization, or the nature of the business, which involved very large numbers of relatively small runs. Small runs mean continual chopping and changing which loses time and hence costs more. The ultimate would be to make only one of each model of shirt at a time, sorting out all the different materials, cutting only one at a time, and so on. Factories are like cars: they are cheapest to run when purring on steadily without stopping and starting.

It seemed unlikely that the modernity of the Eton line alone would enable them to tackle the problems of the European market and I spent a bit of time discussing with Morgan Gustafsson how he saw the approach. One of the problems that faced Double Two was to decide whether they were going to try to sell the English look to a small up-market niche in several European countries, or whether they were going to continue to design different products and sell all those different products into each of the different European markets. Morgan was very strongly of the same view as myself, that each market in Europe is different, and that only a small common market will exist, even for very high quality products such as Gucci bags, or pieces of Louis Vuitton luggage. I was still looking for the unique edge which would be the basis of Ricky's attack on Europe. My next visit was to the warehouse. This was the first time I felt that I was beginning to get close to the philosophy of the Double Two shirt business.

I was shocked to find that the warehouse was carrying 277 000 items, of which 164 000 were shirts. I would have expected the warehouse to be carrying one month's stock at most. And the bulk of the shirt stock was special range stock. They were trying to meet most orders from stock, and dead stock was kept until the following season, so that when a year's holding cost was added, and a discount subtracted when an item was finally sold from dead stock, their margin was much reduced. Christine Brooke, the warehouse manageress, explained that she was endeavouring to ensure that she carried no more than six months' stock, but the clearing section, which supplied the special offers from dead stock, was in addition to that. Yet again the amounts and variety of stock really shook me. They seemed to go on for ever. I had already seen a bit of the computer programming system, which seemed reasonably efficient, but now I asked if I could see some typical orders, and where they were made up. To my amazement I found that they were processing orders for one or two shirts at a time, and very frequently orders of just five shirts at a time. Although they put on a handling charge of £2.50 to compensate for the extra work involved, I know from experience that £2.50 is highly unlikely to cover the additional cost of such small orders, and there appeared to be a large number of these special orders. When I asked Christine about this she explained that Double Two's aim was primarily to supply small independent drapers and men's outfitters which still existed around the country, as well as supplying shirts to gift shops etc., where they wished to stock a few shirts for visiting trade. Apparently there are some 5000 of these outlets whose orders make up 80% of Double Two's output. It is a niche in which Double Two feels comfortable, although it is a decreasing niche. Double Two aim to provide a good service by speedily supplying even the smallest order from stock. I could readily understand the advantages that such a customer base would offer since it would be extremely difficult for a competitor to penetrate but, almost by definition, it was an expensive operation to service. I felt that I was beginning to understand why Double Two was losing money. Their whole service was being provided inside what was, at best, a moderate price level. Double Two was selling in an intrinsically expensive way, and not obtaining the price required to service the business.

There did not seem to be much point attempting to tackle the European market if they were making losses at home, and however they went into Europe it was likely to be slow and, initially, expensive. Of course a private company can manage its affairs more or less as it likes, within the limits of its financial capacity, but it did not seem to me that going into Europe would make very good use of the available money at least until they reestablished their presence in the UK market. I had begun to question the philosophy of the Double Two approach. I resolved to tackle Ricky on this when I met him later in the day.

My next port of call was a marvellous pub called the King's Arms, where I met Brian Curzon-Tompson, the deputy managing director of Double Two, Kevin Burton, the sales director of Sugden's jeanswear and Ken Birch, the sales operations director and chief executive respectively of Sugdens' Topflight and Threadneedle corporate clothing. I wanted to talk about the broader business areas with them. I was particularly looking for the areas where the businesses reinforced each other, and I speedily came across the first. The design facility was shared by all four divisions, and when corporate wear were asked for a new product they were able to utilize the design skills which had already been acquired in jeans and shirts – something which gave them a real advantage against their competitors. Ken Birch was as dedicated as everybody else to the concept of trying to add more value to their products. He saw corporate clothing as a real growth market. It is not only the Japanese who want everybody to wear an identifiable range of corporate clothing in their factories. It is now generally accepted by many companies that it gives a much more professional image to the whole operation, as well as adding to the morale and team feeling of their employees. This concept of adding value has been developed very largely with British Telecom (BT) who have been a substantial customer for eight years. The contract with BT has led Ken's businesses into the distribution and management of corporate clothing. The costs of distribution, packaging and, in Threadneedle's case, the hotline, are all included in the price, which is inflated to allow a good margin to cover these additional costs. Over and over again it has been shown that people will pay for a service, and the more I heard about the Threadneedle concept the more I liked it.

The jeans business is a relatively small one in relation to the other businesses in the group, and so far I had not really looked at it at all. The jeans are sold under the brand name of Jet and have been positioned at the top end of the UK market. Some 6000 pairs are made a week (Levis make 50000 pairs a week and brands like Pepe and Wrangler make about 20000 a week) and, as well as providing their own brand, they make jeans on contract for high street retail customers, such as Next. The factory is running at full capacity and, despite the recession, has managed to do so for the past two years. They have not found it easy to obtain the quality they require by subcontracting, so the business is more or less at its optimum size unless they expand into a new factory. They are increasing their profitability by starting to move away from their contract customers and concentrating more on their own brand. They have recently done a deal with Rifle, the largest, and most prestigious, Italian jeans manufacturer, and the biggest independent producer of jeans in Europe. They have agreed to distribute the Rifle brand in the UK, with the ultimate aim of Rifle handling the British product – Jet – in Italy. This seemed to me to be just the sort of sensible alliance which should work to the advantage of both parties. Even the Italians have been finding it hard to compete, and have moved much of their production to Morocco and Tunisia. In terms of cost Kevin believed that they could compete with the Rifle products which were made in Italy, but not with those made in North Africa, which gave Rifle a 25% cost advantage. That is a great deal to try to make up for through designer marketing.

Brian Curzon-Thompson the deputy managing director of Double Two, used to work in the shirt business at Carrington Viyella in the days when I was there. He came to Double Two from Carrington Viyella. He believes that Double Two has had the most difficult task of the four divisions in the group. Pressure on the shirt market from imports has been unremitting for the past twenty years and he was worried about the large range of the Double Two product and their determination to continue launching up to one hundred new shirt designs a year. He said it was difficult to see much in the way of growth in the market for men's shirts, and he blieved it was necessary for Double Two to try and go more up market. Brian did not believe that they were ready to tackle Europe until they had succeeded in rationalizing and repositioning their shirt business in the UK. The small amount of business they had done in Spain, France and Germany had not been profitable, and had caused disruption in the factory. All three men felt that the group was not using its management strengths effectively. Jeanswear operated as a totally separate company and, apart from the fact that it linked very well with other parts of the company, they believed that its manufacturing strength represented a real competitive advantage. But all of them believed that the group had become a lot more cohesive during the past two years.

I was impressed with all three managers. They seemed to me to be very dedicated, but they were rather less in the picture about what was going on than I had expected. They all shared common views of the problems that were facing the group, and they were certainly dedicated to winning the competitive battle. But all of them gave me the impression that they were not really running free: they were constantly looking over their shoulders to see where Ricky was. I was looking forward to meeting Ricky more and more because apart from his shadowy omnipresence, it was far from clear to me how each part of the group was adding value to the other, although it was apparent that things had been moving much faster in this direction in the last two years. I sensed a certain amount of dissension between the corporate clothing businesses and Double Two, but the jeans business seemed to me to be glad to be out on a limb of their own: they had an absolutely clear way ahead and were very happy with their Italian partners.

It took a few minutes to try and sort out my ideas, before going to visit the design department at the Double Two headquarters. I still had a number of questions in my mind. I was worried about the uncompetitive costs of production in the Double Two shirt business, and I wondered how long they would be able to survive against import competition. It has always seemed to me that you can only beat low cost imports by better indigenous design and service, and by running the business more tightly in a financial sense. I was concerned about the design levels in Double Two, but I would be the first to admit that I am not necessarily the best arbiter of good design, so I made a mental note to check this with an outside designer. I was concerned about the way in which the group as a whole operated: it seemed to me to have many of the disadvantages of a large company, without necessarily having the advantages of a small one. There are a number of good quality managers who had been brought in from outside, but the whole operation has not been brought together with the strategic clarity that I had expected. To my mind there was evidence that many of the operations were not as closely managed as they should be.

I went to meet Shirley Boott, the merchandise manager in charge of the design studio, and was surprised to discover that she had not trained as a designer, but had been Ricky's secretary for many years. I discovered that 90% of their designs are self-created. The design studio had a number of advantages. They were all working together in one room, and so could exchange ideas very easily. They had some very modern technology and, in particular, a computer design system for producing shirt designs virtually while you wait. They demonstrated to me how they could play with endless variations of shirt colours and cut. Another member of the design studio – Lynn Jones, the group fabric designer – had come, some three years ago, from Loughborough, having studied textile design there. However, I did not feel that their designs for Double Two's shirts were different enough to enable them to compete with the likes of Van Heusen and Peter England. But their approach to corporate clothing and uniforms, however, seemed to me to be pretty unique, and they had a sureness of touch in this area which differentiated them from their competitors.

It was almost time to meet Ricky and I felt that I had enough first impressions of the business as a whole to be able to contribute positively to our conversation. I do not know quite what I expected, but his omnipresent shadow over the factory, and the managers' constant references to him, made me think. I already knew that he was an extremely intelligent manager. I was surprised, when we did at last meet, by how much less confident he appeared, and how much more defensive, than I had expected. However there was absolutely no doubt about his intelligence. His mind moved very fast, but I was not sure how open he was to new ideas about his businesses. I felt that he spent more energy in defending the positions that had already been taken on most subjects that I raised with him, than in trying to move on and create new opportunities. And I was rather shaken by the influence that Harvard had obviously had upon him. I have nothing against the Harvard Business School as a training ground, but it can produce an approach to business and a use of jargon which is best described as Harvard-speak. Harvard graduates who swallow Harvard's teachings 100% talk about, and approach business, in a surprisingly similar way.

In Ricky's case I was particularly struck by his conversion to Harvard-speak, because he had been brought up in the business and plainly took tremendous pleasure in his detailed knowledge of every facet of the factories and of the operations. He seemed to have almost every advantage that his position in the business required. He had a full theoretical grasp and had been carefully groomed with practical experience in all the operations. He knew the world markets and was as at home in Japan and Europe as he was in the UK. If anybody was able to lead the business ahead he seemed to be the right man. He appeared to have all the right ideas, and yet I felt that something was missing.

Ricky explained why he had decided against Double Two supplying Marks and Spencer: he did not want Double Two to rely solely upon one large customer, he wanted to keep Double Two's customer base well spread in order to minimize the risk should a customer cancel a contract. Ricky had been visiting licensees in Japan, and obviously took tremendous pride in the success of the Japanese operation. However, he took a rather different view of the contribution of Double Two to the licensees than the views that some of his managers had given me earlier in the day. Ricky felt that Double Two had taught the Japanese everything they knew, whereas the other managers felt that Double Two's primary contribution had been in making its name available in Japan. I had some experience of the Japanese textile industry in the 1960s and I found it surprising that Ricky considered Double Two's production technology superior to the Japanese technology. But, obviously, I could not judge an entire nation's textile industry from the rather limited areas which I had known. However, the other managers had told me that the designs were all chosen by the Japanese, and were specifically aimed at the Japanese market, whereas Ricky gave me the impression that much of the choice was made by Double Two themselves. I would very much have liked to visit the Japanese company in order to check out some of these differences of opinion for myself, but time and the BBC *Troubleshooter* budget unfortunately did not allow such an interesting diversion.

I needed to discover why Ricky was so concerned about the

European situation, and what his aims were. His views were exactly the same as mine, that the European market is an opportunity as well as a threat. Plainly there is a very large market in Europe if a way of tackling it could be found, and if he did not tackle it and establish a position in Europe, and if he failed to strengthen his UK position, then he would be wide open to European competition in his home market. Ricky was particularly concerned about the impact of the Germans on the UK market, since many German manufacturers were having garments made up in the cheaper labour markets of Eastern Europe and North Africa, which gave them a cost advantage that would be extremely difficult for Double Two to compete with. Curiously enough the Germans have not made much of an impact on the shirt business, but Ricky was determined to be able to counterattack on German soil. He did not feel that he had problems with design or cost, but he was concerned about distribution. He had sought agents in Europe, but had discovered that an agent in Germany does not have the same responsibilities as an agent in the UK. Agents in Germany do not give exclusivity as they do in many European countries, and Ricky was deeply disappointed at their failure to push his products. He still felt that the products should sell as they were, and that the only problem was that they were not being adequately sold in the targeted areas. He was very proud of the alliance that their jeans business, Jet, had made with Rifle, and he was frustrated that he had failed to repeat that experience in the shirt business. Ricky agreed that it would be necessary to tackle Europe market by market, and he appeared to feel that they should concentrate on one country at a time.

At the end of my day I found myself with a number of questions which needed checking, and a number of impressions. The overwhelming impression was still that the Double Two shirt and ladies' wear business was not sufficiently soundly based to warrant a major attack on Europe. In many ways British philosophy has been the exact opposite of the Japanese just in time philosophy where garments are made to order just in time for delivery and no finished stock is held. While it is a perfectly permissable business tactic to invest heavily in stock and to supply from it, you have to be sure that the ultimate price received is enough to compensate for the large amounts of money that are tied up in the stock held. This is particularly difficult during times of high interest rates, and I found myself with real doubts about whether the Double Two business was managed tightly enough and whether the correct sums had been done. I made up my mind to enquire more closely into that area of their activities. The potential key to Europe seemed to me to lie in the corporate clothing business.

I talked to Campbell Freeman, the group company secretary. Campbell had recently taken over responsibility for the accounts of Double Two. I asked him whether he could find me some data on the amounts of money tied up in stock, including fabric, goods in transit, work in progress, and finished goods, and what their costings were for handling small orders. I also asked him to give me some idea of the amount of dead stock. However, Campbell said they did not have dead stock. Like others, he plainly thought it wise to check his replies with Ricky. Indeed very shortly afterwards, a series of explanations about why stock levels were deliberately held high arrived from Ricky. I began to get rather contradictory stories about the high stock levels. Ricky stated that, as a matter of policy, he bought in bulk because of the advantageous discounts that he obtained, which more than offset the carrying costs. But I could not find any figures to demonstrate such a desirable outcome. Ricky also stated that a deliberate decision had been taken to carry the stock, in order to maintain employment during the recessionary period. This of course is just the sort of action that family firms can take, albeit at a cost to themselves, in order to support their workforce. But even a family business must never support its employees to the point where everyone loses: when stock is piled so high and orders have fallen so low that the business dies because of the original kindness of the employer to the employed. And the total stock values during the years did not seem to reflect this decision. I could not find the large increase in finances tied up in stock that should have ensued. I found myself more and more uneasy about the clarity of the management in these areas.

My next meeting was with the Sugden brothers, John and David, at their Barnsley factory. I wanted to form a better impression of the strength of their fighting position, and whether it was realistic to try to concentrate the group's aims for Europe on the corporate clothing and Threadneedle concepts. I asked David Sugden whether he could produce data for me on the European market, and was delighted when he produced volumes of comparative studies about the corporate clothing market, particularly in Germany.

I had no difficulty understanding what John Sugden did, he was production director responsible for the Barnsley factory, but David, who trained as an accountant, was described as joint managing director, with Ricky, of William Sugden and Sons. I was not too clear what role he played in the group as a whole, or how he related to Ricky. I took to the two Sugden brothers immediately. They were thoughtful, and very deliberate, and knew their business backwards. They were very highly customer-orientated and, it seemed to me, had a well developed sense of what they were trying to do. There are really very few similarities between the nature of the William Sugden businesses and the Double Two shirt business: they operate as separate businesses. The common ground lies in the areas of production planning and quality, but the whole commercial orientation of the William Sugden businesses is different. David Sugden recently became a director of both Double Two and the group holding company, as well as being jointly responsible for the William Sugden businesses with Ricky, but Ricky remains in overall charge. Apparently he plays a strong role in each area.

John trained as a production man and plainly the Sugden family prepared the two brothers very carefully so that they had all the necessary skills to run their business. David and John are fourth generation Sugdens: the business was started by their great grandfather in 1869. Double Two originally bought William Sugden and Sons to provide additional manufacturing capacity for shirts. Sugdens agreed to the purchase because they were in financial trouble. However, almost as soon as the company was bought, the level of imported shirts sold in the UK increased rapidly as the emerging textile industries of Hong Kong and the Far East, with their low labour costs, started attacking the UK market. The challenge was to find another business to load up the factory. The Sugden brothers were given almost limitless freedom to follow their own hunches and William Sugden and Sons became involved in the uniform shirt business. The company – Topflight –

now supplies many of the UK police forces, as well as the fire, security and ambulance services. This is not such a simple enterprise as it might appear. Although it seems, at first glance, that all policemen wear the same sort of shirt, there is a great complexity of styles. In fact the various police forces around the UK wear no less than twenty-three different styles of blue uniform shirts. Each force is very dedicated to its particular favourite, and defends its own preference with the determination of a mother tiger defending its young. I asked whether Sugdens had made any attempt to try and rationalize this production and the brothers were shocked at the thought. When I reflected for a moment I realized what a stupid question it was. Obviously the more different styles of shirt the brothers supplied, the more difficult it was for a competitor to move in, and the more the customer was prepared to pay for those different styles.

William Sugden and Sons have an in-house design service which seeks to differentiate basic products in a variety of thoughtful and attractive ways, and I was shown some of their designs. David explained that the uniform customers expected a five day turnaround and it was therefore necessary to carry a fair amount of stock. They compensated for this by making garments in only two colours, although obviously the customer could specify other requirements. Sugdens had also introduced an Eton line at the Barnsley factory without the prolonged teething troubles which Double Two had had at Wakefield. The Sugdens learned from the Double Two problems: they also bought their Eton line system secondhand but they installed it in a larger space. I suspected that this might mean that the Barnsley factory was more closely managed and scheduled in the first place.

John and David continuously pointed out that they looked upon themselves as providing a service rather than as manufacturers. Manufacturing was only a part of providing an overall service to their customers, and Sugdens had recently extended this whole idea with the Threadneedle concept. The more I heard about Threadneedle the more I admired the idea. It was developed as the size of Sugdens' uniform contracts became larger and larger and the business managers put their heads together to work out ways to add value to their service. In Threadneedle they have designed a business which greatly reduces the time it takes an employer to provide uniforms and corporate clothing to its employees. Catalogues are provided directly to the individual employee, who can order from a choice of items which are then supplied directly to the employee. Threadneedle also provides a hotline for its customer's employees, so that any individual who has a problem can be dealt with personally, by Threadneedle, without bothering their own company at all. One Threadneedle employee services each customer account. The employing company is billed on a bulk order basis, so the customer time spent is reduced to an absolute minimum. It seemed to me that they had a different philosophy from the Double Two Wakefield factory and an idea that could well be developed into the European market.

There was no question that both the corporate clothing business and the Threadneedle concept were very carefully thought out and administered. In particular they had always been managed with a view to retaining competitive advantage, both in quality, design and service. The description that the Sugden brothers had given me, of the business being a service business and customer led, was supported by what I saw. The factory also showed signs of being more tightly managed. In particular the Eton line had been put in with relatively few hiccups, and it was more than paying its way. They had clear aims about what they were trying to achieve in terms of work in progress and levels of stock. They had fought hard to limit the rate of expansion of their customer base so that they did not reduce the level of service to each customer. But now they planned to double their customer base. I was very interested in their willingness to encourage customer choice and difference in the products they made, even though, on the face of it, their margins would be reduced. The costs that they added for the service they provided seemed adequate, when looked at against the additional costs that that level of service incurred. Certainly the profit figures of the business as a whole justified their policies. In particular the Threadneedle concept made them extremely difficult to dislodge. Once they were handling a company's corporate clothing orders directly with that company's employees, the entry cost for any competitor would be substantial. Moreover, barring a catastrophic failure in the service Threadneedle provided, it was difficult to see how they could fail to respond to their customer needs.

I enquired whether there was any chance of developing into Europe on the backs of some of their existing international UK customers. It appeared that there was a chance that they could do so with some of the oil companies that they were beginning to serve in the UK, such as Esso, BP, Shell and Texaco, and the Sugdens and their employees were all cock-a-hoop, having recently obtained a very large order – worth £2m – from the DHSS, which opened up major opportunities for the future of their business. The corporate clothing business developed from 1970, when it was very much the poor relation to the customer shirt business, although it benefited from it. One of the areas that I failed to grasp immediately was the strong feeling that corporate clothing still benefited from the Double Two branding. The fact that the corporate clothing was linked to what they thought of as a quality product being sold in the high street gave the recipient the feeling that he was not being fobbed off with some cheap import.

John and David Sugden are very proud of the fact that their approach to the uniform business has been anything but uniform. They have never tried to make a standard product which they then sold to their corporate customers. They have deliberately sought out medium-sized customers and developed the ranges in collaboration with them. This whole process has been facilitated by a growing trend towards awarding three year contracts, or longer, for the supply of corporate clothing; previously contracts were always limited to one year. And Sugdens' corporate customers realized that they could make immense financial savings by cutting the levels of stock which they held. I learned, with incredulity, that the Metropolitan Police had at one time carried a two year stock of uniform in-house: this has now been cut to six weeks. A change of that size is only made possible by a very close relationship with the supplier.

Sugdens have now extended their service to buying in any items which they themselves do not manufacture or supply: this has taken even more of the hassle away from the customer. With pride they showed me some of the unique machinery which they designed and made themselves in order to solve particular problems such as epaulettes for uniform shirts.

They were very proud of their long service employees, and I was introduced to Jean, who had first started working at Sugdens in December 1946. Jean was initially so unhappy that after the first week she tendered her resignation, but her mother made her retract it and now she is an absolutely staple part of the Eton line, which has increased productivity by nearly 50%. The corporate clothing production is very high quality. They aim for a standard shirt of the same quality as Marks and Spencer's general range of shirts, ie, a good quality everyday shirt, not a typical cheap uniform shirt. They also have a super quality cloth which is slightly denser and heavier, lasts much longer and can stand up to repeated laundering.

The more I talked to the people in the corporate clothing business the more convinced I became that they were the part of the business which had the best chance of fighting their way into Europe. However, the British Clothing Industry Association's (BCIA) report in autumn 1991 made it very clear that this was not going to be an easy move because of the strength and cost base of the entrenched competition. The concept of corporate clothing in Germany is a much less developed one than it is in the UK, but the corporate clothing that is bought in Germany is very largely imported, and based on cotton rather than polyester cotton blends. As far as I could see there was nothing like the Threadneedle concept in Germany. Because of its large numbers of medium-sized companies, Germany seemed the obvious first target, but it would take persistence, money, and a helpful entry point. They would have to try to persuade the market to see the advantages of the way in which The Wakefield Shirt Group of Companies conducted their business. My own experience of fighting into the German market has been that, although it is a hell of a battle to get in, once you are there the buyers are very quick to see the true economics of the overall situation, which in Threadneedle's case are the savings in administration costs, orders and complaint handling from which the customer company can benefit. I felt that Sugdens were providing such a large element of service that, once they had achieved entry into the market, they would be likely to establish themselves quickly and to prosper, and they would be helped by their responsiveness to the customer and their insistence on very high quality. The experience of visiting Sugdens cheered me up considerably. I began to feel more comfortable that the group had a field of unique strength which they could use to achieve the strategic aims which Ricky and the rest of them were, quite rightly in my view, so set on.

I wanted to discuss Double Two's design quality and the degree to which it would be possible to reposition Double Two in a different part of the market, through better design, so my next port of call was Paul Smith, the British designer who is a legend in his own right. Paul Smith is one of the few British designers who has established himself internationally and now has shops selling either his own products, or products made to his own designs, in London, Paris, New York and Tokyo. His whole range of products is based on his own taste in design matters. He is also extremely interested, as practically all British designers that I have met are, in trying to improve the quality of design in British products. He is design consultant to a major British high street retailer; he is renowned for the bluntness of his views and he understands world markets. I wanted a second opinion from inside the industry and I asked him to look at a number of the Wakefield Shirt Group of Companies' products, literature, and overall design strategy.

It is a sad fact that the UK produces more trained designers than the whole of the rest of Europe put together, and yet we make extraordinarily poor use of them. Their world class skills are more than demonstrated by the fact that so many top-class European products, renowned for their fine design, have been worked on by British designers. The sadness is that so many designers have to pursue their skills outside the UK because the British market is so small: not nearly enough British people are willing to pay the necessary premium for good design.

I was sure that Paul Smith would express clear opinions about the Double Two range, and what needed to be done. To my absolute delight his views complemented my own. He took a very depressing view both of the shirts, and of the new ladies' wear range on which many of Ricky's hopes for Double Two were pinned. To my delight, however, he was extremely enthusiastic about the design content and quality of the corporate clothing. Of course one is always particularly receptive to very high grade professional advice when it happens to coincide with one's own views, so I had to be careful not to allow the increased confidence in my own judgment – which Paul's endorsement gave me – to affect me too strongly. Paul Smith's shop in Covent Garden, where we did the filming, proved to be every bit as interesting as his own views and I ended up buying two beautifully designed shirts.

By now I felt that I had accumulated enough information for my final session with Ricky. But I was still concerned about Ricky's attitude to my advice and suggestions. There was a degree of defensiveness in Ricky's approach to his business and to his people, but, when I began to think about it, I sympathized with him quite strongly. It must be very difficult to take over a business from such a successful father as Isaak. No matter how well trained you are it takes a tremendous amount of self-assurance to be consistent and confident about your own views, and to accept the responsibility of delegation, particularly when the old man is still involved in the business every day. Delegation in a company is one of the most important management skills, but it is never easy. It is obviously both a tremendous waste of money, and highly demotivating for the managers if, having hired them because they are able managers, you then spend your time second-guessing them. Indeed good managers will not stay long under such circumstances. I came to the conclusion that it was essential for me to speak to Ricky about this frankly if I were to be of any real help both to him, and to the company. I felt that he needed to view the business in a more detached fashion. It is all too easy for the employees of a family concern to shrug off their own responsibility for the future of the business by taking refuge in the fact that it is actually the family's concern. However, it is in everyone's interests that family businesses are run both effectively and competitively.

My final meeting with Ricky was arranged on neutral ground at an old manor house hotel called Walton Hall. It was spring and the daffodils were out. I expected a pretty rough session with Ricky, where I would have to argue every point in great detail. I was worried that he would be so anxious to justify the group's present position that he would be blocked from considering the very real points that I thought it highly necessary to make. I began the meeting by addressing the structure of the group. Here I expected a mushroom cloud to erupt.

I told Ricky that I thought that he was too dominant in the business. I understood how it had occurred, but thought that he must accept that, as the son of the founder as well as the managing director, he was inevitably going to be in an extremely dominating position over his managers anyway, so he must make a determined effort to leave his managers alone to run their own businesses. He had attracted good management in the various areas of the business, but I knew that they were looking over their shoulders all the time because Ricky was closely involved in all decisions, even on points of detail. I appreciated that they were now starting to band the businesses together, but I felt this was overdue since the essence of the group had to be that it was stronger than the sum of its constituent parts. Ricky either had to reduce the level of management, or to stress them up more in terms of performance, and direct their energies more firmly outside the company. Either there should be fewer managers, or bigger businesses for them to run. I was not happy about the financial accounts for the group, although I realized that Campbell Freeman had taken over responsibility for them relatively recently. I felt that the accounts could produce a better basis for control and direction of the business.

Then I turned to the main problem that Ricky had asked me to look at: the group's entry into Europe. I fully supported his basic reasoning about the need to try to exploit the potential of the European market if he was to have growth opportunities for the future, as well as providing himself with a defensive position. I was concerned, however, that he was underestimating both the time it would take to get into Europe and – since time is money – the potential cost. However he approached the European market, the money invested would be patient money, and would depress his overall profitability for some time. I therefore felt that it was absolutely vital that he attempted to tackle only one country at a time, and from one basic business position. Plainly Germany was the most important single market. If he could crack Germany he had a good chance of moving into some of the other European markets. I then turned back to what I felt was the most tricky area from Ricky's point of view, namely the Double Two shirt business. I pointed out that Double Two had incurred a loss for three out of the last five years, and therefore I did not feel that it was a good time to try to enter the European market with Double Two.

I had real concerns about the philosophy upon which the shirt business was run. Essentially it was based upon ensuring access to a very large number of retailers by offering reasonably priced, branded, ex-stock delivery. The snag, in my view, was that there were not enough points of difference to attract the retail customer. I told Ricky that I had taken some advice about this and felt that more original design and more originality in fabric ranges would raise the profile of the shirts and be a major selling point. They were in the worst of all worlds at the present time. The size of the range that they were carrying, together with the necessity to supply ex-stock, *and* at a medium price point, all added up to a very high cost business. They needed to move their prices up, and that meant going up market. I felt that it might well be necessary for them to buy their shirts in at some stage. However, if they managed the business with the care and concern for their people which they had shown so far, they should be able to run down the shirt manufacturing in the UK at the same time as the corporate clothing business moved up.

I was quite happy and relaxed about the strategic approach to jeans, which I thought was sensible, but I hoped that the Rifle agreement to sell Jet jeans into the Italian market would be operating soon.

I explained that I had looked carefully at all the businesses, and that I felt that to try to launch an attack on Europe with the men's shirt business would prove extremely slow, and very difficult. I was very impressed by the unique selling proposition of Threadneedle, with its attention to individual employee service, and I therefore felt that the approach to Europe should be through Threadneedle and corporate clothing, hopefully bouncing off one of their existing UK corporate clothing customers, such as one of the oil companies. Ricky must appreciate however that, because he was attempting to introduce a new concept into the European, specifically the German, market, it would inevitably take time. He could not expect to establish a position as quickly as he had in the UK. I reminded him that the corporate clothing market in the UK has been evolving over a period of twenty years. I thought that this would give him some idea of the sort of period that it would take to establish a really strong position in Germany.

To my great surprise Ricky appeared, at this stage, to agree to my strategic assessment, although he rejected my arguments about the management structure. Essentially he told me that they were already doing most of the things that I had in mind. However, I am bound to say that if they were, neither the employees, nor what I had seen of the businesses, confirmed that they were. Our meeting was somewhat strained but I expressed a strong wish to go back at some later stage to see how they had progressed.

The irony of the situation from my point of view is that The Wakefield Shirt Group of Companies has genuinely achieved a near miracle in surviving so long and so well. They have a perfectly splendid business in the corporate clothing business, and they have inherent skills and a knowledge of the shirt business which should enable them to prosper. However, in the tough shirt business they do not have enough points of difference: the Double Two shirt business is at present depressing the results of the rest of the group. A privately owned company can withstand this for a surprisingly long period of time, and the financial strength of The Wakefield Shirt Group of Companies is superb. They have hardly any borrowings, and they have the potential financial headroom to undertake almost any course of action they might be inclined to try. The company is very strong, and the UK needs companies like that for all our sakes. I am certainly looking forward to buying and wearing Double Two shirts again, and I shall watch with great interest to see whether, when my views have been digested, the company decides to change or not. I certainly hope they do, for they are performing considerably below the potential of the business, and of its people.

I had a further meeting with Ricky Donner and David Sugden at the end of July. It was a pleasant surprise, for they had accepted far more of my points than I had expected. They had worked energetically at reducing stocks in the shirt business, and although they had decided that they must try to hold their middle of the range position in that business, they had clearly made efforts to move the whole market up, and consequently improve their margins.

In Europe they had accepted that their attack should be spearheaded by the corporate clothing businesses and not by Double Two's shirt business and, apart from exploiting any opportunities that came their way, they had made the export of shirts a lower priority. They had developed a relationship with a German firm, with whom they hoped to form an alliance, and had also looked at Italy. However, they had not liked the market there, and were now seeking opportunities in Spain instead.

Once more I cautioned them against trying too much at once, but I left feeling that my advice had been of some practical help. I felt that they had made some changes that would help put them back on course to equal – if not better – the success of the original Double Two company in its heyday.

POSTSCRIPT: JUNE 1993

Despite my initial misgivings, things really do seem to have changed at Double Two. Once Ricky had accepted that a change in his management style and his priorities would benefit the business – and that cannot have been easy – he really did take the bull by the horns.

I was delighted – and relieved – that he took my advice on the need to really *focus* their attack on Europe with the workwear. Since the programme, they have built up a relationship with a German distributor for the corporate clothing system, and orders are beginning to flow in.

They have also achieved an indirect entrée into the continental market by selling the Threadneedle system to UK-based multinational companies which have divisions in Europe, such as Thomas Cook and Ladbroke Betting, which has brought in £250,000 of new business.

Although I had recommended they select Italy as their second European market, Ricky and his managers initially opted for Spain. But due to the rapidly deteriorating economic conditions in Spain, they have switched their attentions to Holland, where two distributors have been secured for two different customer types and business has started to flow.

With the revamping of the Double Two men's range, and the acquisition of two ladieswear companies – Saveena and Refsons – the shirt business looks to have turned the corner. Double Two's turnover has risen by 25%, with a respectable 3% profit on sales.

Undoubtedly it is the corporate side of the business which is showing the most growth, and they are using this to fill any spare capacity in the factories. Double Two seems to have taken its rightful place in the hierarchy. It is no longer the overstocked member of the group and its stock turn is rapidly approaching that of the workwear and corporate clothing side. So confident is Ricky of reaching the 1994 profit targets which we discussed in our final meeting, that he has already reserved a table at the Ritz for the autumn of the year! If they do hit the figures, I shall indeed be more than delighted to buy the champagne!

CHAPTER TWO

THE TOLLEMACHE AND COBBOLD BREWERY

TROUBLE SHOOTER

The heroes of this story, Bob Wales and Brian Cowie, have bet their own money and risked their personal future stability to realize a dream: the resurrection of a traditional British brewery and a brand of beer which they love. But they face considerable odds. Both the brewery – the Cliff Brewery in Ipswich – and the beer – Tolly Cobbold – inspire fierce local loyalty and affection, but in the 1990s the British brewing business is truly in a state of turmoil and change and it is far from clear, even to the people within it, what ultimate form the business will take.

The Cliff Brewery and Tolly Cobbold beer have long East Anglian histories. In 1723 Thomas Cobbold began brewing Cobbold beer in Harwich, but the Harwich water was too brackish for his beers and by 1727 Cobbold was shipping clear spring water to Harwich by barge down the river Orwell. Cobbold's pure water supply came from the Holy Wells on an Ipswich estate owned by his family: the Cobbold brew sold well and the Cobbold family prospered. In 1746 Cobbold decided that it was no longer economic to ship the water for his beer to Harwich so he shipped his brewing business – and his family – to a site on the Cliff, beside the Holy Wells at Ipswich. There has been a brewery on the same site ever since.

Today's Cliff Brewery – a gravity fed brewery whose tall tower construction eliminates the need for pumps – was rebuilt in 1896 on what is now called the Holywell Estate on the banks of the river Orwell, and although the Holy Well no longer looks as romantic as I had hoped – it is just a hole in the ground with a fluorescent light at the bottom and its water is contaminated – it is still there and Bob and Brian own the rights of abstraction.

In 1957 the Tollemache family (a Suffolk family who became brewers in the late nineteenth century), and the Cobbold family, merged their brewing interests to form the Tollemache and Cobbold Breweries. Tolly beer was well established in Cambridge and had a national reputation. For some years the business looked set for continued expansion and a bright future.

At that time Tolly Cobbold differentiated themselves from other British breweries largely by the proportion of bottled beer which they produced which amounted to between 60%–70% of their total output, (the remaining 30%–40% was cask conditioned). And there was a constant stream of innovation: numerous new brews and different brands were developed, and many of the present owners' hopes for the future are based upon the recipes which were developed then. Tolly Cobbold expanded into pubs and off licences, and owned nearly 500 retail outlets of one sort or another, mostly in East Anglia with a few in London. The brewery remained a family business with members of both families investing in the business and working in it from offices based in Cliff House on the Holywell Estate, the house which had once been the Cobbold family home.

But since 1957 the British brewing business in general, and Tolly Cobbold in particular, have seen great changes. In the late 1960s breweries rapidly concentrated into larger and larger units – mega-breweries – as the economies of scale, and the application of modern technology to the centuries-old craft of brewing, began to make a greater impact. Brewing processes became automated and more and more elaborate systems of process control developed, so that at one stage it looked as though the ancient craft of the head brewer would disappear altogether. The new mega-breweries began to resemble chemical processing plants rather than traditional breweries, and their beer was pasteurized and delivered to the pubs in kegs. Keg beer is much easier to distribute than 'real ale' and it has a much longer shelf life. The existence of small brewers of real ale, like Tolly Cobbold, was under threat.

It was at this stage that British beer drinkers began to revolt. The Campaign for Real Ale (CAMRA) was set up in March 1971 and campaigned vigorously for a return to old fashioned natural cask conditioned beers. Real ale, or cask conditioned beer, has a very limited shelf life, and demands skill and attention on the part of the publican because it leaves the brewery live and continues to ferment inside the cask. When cask conditioned beer arrives at a pub it must be kept at a carefully controlled temperature and the publican must be experienced in order to know when the beer is ready to serve. Real ales vary because they are alive; keg beers do not because the yeast is killed by pasteurization, or other chemical processes, before the beer leaves the brewery. But devoted British beer drinkers – and CAMRA campaigners – consider real ale to be the only real drink.

There is a second, international, threat to the British real ale market. The ubiquitous lager, which originated in Germany and also has a long shelf life (lager literally means to store), has taken a near international hold. During the 1970s and 1980s the sales of lager steadily encroached on the sales of traditional British bitter and mild beers, and there appears to be a trend towards the internationalization of brewing, with a number of the mega-brewers envisaging worldwide branding and worldwide businesses.

Inexorably mega-breweries established themselves in the UK and brewing became a capital intensive business. The vast numbers of tied (or owned) houses – a peculiarly British system – which these mega-breweries now own guarantee them thousands of outlets for their beer through direct or indirect ownership of those houses. (Direct ownership is known as the tie. Indirect ownership, where the brewer lends money to the publican to enable the publican to buy the pub, is known as the loan tie.)

By the mid-1970s Tolly Cobbold simply could not compete against the mega-breweries, and in 1977 the families decided to sell out to Ellerman Lines – a shipping company looking for sources of diversification. It was to prove an unfortunate choice and a game of corporate pass the parcel ensued. For a time Ellerman Lines injected funds into the brewery and its pub estate, but the recession in shipping finally forced them to sell out. David and Frederick Barclay bought Ellerman Lines in 1983, but they saw their purchase primarily as an opportunity for a property play, and they quickly sold the Cliff Brewery to Brent Walker, George Walker's fast-expanding property and leisure group. Members of the Tollemache and Cobbold families (who had become non-executive directors of the company when it was sold to the Barclay twins) resigned when it was sold to Brent Walker and with their resignations went the history of the company. Some investment was made in the brewery but it was a time when, elsewhere in the industry, massive amounts of money were being ploughed in. Gravity fed breweries were rapidly becoming a thing of the past and the size of the batches brewed at the Cliff Brewery were uneconomic.

During this period the quality and reputation of Tolly Cobbold beers was not as high as it had been and the brands were felt by some to be trading very largely on their past reputation rather than their current quality.

The coup de grâce for Tolly Cobbold came when Brent Walker announced plans to demolish the Cliff Brewery. The brewery was operating well below capacity and Brent Walker – who had also bought the Cameron Breweries in Hartlepool from the Barclay twins – inevitably decided that it was not economic to keep the Cliff Brewery open. The Cameron Breweries were much larger than the Cliff Brewery, and more efficient, and there was enough spare capacity to swallow the Tolly production. However the Tolly Cobbold brand name still had considerable value, so Brent Walker decided to retain the brand name and transfer the brewing to the Cameron Breweries, supplying the East Anglian market with Tolly Cobbold beer brewed in Hartlepool, some 250 miles to the north.

Although there is little doubt that from a purely business point of view this was the right decision, Brent Walker severely underestimated the reaction of the East Anglian people, particularly the people of Suffolk, and the determination of some of the management of Tolly Cobbold to keep the Cliff Brewery going, if at all possible.

Bob Wales, who was then the finance director for Tolly Cobbold, and Brian Cowie, who was the sales and marketing director, were determined to save the brewery and they started trying to put together a management buy-out. In this they showed considerable courage, since management buy-outs in this sector are often difficult to achieve: Bob and Brian might well have found themselves outbid by a mega-brewery with much more cash at their disposal.

At approximately the same time, the British government, in their belief in free markets, introduced deregulation to the brewing industry as a result of a report – *The Supply of Beer,* March 1989 – which they commissioned from the Monopolies and Mergers Commission (MMC). But the deregulation was so complex and the brewing industry opposition to it so great, that a lobby of powerful brewers, backed by several MPs, succeeded in obtaining a series of compromises and the deregulation which was introduced, with much publicity about cheaper beer, more competition, and better access to different brands, has, in fact, had precisely the opposite effect. There is now an unparalleled concentration of brewing power and the industry has polarized into large groups of controlled pubs. There has also been a sharp increase in the price of beer and many small brewers and breweries have closed, or have been amalgamated into large groups which have, in turn, carried out sweeping rationalizations.

It is in this exceedingly unsettled – and apparently unfavourable – business climate that Bob and Brian are attempting to turn their dream of resurrecting the Cliff Brewery and brewing old fashioned real ales, into a reality. Brent Walker closed the Cliff Brewery on 14 July 1989, and a final Tolly Cobbold brew was made to commemorate the sad day. The local CAMRA group held a wake in a nearby pub to mourn the passing of yet another famous traditional English beer and its brewery.

At this point a piece of good fortune helped Bob and Brian. Ipswich Council had ambitious plans to redevelop Ipswich docks as a tourist and leisure centre. Tolly Cobbold's superb Victorian buildings lay right at the heart of the proposed redevelopment area and Bob and Brian had a good relationship with Ipswich Council, having already discussed ideas for buying the Cliff Brewery and developing it as a working brewery and museum. These ideas fitted beautifully with Ipswich Council's own ideas for the redevelopment of the area.

When Ipswich Council realized that Brent Walker intended to demolish the brewery they immediately listed the brewery buildings (and all the plant and machinery inside it) as Grade II. This not only prevented demolition, but also stopped any ideas Brent Walker had for redeveloping the site, forcing George Walker and his team at Brent Walker to look for buyers who would guarantee the continuing existence of the buildings – and the plant and machinery inside it – in some form or other.

This was not entirely a matter of fate smiling upon Bob and Brian. I believe that they created this piece of good fortune – or luck. Successful businessmen very often do this. Sometimes it is genuine luck, but more often what appears to be luck has been worked for and is achieved by the early recognition and nurture of potential partnerships, opportunities, and possibilities. I suspect that both Bob and Brian would have liked to go it alone if they could have done so, but in practice, without the active involvement of Ipswich Council, and numerous others in the Ipswich area, they could not hope to succeed.

When I met Bob and Brian, I thought they were an unlikely couple of partners: Bob is an entrepreneurial risk taker; Brian is more cautious and sceptical. Curiously neither originates from Suffolk, and their skills and characters appear to be as different as you could imagine. Bob Wales trained as an accountant, and he is quick-witted and voluble. He comes from the north east of England and, despite a strong streak of romanticism, he is a very practically minded man. Brian Cowie is a large Glaswegian, designed physically rather along my own lines. He is a splendid marketing man who writes poetry, and has been known to exhort his sales force in verse. He has an underlying streak of romanticism and passion, together with a dry sense of humour.

Both men are truly inspired by their dream of owning their own business and building something for the future out of the past. They agreed from the beginning that, if they were successful, they would operate as joint managing directors. This is a system that generally only works under the direction of a strong and independently minded chairman who will step in to ensure that progress is not held up through irreconcilable differences of opinion. While, in the event, they managed to find an eminently suitable chairman, in the shape of the Hon Sir

Peter Strutt, who is a member of the Tollemache family, and who therefore brings the support and continuity of one of the original brewing families with him; in practice, I discovered, Bob and Brian operate by each having a power of veto over the other. In due course this may be a limitation on Tolly Cobbold's ability to move fast. Speed of reaction is one of the in-built advantages that a small operation has. It is essential that they retain this ability if they are to take advantage of the opportunities that are opened up by the more lumbering approach of larger operations.

Now that the Tolly Cobbold brewery buildings were protected by law from demolition, George Walker began to discuss the future of the brewery with Bob and Brian in a serious way. Meanwhile Bob and Brian were working hard to find out how to set up a management buy-out. Although there are some commercial lawyers who have a great deal of experience in this area, and even though the path is such a well trodden one, constructing a deal of this sort is always more complex than it appears. Bob and Brian started reading up everything they could find on the subject and, with characteristic resourcefulness, Bob managed to obtain a copy of The Economist Intelligence Unit's publication, *The Guide To Management Buy-Outs* (published in 1991, price £85) for nothing. They followed its advice almost to the letter. The next stroke of luck was to find a really splendid firm of commercial lawyers. In this case it was indeed luck, because they thought that the lawyer's role in the buy-out would be a relatively small one. In actual fact lawyers play a much wider role in a buy-out than merely ensuring that the paperwork is correct, they often also find themselves acting as advisers, as a think tank or as a sounding board, as counsellors and as friends. The two essential ingredients for a management buy-out are good commercial lawyers and really top-flight accountants.

Bob and Brian produced their business plan almost exactly on the model of the buy-out guide. They limited the business plan to thirty pages, they produced five year financial projections, and they set out their ideas about how and why they believed they could make money out of the operation, where others had failed.

Briefly, the basic philosophy of their business plan is:

To build a future for the historic Cliff Brewery and its traditional

Tolly Cobbold beers. To aim for quality and excellence in everything they do.

and the business plan divides into three main types of operation:

1 To brew the highest quality flavoursome old fashioned cask conditioned ales and bottled ales
   (a) by using only the best natural materials, without using chemicals, additives or colourants
   (b) To increase the annual throughput from 20000 barrels a year to 80000 barrels a year
   (c) Only to supply outlets which would handle Tolly Cobbold's cask conditioned ales correctly
   (d) To develop Year Beers, using old recipes from the past
2 To develop the distribution business
   (a) To service licensed trade customers with lagers, wines, spirits, soft drinks and beers, as well as distributing Tolly Cobbold's own products, both to tied and to free trade outlets
   (b) To concentrate on the six main conurbations in East Anglia which account for one third (600000) of total East Anglian adult population
3 To develop the company assets:
   (a) by developing the Cliff Brewery as a working brewery and museum
   (b) by developing the Cliff House offices into a pub to be called The Brewery Tap

From my point of view their business plan gave me the fullest description of what they were aiming for that I have ever had from any company I have visited with *Troubleshooter*, but people who put money behind management buy-outs are a very hard headed lot. They almost always want to see a relatively swift exit route, so that they can recoup their money (as well as a nice capital gain) within a predictable time period. This was a particular problem for Bob and Brian. Unlike many managers, who go into a management buy-out with the aim of managing the business for a few years, establishing a turnaround, and leaving with a large amount of money, their ambition was to ensure that Tolly Cobbold was still running as a business well into the future. They even hoped that their families might be interested in joining the business. It would plainly be impossible to earn enough money to buy out the investors who had supported them, within a reasonable time frame. Almost immediately there was a conflict of interest between Bob and Brian on the one hand and potential capital investors on the other.

At this stage Bob and Brian thought they needed about £4m, a very large sum of money to advance to two professional managers who, apart from part ownership of their own houses, had only limited resources and also wished to retain some measure of control over whatever they set up. The clarity of their thinking helped enormously in raising the equity. Since their objective was to continue the future existence of Tolly Cobbold as an entity it was important to ensure the involvement of members of the various families, as well as some of the key publicans. They also thought it desirable to have some injection of equity from other members of the management whom they wished to be involved in the venture.

Through all of these means they managed to raise an equity capital of about £450 000, while still retaining a controlling interest of 51% between themselves. Other shareholders include Patrick Cobbold, Lord Tim Tollemache, local pub landlords, local businessmen and senior managers of the new Tollemache and Cobbold Brewery Limited. Of course there was still a massive shortfall of money to be raised if they were to have any chance at all of putting together a deal which Brent Walker would accept. They tried various British venture capitalists, but were turned down because of the risks involved in their projections. Then Brent Walker themselves introduced Bob and Brian to Svenska Handelsbanken, a Swedish bank which operates its venture capital department and lending facilities as separate organizations under a single roof. It looked as though this would be the solution to their problem, although eventually they benefited very largely from a quirk in the way in which the brewing industry finances its business: for many years brewers have lent money at beneficial rates of interest to their customers and in return those customers sell agreed quantities of the brewers' products (the loan tie). The money itself is usually supplied by a bank, which appoints the brewer to collect repayments from the customer on its behalf. This is one of those wondrous financial arrangements which seems to benefit everybody. The brewer is financed off balance sheet, and all he picks up is the bill for the amount of interest subsidy he provides for the customer, but the brewer treats this as the discount – in his accounts – that the customer would have benefited from if he was buying from the brewer free of the loan tie. Through good negotiation Bob and Brian managed to persuade Brent Walker to provide such a loan from its loan tie resource. In the event Brent Walker's loan represented over 60% of Bob's and Brian's total bank borrowing, so that their need for money from Svenska Handelsbanken was limited, and well within the limits of risk that the bank were prepared to accept.

Meetings continued with Brent Walker over a period of about three months and, perhaps propitiously, it was Christmas Eve 1989 when Bob Wales received a message from George Walker to say that they were prepared to go ahead. It must have been a very jolly Christmas, but it still took six months before the deal could actually be signed up. The arrangement was that the brewery itself would be sold to the new team, but only part of the site, although Bob and Brian had the right to lease certain parts of the site from Brent Walker. Brent Walker also undertook to take beer from the brewery for a five year period and, in addition, placed a delivery contract for distribution to the 600 Brent Walker pubs in Suffolk and Essex. Brent Walker retained a small shareholding in Tolly Cobbold, but actually acted in a very open and supportive way to Bob and Brian once the deal was done. It was not until 22 June 1990 that the joint managing directors became the half owners of the Tollemache and Cobbold Brewery Limited, and, of course, it was to be only the beginning of their travails.

Just reading what had happened so far convinced me that Bob, Brian and their team were people of unusual commitment and imagination, who had succeeded in firing the enthusiasm of their customers and of the locality. The files and newspaper reports on what had been achieved showed me the depth of emotional feeling that existed in Suffolk for the rescue attempt. This tremendous local goodwill was shown by the way that Ipswich and its inhabitants had rallied round when the brewery was threatened. The question was, were the resources adequate, particularly since they were trying to get their operation off the ground in the middle of a recession? This obviously imposed trading conditions which they could hardly have been expecting to bargain with. The numbers in Bob's and Brian's business plan had already been poured over by those who were backing the concept with their money. This gave me the comfortable feeling that I was not entering a game of blind man's bluff where I would have to ascertain the realities of the business situation. And the fact that Bob was an accountant, and that everything he had achieved had been committed to the company, gave me confidence that he was unlikely to be taking stupid financial risks.

However the irony is that in a management buy-out you have to take risks. Time is not on your side because in business time is money, with real costs, and Bob and Brian had already had a foretaste of this in the time between the closure of the brewery and before they started earning. Moreover, as well as the continuation of the recession they had suffered a setback over which they had no control. The much publicized collapse of the Brent Walker empire meant that a number of the players with whom Bob and Brian had negotiated, in particular George Walker, had disappeared from the scene. Many of the proposals which had been negotiated with Brent Walker would now have to be honoured by other people, in other organizations, and I could not be sure that they would feel the same commitment to helping the dauntless duo that Brent Walker had. As if this was not enough, they were also operating against time constraints in other ways. The lease on parts of the property was about to expire and had to be renegotiated, and the Brent Walker agreement to take beer from Tolly Cobbold was only for a five year period: although five years sounds a long time, if tied sales represent 100% of your initial business, it can be very difficult to find replacement volume in five years.

The brewery itself was in need of investment and, although there was some provision for new investment in the forward plans, I was concerned about whether it would be enough to allow them to compete in a very tough world. Although Bob and Brian have been in the brewing business for many years, they have been managers rather than principals, and now they would have to deal with the top brass of very large companies on an equal basis. None of this was going to be easy, and yet they appeared to have many of the ingredients necessary for success. Between them they had sound commercial and accountancy skills and, provided they had chosen the right head brewer, they would have technical competence as well. Above everything, their dream to build something for the future out of the past, to resurrect the brewery and to produce the highest quality old fashioned beers, certainly appealed to me and I felt it would be likely to appeal to their customers, their employees and their backers as well. Bob and Brian had involved their customers, the descendants of the founders of the brewery, and the local community in a most open and far sighted way. It was therefore with great enthusiasm that I looked forward to my first visit.

As their business plan makes clear, there are three types of operation: the production of quality cask conditioned and bottled ales; the development of the distribution business which was designed to service licensed trade customers in Brent Walker pubs and the development of company assets. Bob and Brian had a licence to brew the brands, and they had an option to purchase the brand name at the end of the third year. They had raised £3.6m to buy the Cliff Brewery and its associated buildings and they had renegotiated their agreement to supply 20 000 barrels of Tolly Cobbold beers per annum to Brent Walker pubs for a five-year period. They had also obtained Brent Walker's free trade – as opposed to tied – customer list which they could service through their own distribution system. They were aiming for a ferocious return on capital, no less than 30% – most people would be happy with a smaller return – and an average trading profit of over £1m a year. They had the support of Peter Strutt of the Tollemache family as their chairman, and their business plan made it clear that they would concentrate on the six main conurbations in East Anglia which, as well as having very fast growth, cover almost a third of the total East Anglian adult population. By concentrating overwhelmingly on these towns they would reach a large market in the most economical way possible.

The whole operation was underpinned by the supply agreement to Brent Walker, which involved selling Tolly beers into some 600 pubs for five years, until 1995, but the number of barrels this agreement represents is only a small part of the potential capacity of the Cliff

Brewery, and it is absolutely essential that free trade sales are built up at the same time. This part of the original deal was not made easier by Brent Walker's problems. However many of the Brent Walker pubs are now in the Pubmaster Estate, a separate company created to own and run Brent Walker's pubs when the Brent Walker empire collapsed, and it was the new Pubmaster management with whom Bob and Brian renegotiated their seven year agreement, so there is a reasonable chance that this agreement will remain secure.

Perhaps the most critical part of Bob's and Brian's five year plan lies in the finance and repayment schedule. Interest of approximately £450000 per annum has to be met from year one, and repayments, scheduled to begin at a rate of approximately £200000 per annum, are to start from year three. This is the closing door through which Bob and Brian have to run. Their plans involve profit contributions from both the brewing and wholesale side rising, by year four, to roughly £700000, with a contribution from the retail side as well. Plainly this whole operation is only possible with very tightly controlled central administration costs, which the two men clearly have in mind.

I was, of course, thrilled to be invited to look at the business and to see whether I could offer any help and advice. I very much admired the risks that the duo had taken, the determination they had shown and, above everything, I admired a management buy-out where the intention was not to make a quick return and get out, but where there was determination to try to grow and enhance a business which they clearly loved. However I was uncomfortably aware that their policies, and the products that they were trying to sell, were going to be in head-on competition with two of the finest makers of real ales in the area – Adnams and Greene King. The problem with a management buy-out is that time is everything. Inevitably the business is undercapitalized and tends to have over-borrowed. The management of cash and achieving profit within the time forecast is absolutely vital because there are few, if any, reserves, and failure to perform can result in very speedy closure.

On my trip to Ipswich by train I felt more confident about the rough picture I had of the business than of any other I have visited with *Troubleshooter*. Moreover I was encouraged because, as well as wanting the publicity which the *Troubleshooter* film would inevitably produce for them (publicity they could ill afford to pay for), it was apparent that Bob and Brian were actually interested in discussing their plans with somebody outside the industry.

Bob and Brian have thought their way through the forms of business they want to follow, and these were clearly laid out in their business plan. They were determined not to go into keg or lager beers and they did not wish to run their own bottling facilities. They were also determined, as far as possible, to ensure that they only supplied outlets which would handle their cask conditioned beers correctly. This is always a problem for the manufacturer of real ale. It is plainly easier to control if you own the outlets, because bad handling of real ale at the pub can severely affect the quality for which the brewer has worked so hard. But the sheer scale of resources needed to purchase their own outlets was such that they could not hope to develop in this way.

Bob and Brian were determined to restore the reputation and the quality of Tolly Cobbold's products. They deliberately sought to differentiate themselves in every possible way. They were absolutely determined that their beer should be more flavoursome than before: they would use only the best natural ingredients available and utilize 100% malt in all their brewing processes. They also decided to increase the strength of their beers by a degree or two and they carried out numerous test brews. They were helped in this process by the local pub landlords, some of whom were already shareholders, and who formed their tasting panel. It was September 1990 before they were ready for a commercial brew, and remember that during the whole of this period they were having to pay interest on their initial loan. Brent Walker had decided to shut down their own distribution department, and to transfer the responsibility to Tolly Cobbold. And, as part of the buy-out agreement with Brent Walker, Bob and Brian had agreed to manage the closure of Brent Walker's central warehouses, and to set up a new operation with drivers and warehousemen from the closed Brent Walker operation. They decided to retain just over half the Brent Walker warehouse workforce and to operate from a warehouse on the Cliff Brewery site.

By the end of September 1990, after frenetic activity, Bob and Brian had assembled a brewery team of sixty-nine, sixty-two of whom were re-employed from the old company. (Brent Walker made the entire workforce redundant when they closed the Cliff Brewery in 1989.) This new (old) team of sixty-nine constitutes the workforce that represents the future of the Tollemache and Cobbold Brewery Limited. Those who were re-employed after their redundancy the year before must have had a considerable shock when they saw the way in which the new company was to operate.

I first met Bob and Brian outside the customs house on the Ipswich docks. In many ways it was a splendidly symbolic meeting place and I thought about Thomas Cobbold shipping his pure spring water by barge along this very river. Bob and Brian were much as I had expected them to be, but in one important aspect they surprised me. I had expected to see some evidence of the weight of the responsibility they had taken on. While there was no doubt about the professionalism of their approach, they also seemed to be pacing themselves extremely sensibly. Well managed businesses are businesses which have thought through everything and are not surprised by the turn of events: these have been anticipated, and the reactions are pre-planned. Both Bob and Brian seemed to me to be thoughtful, and quite clear about what they wanted to do. They were not falling into the trap that swallows up so many businessmen: they were prepared to dedicate time to thought as well as to action. However, they did seem to want to do an awful lot of things at once. From my initial reading of their financial position I rather doubted whether all of their ambitions were achievable – and certainly not in the time frame that they envisaged. One of the problems of business is that even the best organizations need to concentrate their efforts and be very clear about their priorities.

Bob explained the financial position of the business and in particular their dream of running a working brewery museum and converting the Cliff House offices into a pub to be called The Brewery Tap. They believed that the pub would pay its way in its own right, and would also play its part in attracting tourists to the brewery itself. They were actually brewing when I arrived and I was very keen to see the brewery working. The partners speedily introduced me to Chris Gregson, their head brewer who joined the Tolly Cobbold team in early August 1990. Chris is a small man but he certainly packs a big punch. He trained originally as a biochemist and then worked his brewing apprenticeship with Grand Metropolitan. He is in his mid thirties and, as well as being a bundle of energy, plainly loves his job. The head brewer is the man who really creates the product, but in the case of the newly constituted Tollemache and Cobbold company he has to do a great deal more than that. Chris is totally dedicated to the production of real beers and has a vast experience to back his abilities. In addition to that he is running one of the smallest brewery teams in any operation in the UK which means he has to have strong leadership abilities and be willing to turn his hand to anything and everything. These are all rare attributes, but I realized that Chris had them and it was Chris who conceived the idea of going through the old recipe books and producing an annual special brew – to be known as a Year Beer – building on the historical connections of the brewery. Cobnut, an old Tolly Cobbold recipe, was Tolly's second Year Beer, successfully launched at the end of 1991.

The actual policy for brewing was clearly agreed by all three of them. They knew that they lacked the resources to compete head-on with the big boys, although the more I looked at it, their cost situation did not seem as unfavourable as I had feared. They were absolutely determined to use the best natural materials and eschewed every form of additive or colourant. They were determined to make beers in the way that they had been made in the old fashioned Tolly Cobbold brewery, and they believed that the results would speak for themselves. They were fastidious in the extreme about the raw materials they used. Indeed, when Chris showed me the hops they were using he was extremely apologetic that they were hop pellets instead of the loose variety. Hop pellets do not require the special storage conditions that loose hops require, they take up far less room than loose hops, they are easier to handle and they can be kept more or less indefinitely. It is also possible to have hop pellets made up to particular specifications. This was the closest to a compromise of their ideals that I saw during my whole tour of the brewery.

I entered the brewery passing the marvellous 1700s Cliff House – Thomas Cobbold's house – and as soon as I entered the brewery I felt wrapped up in the history of the place. One of the first things I came upon was the Holy Well itself. Because the well is contaminated the brewery has been running on the town's water supply, but they have been working on the Holy Well and have, as a sort of twinkle in their eyes, an idea that at some later stage they may be able to bottle and sell pure spring water from the Holy Well. Next to the Holy Well there was a marvellous old steam engine which used to produce power for the whole brewery. One of the men, Doug Woodgate, who was manning the boiler which now supplies the brewery with its power, had worked for ICI and I met him some years ago when I visited his works. He and his colleague Bob Gilbert represented the total maintenance force for the power supply for the whole brewery and they were prepared to turn their hands to anything.

By the time I saw the Cliff Brewery it had been lying dormant for nearly twelve months before it was recommissioned. Brent Walker helped the new Tollemache and Cobbold company to recommission the Cliff Brewery by seconding the head brewer from the Cameron Breweries to the Cliff Brewery for three months, until Bob and Brian had recruited their own head brewer. The position of head brewer is key, and Bob and Brian were lucky that they found such an inspired candidate as Chris Gregson. And I have never been inside a company where there is less division between us and them: the staff's commitment to the new company is total and so far personnel turnover has been nil. The spirit is absolutely tremendous, but so are the requirements, for the willingness to muck in is an essential part of the new way of working.

I entered the brewery building itself and started the long climb to the top, past great copper vessels and brewing paraphernalia. When we eventually reached the top of the tower I had a really clear view of the whole site. One glance showed the higgledy-piggledy way in which the place had been developed over its latter years. Any available space had been used for new plant in an apparently haphazard way: there was little logic to the whole set up. The boiler house, in particular, represented a real problem for Bob and Brian. It was stuck out on a limb of land which they leased from Brent Walker because they could not afford to buy all the land in the original management buy-out. The land lease is up for renewal and the boiler is old and energy-inefficient. Bob and Brian must decide soon whether to move the boiler and refurbish it or buy a new boiler and put it on land which they own, or renegotiate the land lease with Brent Walker leaving the (refurbished) boiler where it stands, and continue to pump power across the whole site from the boiler's present position. It is the sort of decision which in an ideal world they would be taking when they had much more operating experience, but unfortunately it is something which must be decided quite soon because of the age of the boiler and the possible pressing need to renegotiate the land lease. Chris explained to me some of the possibilities that he had been looking at and I suggested a few other approaches that could be made but there is no doubt that, whatever they do, some of their restricted cash must go into replacing the power supply to the brewery.

The sixteen people who are employed in the brewery itself are the most tremendous bunch. When they are not brewing they are painting and preparing the brewery for its future role as a working museum. The place was already beginning to show the effects of so much loving care. It was mostly surprisingly tidy and well laid out, but the antiquity of some of the plant really shook me. When we visited the copper area – where the wort (malt, water and sugars) is boiled – I saw the original eighteenth century vessels still working. The sugar vessel has been in use since 1723 and was described by the Science Museum as 'the oldest piece of bio-technology in the world.' It looked very much as it must have done in 1723. It is not difficult to see that the brewery itself comes from a bygone age. As we walked round the plant the reasons why Brent Walker had decided to shut down became clear. When we reached the fermenting room there were six vats that, as far as I could see, had not been used for many years, and five which were barely in use at the present time. However, the vats were of very varied capacities and so had considerable flexibility in the size of brew they could make. The total potential capacity of the brewery is 150 000 barrels a year but that would require additional manning and would be far outside their existing potential sales. At present they are only selling 20 000 barrels a year but with their existing team, even when they are manning their museum tours, they could reach 80 000 barrels a year at little additional expense. The key to the future of Tolly Cobbold's brewing must lie in trying to get this increased volume, but it was quite apparent that it was not going to be easy. Their salesmen are working hard to develop their off licence business, but this was moving slowly. I was immensely impressed with the people I met. Most of them had been in the business for a very long time and were as enthusiastic about the ideas for the future as Bob, Brian and Chris were.

It was when I got down to the washing and filling area that the limitations of the brewery became more apparent. The arrangements were pretty primitive and makeshift. Moreover, as I went through the brewery it was apparent that there was very little in the way of process control. Although they were so insistent upon quality it depended almost totally on the dedication of the operators and in particular of the head brewer and of the foreman, who puts the brew to bed every night in the time honoured way. For absolute consistency they will need some micro computers to test and analyse the brews automatically, but across the piece I was really quite cheered. The actual capital employed in the brewery is, by definition, very low indeed. Given the old fashioned nature of the brewery it seemed to me that their labour costs are pretty low too. This is only achieved because of the willingness of every member of the workforce to undertake every sort of job you could think of. Chris confirmed that he did not think that they were at any cost disadvantage with other organizations producing small batches. The problem, therefore, has to be to increase the throughput of the brewery to the capacity of the existing team. It is tempting to think that this could be done by contract brewing – brewing real ale on contract for other companies. I was subsequently to find out that the whole area of contract brewing, with the responsibility of trying to raise other contracts, was somewhat ill defined in Bob's and Brian's business plan. Of course if contract brewing were possible it would in any event be at a very low price because companies will not pay over the odds, but at least it would fill up the brewery and make a contribution until such time as the sales team could manage to develop their own free trade business.

In the afternoon I went to see John Artiss and the distribution business. John started his working life as a drayman and is living proof of the fact that experience can make up for any amount of theory. The distribution business seemed to me to be a lot more secure than the brewing business. The distribution business employs forty-five and is operating from leased buildings on the site, the lease on which soon expires. They have eighteen drivers, and twelve warehousemen and again their tremendous flexibility became abundantly clear. They reckoned that they could multiply their distribution business by a factor of four, and were particularly proud of the fact that they paid their delivery men on the basis of tons delivered, rather than by piecework estimates for entire jobs. This means that work completed, rather than time taken to complete work, is paid for and it gives the employees immense flexibility. All these employees are union members and it was good to see the union, the Transport and General Workers' Union (TGWU), allowing such flexibility and acting so supportively – a far cry from the popular picture of how unions work.

The delivery drivers and warehousemen were paid at a different price per ton but all pay is directly linked to throughput. John Artiss and his fellow managers all went out on delivery rounds themselves and so knew the conditions at first hand. The whole system was totally dedicated to ensuring a really good service to their customers, who could get what they wanted at quite short notice. There is no doubt in my mind that the warehouse is an extremely efficient wholesaler and distributor. John was very enthusiastic about the results of the buy-out. He thought that the new company was much more open and there was a tremendous feeling of teamwork, which you could practically touch. The drivers, supervisors and John himself all knew that their future lay in their own hands, and that no one else was going to bail them out. It was good to see just what people are capable of when they are given the opportunity and have absolute clarity about where their interests lie.

I had a lot to think about and there was a lot more to discover. I had now seen the production side of the business, but not the market end, and I was far from clear yet about what the museum idea would involve. I had a brief talk with Sheila Moll, the accountant and office manager, who joined the business from the record industry. Like all the others I had met, the head office team was willing to turn a hand to any job, and had a real sense of priorities about what they were trying to do. Bob and Brian's control of the whole operation and their indispensability was also painfully apparent. I ended the day by sitting down with them in order to hear a bit more about their plans – both on the marketing side and for the museum. They had gone to a lot of trouble to check what they could expect to charge for their museum tours and had thought hard about the attractions they could produce. They had already managed to find a number of the old pub signs and one of their employees, John Wragg, who worked in their warehouse, was an expert on local history and knew many anecdotes and legends about the pubs and the beer. Their views on the museum were that it was a means of selling the beer and they also had plans to produce a large amount of memorabilia to sell in the museum itself.

Brian had thought through the whole of his marketing strategy very carefully and had ensured that everything, including the badges on the beer pumps, supported the overall picture they were trying to project. They hoped to have 100 000 visitors a year and believed that, as well as selling more beer to the museum visitors, the museum itself would make a significant contribution to revenue. From my experience as chairman of the Wildfowl and Wetlands Trust I had some idea of the problems of running this sort of operation. I knew about the expense of ensuring that members of the public are properly looked after (paying guides, obeying by-laws and making sure that the company's responsibilities in terms of public liability are covered etc.), and I also knew what one could expect in terms of income. It seemed to me that Bob's and Brian's approach to the museum concept lacked a degree of focus. I could understand that bringing people through the brewery might be a means of selling more of their products, but I was not by any means sure that the business would be a good one in its own right.

We then talked about the marketing plan. Both Bob and Brian were convinced that they needed to buy pubs, and felt that this was a good time to contemplate a move in this direction. They had not been able to afford to buy any of Tolly Cobbold's outlets in their management buy-out. I certainly agreed that there were many pubs available on the market at the present time because, under deregulation, brewers may not own more than 2000 pubs apiece after 1 November 1992, but I was concerned about the drain of money involved. Whatever they did, Bob and I were quite clear that they must manage inside their existing monies and avoid borrowing more money at inevitably high interest rates. Prioritization of their ideas was therefore absolutely key. It seemed to me that it was essential to ensure that any proposed expenditure would either have a very quick payback or was totally critical to the future of the business. It had been a long day, and although I was fascinated with the business, I was glad to stop soaking in new impressions and have a little time to think about what I had seen.

I had arranged to meet the commercial manager of Tolly Cobbold, Keith Blyth, the following morning. He is responsible not only for the development of free trade sales, but also for the wholesaling operation, and I wanted to find out a bit more about his ambitions and ideas. I also wanted to meet one or two of the customers and publicans to see how they felt about the Tolly Cobbold products. So bright and early the following day I was at the Butt and Oyster pub, one of the UK's most celebrated waterside venues. I had known the pub from my time in East Anglia, and it was a pleasure to see how little it had changed. When I arrived Keith was already busily selling some new ideas to the publican, Dick Mainwaring. Keith was very clear about his aims. He felt that it was necessary to raise the number of customers from the existing 150 to over 500, and to try to reach a level of 35 000 barrels of free trade beer as soon as possible. The more I questioned him, however, the more apparent it became that despite the fact that he was selling an additional two to four barrels cumulatively each week, the specific advantages he was selling were so slim, and the financial limitations such that I thought it unlikely he could increase the free trade business at more than 10% per annum. Even that is a pretty ambitious plan for sustained growth in market share against tough and established competitors. A few sums on the back of an envelope showed that this would leave a considerable shortfall in the capacity of the brewery. He was very confident about the wholesaling business, but concerned at the speed at which he could develop, and he was hoping that some investment to buy their own pubs could be managed. He did not think it would be possible to develop the brand at the rate that was needed without the assistance of owned pubs.

When they were setting up the company Bob and Brian had involved a number of free trade publicans as shareholders in the company, who also sat in on the ideas for the development of the brands. The problem facing the whole marketing operation is that there really is not enough money for expensive branding, or any wholly owned pubs. Just as in everything else in this management buy-out it was a problem of making bricks without straw or, I suppose, beer without malt. We briefly discussed the prospects of exporting the beers, and agreed that at the present moment it would be too expensive and a diversion of effort. Understandably, however, Keith was extremely conscious of the strength of the East Anglian competition from Greene King and Adnams and, in particular, Greene King's distribution advantages. (Greene King are members of a consortium of East Anglian brewers who distribute their beer in London.)

The overall distribution strategy of concentrating on the six major conurbations had been carefully worked out by Keith and John, and there was certainly enough scope within the areas they were serving to reach the sort of free trade sales that were needed. But could they be made in time, especially when the whole nature of the beer business was changing, as well as the relationships between the companies and their pubs because of deregulation? But I was cheered by my meeting with Keith. He was a real professional, who had previously been a publican, and had worked for Coca Cola. He was another example of the openness of the whole team and I was impressed with the relationship between Brian and Keith. Keith defended his own area like a tiger, but I was still worried about who was actually dealing with the problem of contract brewing. It was clear that Keith himself was not, and I was not too sure how high contract brewing was on Brian's list of priorities.

I had arranged to have lunch with Roger Protz, the editor of *Brewing News*, a leading UK journalist and author, and a considerable expert on beer in his own right. He is also a spokesman for CAMRA. Since 1971 CAMRA, which began as a small group of enthusiasts wishing to protect traditional beers from the ever increasing encroachment of the big battalions, has been the most astonishing success. It is now a highly efficient organization and an acknowledged expert in its own field. Something like 15% of total beers sold in the UK are now real ales and both their availability and reputation are largely due to CAMRA's efforts. Roger and CAMRA strongly supported the management buy-out from the beginning, so I was not surprised to meet an enthusiast on the subject. Roger is very keen that Tolly Cobbold should continue to increase their range of real ales, and in particular that they should use some of the historic names that were used in the past. He believed that contract brewing for larger organizations should be possible, particularly for those who did not find it economical to meet the rather more limited demands that existed for the sort of products that Tolly Cobbold were already making.

Roger also thought that it might be possible for Tolly Cobbold to brew special beers directly for some of the new pub chains which were now being set up independently of the breweries, as a result of deregulation and the breaking of the tie. He also strongly advocated the need for outlets in Cambridge, which had always been the historic home for Tolly beers, and he thought they should have some outlets in London. He felt that Tolly Cobbold needed flagship pubs of their own if they were to succeed, although he did understand their current financial limitations on this front. Roger is a tremendous and lively enthusiast for beer, and a fountain of bright ideas. I was delighted to see how well he and Keith got on. Before lunch I did a bit of random market research myself in the Butt and Oyster to see what the locals felt about the new Tolly Cobbold beers. I was encouraged to discover high levels of enthusiasm for the products.

I ended the day with a further list of queries in my mind. There seemed to be a general consensus that ownership of their own pub outlets was essential, and yet I was sure that they could not afford the capital involved. I was confident that the distribution business was soundly based but they needed to watch it very closely, because it could very well represent the banker for their total operation. I was still doubtful about the position of the museum concept and I was concerned about the problems of filling the brewery to its current potential capacity of 80 000 barrels a year. Even with the renewed Brent Walker contract they were still a long way short of total capacity and if they were to make serious money out of the brewery they should be brewing and selling amounts which were nearer to their total capacity. I felt that everything needed to be moving much more quickly than it was at the present time. I was ever conscious that they were already more than half way through the three year period when they have to start to repay the capital, as well as meeting the interest payments. I had ascertained that, in their second year, they were managing to make a modest profit after paying interest, which was good news, and their cash control was well within the limitations they had set themselves.

I decided that I needed to talk to someone who could give me a broad unbiased picture of the current state of the brewing industry. I therefore went to the brewing capital of the UK, Burton-on-Trent, to talk to Don Marshall of Allied Breweries. I chose Allied because they had taken over some of Brent Walker's interests and they had experience of running a brewery museum. Even though I had expected to see a brewery museum, it was still quite a shock to see Allied's brewery laid out for brewery tours with a number of boutiques selling memorabilia and so on. The brewery has, of course, been fully modernized, and it has an enormous capacity, so they were not offering quite the same historic brewing perspective that Tolly Cobbold were hoping to provide. But just a glance at the operation showed the scale of the competition that Bob and Brian were taking on.

When I met Don I was impressed and cheered at the relationship between Allied Breweries and Tolly Cobbold, and the goodwill that Bob and Brian had engendered. Don has been in the business all his life, and a walk through their sampling room showed the tremendous range of products which Allied Breweries produce, all of which represent competition, in one form or another, for my friends at Tolly Cobbold. I wanted to check a number of points with Don. Firstly, he was very strongly of the view that Tolly Cobbold needed to invest in distribution, and that there they had a real competitive advantage. He knew the brewery and he felt that in order to ensure consistency of quality, which was absolutely key to all their futures, they would need to invest in computer brewing controls and microbiological testing. Such controls would certainly, in his view, be required if they were to obtain any opportunities for contract brewing: to reassure contract customers of the consistency of the brews. He strongly supported the idea that they should not attempt to go outside the real ale business.

But he too felt that they needed outlets in Cambridge and in London if they were to succeed. He was pretty scathing about the museum idea. He claimed that Allied Breweries had never made money from selling their memorabilia and brewery tours, and that it was viewed purely as a loss leader in order to sell the products. Moreover, the nature of the brewery tours was such that they attracted very little in the way of repeat business. Once people had seen a brewery they had seen one, and that was that. But Don was anxious to help Tolly Cobbold and he was confident that their 20 000 barrel a year commitment could be met.

I left the day cheered that my analysis was more or less on line, but I was still wrestling with the problem of the pubs. It was nearly time to go back and see Bob and Brian and to tell them what my views were. As luck would have it I had the opportunity of meeting them aboard a converted Thames barge. These barges have always been a fascination of mine and after the war I wanted to spend my war service gratuity on one. In those days a barge was purchasable for about £150, but I knew that my naval career would take me away for most of the time, and it would be difficult for me to look after a boat adequately, so sadly I did not buy one. Years later I have made up – to some degree – for lost time by joining the Thames Barge Society, but I still hanker after one of these beautiful vessels for myself. Bob and Brian had been discussing ideas with the barge owners who ply the river Orwell, to try to link the barges in some way with the historic brewery concept. Although the barge we were on was marvellous, the weather was appalling. It was bitterly cold and the wind was blowing a treat, so that while the barge motored majestically along we huddled around the stove in what would have been the hold in the barge's trading days.

It was good to see Bob and Brian again and they were both full of enthusiasm and conviction. I started by summarizing their opportunities and saying how much I admired their determination to run the business and to ensure that it had a future. I told them how impressed I was with the way that they had set up the business: how they had involved both their customers and their home market, as well as maintaining a high profile with low expenditure. I explained my concern that they had to successfully negotiate the time trap until they started to repay the capital successfully. I explained that I felt that some of their decisions could have been sharper. However I gave them better than a 50% chance of success which, for a management buy-out, were very high odds indeed (see table below). But it seemed to me to be absolutely essential that they were much clearer about their priorities and their spending than they had been, and I said that the distribution business should have absolute priority over everything else, both in terms of attention, and available money. I was worried that because it was doing relatively well on its own, it would not get its share of management attention. If all else failed, and their brave attempt at the brewing and the leisure business did not succeed, I was sure that the distribution business could continue to stand on its own feet, as long as it was run professionally. I therefore felt that it had to occupy a higher place in everyone's thinking than it had at the present time, indeed it should become their single most important objective.

UK MBO SUCCESS/FAILURE

Year of MBO	Success (exited)		Intermediate (not exited)		Failure		Total	
	No	%	No	%	No	%	No	%
1982	64	27.0	156	65.8	17	7.2	237	100.0
1983	129	54.9	87	37.0	19	8.1	235	100.0
1984	75	31.6	145	61.2	17	7.2	237	100.0
1985	69	26.2	174	66.2	20	7.6	263	100.0
1986	70	22.2	221	70.2	24	7.6	315	100.0
1987	73	21.2	228	66.3	43	12.5	344	100.0
1988	44	11.8	284	75.7	47	12.5	375	100.0
1989	18	4.8	300	80.4	55	14.7	373	100.0
1990	10	2.1	427	88.0	48	9.9	485	100.0
1991	4	0.9	433	97.3	8	1.8	445	100.0

Note: Success (exited) defined as trade sale, float or MBO; intermediate (not exited) defined as 25% refinancings and those which have either exited successfully or not gone into receivership; failure defined as receivership and 75% of known refinancings

Source: Centre for Management Buy-Out Research (University of Nottingham)/BDCL/Touche Ross

The next priority for investment should be whatever was necessary to maintain the brewing operation. We had already discussed the boiler replacement and I had also discussed it with Chris Gregson. I suggested a number of possible opportunities for replacing the boiler at relatively low capital expense. But in addition to focusing on the problem of the boiler they also had to find the money to put in better computer control systems, so that consistency of strength and quality could be maintained. This involved more investment in computers than they had at the present time. This investment in brewing is essential to attract contract customers and so achieve their marketing strategy of filling the 80000 barrel a year current potential capacity of the Cliff Brewery.

I also explained my concerns about the museum concept. Experience elsewhere was not encouraging, and I felt that they should minimize expenditure in this area. I did not feel that the project was likely to be a source of profit in its own right. If they looked upon it as a loss leader for selling the beer, as Allied Breweries do, then I felt that they should compare the cost of that loss with other ways of achieving the same objective. They were so far down the line with The Brewery Tap that I felt that this should go ahead. Indeed they were starting work on it that week, but I believed that thereafter the whole proposition was high risk. I had a number of minor proposals of things which they could do to enhance their opportunities there, but I still believed that the leisure business had to prove itself and that they could well find that it was more of an expense than they supposed. Lastly, in terms of capital expenditure, I was convinced that they could not afford to invest in buying pubs. However I did believe that there were opportunities for leasing, and that the leasing could be carried out in such a way that the leases were able to pay their own way. I had been advised throughout that they needed flagship outlets in East Anglia, but I was convinced that this should not be done through any call on their capital capacity.

Turning to the marketing plans I believed that the overwhelming problem was to fill up the brewery profitably to its current potential 80000 barrels a year. I accepted that it was most unlikely they could build the free trade business up by more than 10% compound, and I thought it essential that next time – 1995 – that the 20000 barrel contract with Pubmaster comes up for renewal, they should try to extend both the period of the contract, and the quantity, if possible. Contract brewing should ideally only be sought in the real ale area, because the Cliff Brewery is only equipped to brew real ale, and it seemed to me that there might be opportunities for contract brewing for some of the new groupings of pubs resulting from the dismantling of the tie under deregulation. However, I believed that they needed more clarity about who was responsible for negotiating the contract brewing, and that this should form a larger part of Brian's responsibility. Everybody I had spoken to was enthusiastic that Tolly Cobbold expand into Cambridge, both in terms of distribution and as an outlet for new brews of beer. There was strong support for the idea of trying to relaunch the old Cantab and Cardinal brands for Cambridge, using their original recipes, as well as possibly trying porter. A number of the people I spoke to believed it was desirable for Tolly Cobbold to have a presence in London, either through a leased pub, or perhaps through ensuring that their beers were for sale at some of the London railway stations. Both Bob and Brian reacted fairly strongly against this proposition; they said that in the past it had been a very expensive operation for very little reward, and now they felt that it would be difficult to service London adequately and that distribution would be too expensive. They also worried about not being able to ensure the correct handling for their cask conditioned ales from a distance. They are, however, looking at the possibility of having a partner in London, which would remove these obstacles.

Turning back to the leisure business I thought that, given that they were committed to trying it, they might look at a number of other minor frills on the basic operation. Perhaps they should set up a club called 'the friends of the Tolly Brewery', to build upon the high level of local enthusiasm and support, and perhaps offer discounts on bottled beers to members. It seemed to me to be highly desirable to establish the brewery. and The Brewery Tap, as a meeting place for local Rotary Clubs, Chambers of Commerce etc., and they should make sure that they had facilities for handling that size of group if they were to be successful. I told them about a suggestion that they spend some money on publicity on local radio, but I personally felt that the present policy of trying to get exposure through the local press, by a constant stream of interesting and newsworthy stories, was both more effective and, in terms of availability of cash, a better use of their limited resources.

Lastly I told them that I believed they needed a slogan or a better sales pitch than they had so far devised, for both the brewery tours and for the beers. I said that they must make sure that this slogan or sales pitch underlined the fact that they were producing old fashioned beers in the traditional way. Something like 'yesterday's real ales from one of the last real breweries' seemed to me to be the sort of line they should aim for. This was, after all, the reality of their position: they were producing real ales in a traditional brewery in the traditional way and I felt that they should make more of a virtue of this, both in the labelling on their bottles, and as a consistent slogan which ran through everything, including the museum tours.

Bob and Brian seemed to accept many of these points, and said they would go away and think about them. Bob confirmed that, although they were trading at a modest profit (after paying interest) at the present time, this was before the major capital expenditure programmes which they would have to begin the following year. However both of them expressed their continuing conviction, confidence and commitment to what they were doing. They and their people are just the sort of business people I admire. They are taking very big risks and backing their judgment with everything they have. Their people are with them, and every man and woman in Tolly Cobbold understands what they are fighting for. They are trying to turn round a business which has been pawed over by too many people who have not had the future of the business or the retention of our heritage in mind. The Tollemache and Cobbold Brewery Limited deserves success and I am pretty sure that, if their success depends on the people of Suffolk, they have every opportunity of preserving the Cliff Brewery, and of brewing real ales for a long time to come; and I am sure that they can look forward positively to a great celebration in 1996 to commemorate 250 years of brewing, since 1746, on the site of the Cliff Brewery beside the Holy Wells at Ipswich.

A postscript: The Brewery Tap opened to an enthusiastic Suffolk public in the week of 22 June 1992, exactly two years after Bob and Brian signed their management buy-out agreement and became joint managing directors of the Tollemache and Cobbold Brewery Limited. And the official launch of the Cliff Brewery as both an operating brewery and a working museum is on schedule for the autumn of 1992. Bob and Brian asked me to open the brewery tours on 16 September 1992, which I was delighted to do.

There are challenges ahead for the Tollemache and Cobbold Brewery Limited, and I am not entirely convinced that Bob and Brian feel the need , as urgently as I do, to fill the brewery to its 80 000 barrel per annum capacity. Filling this capacity is the key to their future and it will set their business on a secure footing. If they manage to achieve this capacity, and I am the first to recognize that it's not going to be easy, I would give them an evens chance of success. They deserve to do well, particularly because their plans (and their dreams) are long term ones which have to do with the preservation of our heritage as well as the future of one of our oldest businesses.

POSTSCRIPT: JUNE 1993

Since autumn 1992, Tolly Cobbold have gone from strength to strength. Despite my misgivings, the brewery tours have turned out to be a huge success – by spring 1993 more than 10,000 visitors had passed through the doors, and on current form they expect to have received nigh on 18,000 by the end of the first year. Ipswich council has even laid on a special bus service from the city centre – the 'Ipswich Tolly Bus' – which takes in the newly created heritage trail around the Docks area followed by a tour of the brewery – culminating, needless to say, in The Brewery Tap pub. They have actually had to expand the pub to cope with demand.

Sadly, a major brewing contract still eludes Tolly Cobbold. The good news though is that Brian has secured a number of small-scale contracts brewing own-label beers for local pubs and clubs – Ipswich Labour Club now boasts its own 'Red Rose Bitter', brewed by Tolly! They have also negotiated a small export order for their bottled beers in Italy.

One of the most exciting developments for me personally was the launch in April 1993 of their new premium bitter – 'Tollyshooter: the beer that means business!' I was delighted to attend the formal launch – for better or for worse, it is I who grace the Tollyshooter label! With characteristic enterprise and ingenuity, Bob and Brian arranged the occasion to coincide with my sixty-ninth birthday – and even laid on a demonstration of hand silk-tie painting in my honour! In the event, they sold out of the first batch of Tollyshooter within a few days, and had to do an emergency brew. They expect to sell some 5,000 barrels a year, which will be a real boost towards that elusive 20,000 barrels that will make the brewery really cost-efficient.

Meanwhile the wholesale and drinks distribution business has continued to expand – they are now selling into London and Kent, and are sole distributors for the newly created Carlsberg Tetley group in the East Anglia area.

I have enormous admiration for Bob and Brian, who, despite my initial concerns, have managed to turn their dream into a reality, without losing sight of the harsh truths of running one's own business. In the end, it seems, the heart has inspired, but the head has prevailed. I am certain old Tom Cobbold would have approved.

CHAPTER THREE

THE BRADFORD HOSPITALS TRUST

TROUBLE SHOOTER

The UK's National Health Service (NHS) is undergoing its most fundamental change since its birth in 1948. Decision-making in the NHS has become a byzantine process and waiting lists for treatment are very long, so the government, believing that market forces would encourage efficiency in hospital management and administration, proposed the creation of an NHS internal market in 1989. The internal market separates hospitals, who become the providers of health care, from district health authorities and family doctors, who become the purchasers of health care, thus creating competition between health care providers for customers, or purchasers, and inevitably making the providers provide a quicker, more efficient, health care service. The more efficient the health care the providers provide, the more patients (and therefore money) the providers will attract, or, in the government's phrase 'money [will] follow the patient'.

At least that was the idea. But at the hospitals trust I visited with the *Troubleshooter* team, it seemed that they were treating more and more patients for less and less money. The government's idea for creating an NHS internal market seemed to me to be such a good one: I was curious to find out why it wasn't working in practice.

Hospitals were invited to apply for self-managing hospital trust status to establish the NHS internal market and, to qualify, they were required to meet criteria laid down by the Department of Health in the government white paper 'Working for Patients', published in January 1989. Trust status was granted to those applicants who showed – among other things – that they would establish a local board of directors, the vast majority of whom would be the consultants themselves. This clinical board would take local management decisions and so simplify decision-making. Applicants were also required to show that they would establish a new financial regime, taking over responsibility for their own financial affairs from the district health authorities, and that they would become directly responsible for providing cost-effective health care services to their customers, or purchasers. The hospitals would no longer report to the district health authority, but directly to the Department of Health, and they would compete for contracts for patient care from their local doctors and district health authorities.

As I have said, these all seemed to me to be steps in the right direction, but there was considerable controversy, both within the medical profession and in media and political circles, about the concept of trust status for hospitals. In Bradford, the home of the hospitals trust I visited, the majority of consultants voted in a ballot against going for trust status. And in a public opinion poll, the citizens of Bradford also voted against going for trust status. However, in April 1991, the Bradford hospitals group was granted trust status, becoming the Bradford Hospitals Trust. Why, you may ask, if the majority of consultants and public were against it? Because the drive to go for trust status came largely from the general manager of the Bradford District Health Authority, Dr Mark Baker – whom I knew from my days as chancellor at Bradford university. He is an extremely dynamic, hard-driving, rather autocratic manager. He believed that being one of the first group of hospitals to form a trust would give them much greater access to funds and support than they could expect from the normal NHS funding systems. Dr Baker pushed the idea through, against considerable opposition, and he became chief executive of the Bradford Hospitals Trust in April 1991.

Before I visited the Bradford Hospitals Trust, I read a copy of their trust application prospectus to the Department of Health and I have to say that it made pretty inspiring reading. It obviously had the same effect on the Minister of Health and I was not surprised that their application was accepted. However it quickly became clear that Bradford's trust application was much stronger on words and promises than on numbers and financial planning. The trust is a considerable business with a turnover of something like £84m per annum, and fixed assets on the balance sheet of around £71m. But despite the size of the business, the trust faces very real problems. Like much of the NHS, the hospitals in the trust have been starved of capital.

The main hospital of the four in the Bradford Hospitals Trust is the Bradford Royal Infirmary which was opened in 1827, and moved to its present site in 1937. The second hospital is St Luke's, built in 1850 and used as a military hospital during the First World War. St Luke's has changed radically since the 1930s; it is currently undergoing a major redevelopment programme, more of which later. The third hospital is Bierley Hall Hospital, built for the military during the First World War. A new hospital was built at Bierley Hall in the mid-1960s and it is now primarily a psycho-geriatric hospital. These three hospitals are in central Bradford. The Bradford Royal Infirmary and St Luke's provide 1052 general beds and 267 maternity beds between them, and Bierley Hall provides 111 beds. The fourth hospital in the trust is Woodlands Orthopaedic Hospital which was built in 1877 and became an orthopaedic hospital in 1954. Woodlands has 94 beds and is fully equipped with operating theatres and an x-ray department, but it is seven or eight miles outside Bradford and so not particularly handy for Bradford's citizens. Woodlands is also a training school for student nurses.

Studies of the funding of health care throughout the world show the UK's NHS in the top echelon of economic health providers, but as far as I can see there isn't a country in the world which has, yet, resolved the problem of guaranteeing its people access to relevant health care, without running into horrendous funding and management problems. The NHS is caught in an inexorable squeeze between advances in medical technology, and the rising expectations of its customers for standards of health care. Overall economic growth has slowed down and, although the funds provided to maintain the NHS are going up in real terms, they continuously fall short of what is needed. By any international standard the NHS – and therefore the hospital trusts – is underfunded. Comparisons show that a smaller proportion of the UK's gross national product goes on health care than in America, Holland, Germany and France.

As I read the trust document I wondered about the proposed management structure which did not clearly illustrate reporting lines and accountabilities, however it did make provision for the introduction of a clinical services board, which I have long believed desirable in hospitals, consisting of fourteen clinical directors (consultants and doctors who represent all the fields of medical activity), a director of nursing and site managers. The intention seemed to be to focus on the clinical operation of the hospital, rather than the administration, and that certainly cheered me greatly.

The management task in health care is one of the most difficult and complex. Although, in theory, everyone is entitled to the most effective treatment that is technically available at any given moment, in practice the supply is limited. Even if the money was available, the facilities and specialists are always in short supply. Whether we are comfortable with the concept or not, the reality of health care is that it is a rationed system. Decisions are continually being made, both on an individual and on a general basis, about how the available sums of money can best be spent to achieve the overall objectives of continually improving the health of the country. Many people have argued that the NHS – the National Health Service – is a misnomer, and that it should be called the NIS – the National Illness Service – because it is primarily concerned with the curing of sick people rather than the prevention of sickness in the first place. Maintaining the balance between funds spent on primary (non-hospital, community based) health care and on acute (hospital) health care is just one example of the invidious choices that have to be made within the management of the NHS.

When I visited the Shropshire District Health Authority during the first *Troubleshooter* series in 1989, I witnessed the NHS management decision-making process: it is like swimming through treacle. It takes so much effort, determination and faith to try to change anything, or to move in any proactive way, that all but the very best, and the most determined, give up the unequal struggle. Of course, the advantage of swimming through treacle is that it is difficult to sink but, because movement is virtually impossible, a sort of crystallized preservation of the status quo is inevitable. So it is not really surprising that many managers settle for maintaining the status quo. This is never a satisfactory situation for any manager in any business, and least of all in health care, where both the technology and the outside environment and expectations are changing at an ever accelerating pace. Moreover the NHS suffers in another respect. Although the demand for care is created by the health of the population, the way in which that demand is met is controlled, very largely, by the decisions of vast numbers of doctors. These doctors take individual decisions about what is best for their particular patients, often without clear knowlege of either the costs, or the availability, of the treatments that they prescribe.

However I also discovered, while visiting the Shropshire District Health Authority, that for many years now UK doctors and surgeons have wanted to be actively involved with the problems of NHS management and administration, rather than remaining aloof from them. They know their involvement is essential in order to provide the sort of service they wish to provide. The clinical services board at the Bradford Hospitals Trust should ensure that doctors are deeply involved in the decisions which so critically affect their own ability to function and, because the doctors are involved, the decisions should be taken much more quickly and the standards of service to which the doctors are so obviously dedicated should be more easily maintained.

The NHS has a genuine need for the best in sensitive, skilled management and, as in most public services, hospitals need to have a sort of licence of support and trust from their patients – their customers – if they are to be able to manage their affairs. Bearing in mind that it takes at least five years to qualify as a doctor in the UK, it is not surprising that those in the medical profession do not feel that there is any spare time to spend on management training. Many of them feel that management is something that anybody can do and that management training is unnecessary. Of course management does not require as long a period of training as medicine, but the idea that management can be undertaken by anyone, of any background, without study, preparation, training and practical experience, is almost as ludicrous as the idea that any passer-by could be summoned from the street to carry out a complex heart operation. Management is an art, and a rare one at that. Just as most of medicine is about dealing with people and their physical and mental problems, so management is about gaining the freely given commitment of groups of people to achieve pre-determined goals. The essence of management is that it must be going somewhere. It is not about the maintenance of the status quo, but about achieving change and continuous improvement.

But I have yet to meet a doctor who does not consider his profession to be a calling, and who does not want to achieve the highest possible standards for his patients. Doctors, like all of us, want to be proud of the organizations they work for and they want those organizations to be effective. The NHS inspires fierce loyalty from its staff and its doctors and fierce emotions from its customers, who are, after all, the people who pay for the service. There can be very few doctors who have taken any pleasure from the parliamentary wrangling over the NHS that has occurred in recent years, although the reality of the provision of medical treatment in the UK seems to me to be substantially better than the picture that is so often painted in the press and in political circles. Trust status should help redefine hospital management and make it more efficient.

There was quite a fuss about the hospital trusts when they were first proposed, and I dimly remembered hearing about an investigation into the Bradford and Guys and Lewisham Hospitals Trusts by the House of Commons Health Committee, so I also read a copy of the Health Committee's investigation document. The investigation into the Bradford Hospitals Trust was sparked off by the announcement, in May 1991, of 300 job cuts and the need to reduce costs by £7m over the next three years. The announcement hit the headlines and Dr Mark Baker was summoned to give evidence to what seemed to me to be extremely hostile questioning from the House of Commons Health Committee. But I am bound to say that my enthusiasm on reading the trust status application prospectus was speedily dispelled when I read the minutes of the evidence. In the first place Dr Baker continually stressed his lack of financial expertise, and the committee took him severely to task for putting in an application which they thought was hopelessly financially over optimistic. Moreover, the Health Committee enquiry drew attention to an apparent mismatch between the plans for the Bradford Hospitals Trust and the intentions of the Bradford Health Authority. The Bradford Hospitals Trust was an acute (hospital care) services trust only. They planned to establish a separate primary (non-hospital, community based care) services trust at a later date. The Bradford Health Authority made it clear that they wished to restrict their expenditure on acute health care in order to try and tackle the problems on the primary level.

Dr Baker resigned his position as chief executive of the Bradford Hospitals Trust in December 1991, just seven months after his grilling at the House of Commons. He went to work for the Yorkshire Health Authority. Few anticipated this change and, together with the problems of capital funding, and the over optimistic figures in Bradford's trust application, the Bradford Hospitals Trust was in trouble almost before it began.

The figures produced about the health of the Bradfordians are pretty horrific. The trust's catchment population is 400000 and there are 310000 visits to the hospitals each year, although it must be said that many of those visits are by the same patient for a course of treatment. Bradford suffers a 17% higher rate of hospitalization than comparable areas elsewhere in England and Wales, and the statistics for infant mortality, heart disease and lung cancer are among the highest in the country. It is apparent that the Bradfordians are not winning the healthy living race.

All in all my preparations for my visit to the Bradford Hospitals Trust left me wondering what I would find. But I was delighted that the trust was in Bradford. I am very fond of Bradford. In my six years as chancellor of Bradford university I had plenty of opportunity to get to know the area and the warmth, pride and involvement of the people of Bradford in the welfare of their city. Bradford university is very much a part of its city, even though only a small proportion of the students come from Bradford itself. The university boasts one of the best pharmacy departments in the country and we developed joint research programmes with the Bradford Royal Infirmary in certain critical areas of health care. I also had some personal experience of Bradford Royal Infirmary. One of my colleagues at the university was treated at the hospital for what proved to be a terminal illness, and I saw, at first hand, the care, skill and devotion with which my colleague was cared for.

Bradford has struggled to cope with almost every form of misfortune that could occur in a major city. Basic industry has largely gone. The days when Bradford and the Bradford wool exchange were the centre of the textile world are long past. And Bradford is a very mixed community: it has acted as a welcoming haven to refugees, or people seeking to better themselves, for more than a century and a half. The inhabitants of Bradford hail from almost every nation in the world: of a total population of 340 000, approximately 20% are from ethnic minority groups.

I knew that Mark Baker had been instrumental in my visit to the Bradford Hospitals Trust. He suggested to Rodney Walker, the chairman of the trust, that I should be invited to assist the trust. It was apparent that the optimistic picture painted in the application for trust status had not materialized. I wondered what I would find in terms of morale and commitment to the trust when I met the people, and I wondered whether the promises of more freedom of operation and access to capital had materialized. It did not take me long to find out.

In January 1992, two weeks after Mark Baker's departure, I paid my first visit to the Bradford Royal Infirmary where I met David Froggatt, director of clinical services, who was acting chief executive until a permanent replacement for Mark Baker was found. I expected to find a man battered and bowed by the responsibilities of unexpectedly running the troubled trust, but instead he appeared to be brimming with confidence. I immediately felt that David was good news, he has a very realistic attitude. David gave me a picture of the overall loading of the trust: it employs 110 consultants – 34 of whom are surgeons who carry out 30 000 operations a year – as well as dealing with 100 000 calls in the accident and emergency departments. Demand increased last year (1991), and the trust felt that they were being asked to carry out more operations – by the health authority – for a smaller amount of money.

David took me to meet Basil Gray, an old friend of mine, who was just about to retire as the director in charge of the trust's seventeen operating theatres. Basil immediately lightened my spirits by the openness of his approach, and his enthusiasm for the things that the trust had already enabled them to do. He particularly wanted me to see the new lithotripter, a machine which breaks up kidney stones by ultrasound technology. By squeezing expenses in other areas, the trust had just managed to buy the lithotripter. Quite apart from the improvement from the patient's point of view (an operation with this machine blasts the kidney stones from outside the body and so does not involve intrusive surgery, thereby avoiding much pain and discomfort to the patient), the savings that the lithotripter made for the trust were dramatic. The lithotripter cost £750000, but patients only need to spend one day in hospital, instead of the normal twelve days for a kidney stone operation. But I was not being shown the lithotripter just to marvel at the machine – the most modern of its kind in the UK – or the savings it made in terms of fewer beds occupied and therefore shorter waiting lists for this operation: the trust had gone one step further. They had bought a lorry so that the lithotripter could be hired out to other hospitals. By these means they thought that the lithotripter would pay for itself within five years. It is difficult to think of a better example of how, when imagination and initiative are allowed the sort of freedom that trust status brings, original and cost-effective ideas can be realized. I saw many others during the day.

Basil described how the trust was performing more and more operations inside a day for all sorts of conditions which had previously taken significantly longer, and therefore been a drain on the hospitals' resources. Since setting up as a trust the Bradford Royal Infirmary had introduced day hernia operations and I thought that they handled the approach to the patient with outstanding sensitivity and understanding. Each patient is nominated a personal care nurse, who calls on them at their home two days before the operation to explain exactly what is involved. The personal care nurse is also responsible for follow-up visits after the operation, and these nurses man a twenty-four hour hotline so that anybody who wants advice, reassurance or attention can ring in at any time of the day or night. I asked how many times the hotline had been used so far, and was told only twice, and that both times the enquiry had been of a routine nature. Basil explained that one of the problems was to convince patients that being treated as an outpatient was not a way of giving them less care and saving money for the hospital, but for their own good: less time on the operating table and less time in a hospital means a quicker recovery for the patient. And it was plainly more efficient for everyone, as well as being more pleasant for the patient, to convalesce at home, rather than in a hospital ward. Nevertheless hospital wards are associated with proper care in people's minds, and Basil knew that it was necessary to ensure that the patients did not feel that they were being fobbed off with inferior service, and less attention, purely so that the trust could meet its financial objectives. It seemed to me that this idea, and other ideas I heard throughout the day, was sound on clinical and financial grounds, but I wondered about the way the trust was – or was not – communicating the good news to its patients.

During the morning I met consultant after consultant, all bubbling over with ideas about ways to improve the service and to cut costs. I met Charles Vize, an ear, nose and throat (ENT) consultant, who was looking for £1m to create a dedicated day case unit for ENT and ophthalmology. He was convinced that the waiting lists for ENT and eye treatment could be eliminated by the use of day surgery, as indeed had already happened with the hernia operations and the lithotripter. At the moment only 6%–7% of ENT operations are day cases, but Charles Vize thought that the trust could perform 50% day case surgery with a dedicated day case unit.

Then I met Shaun Brown, director of resource management in the x-ray department. He was looking for £750000 for an angiography machine. This is a machine which takes x-ray pictures of blood vessels – after they have been injected with a dye – and it is particularly used for detecting blocks in the blood supply to and from the heart. At the moment the Bradford Health Authority have awarded the contract for coronary angiography work to the United Leeds Hosptials Trust, and Bradfordians who need angiograms are being sent to Leeds because the Leeds Trust has an angiography machine. If Shaun could raise the necessary £750000, he would have a chance of competing for this contract from the Bradford Health Authority. The contract is worth £350 000 per annum.

Most of Shaun's existing machinery is hopelessly out of date, and always breaking down, to the extent that the x-ray department is often the bottleneck which delays all sorts of other treatments.

There is no doubt that the Bradford Hospitals Trust has earned the commitment of all the consultants I met. It has also been responsible for a very welcome release of entrepreneurial spirit, and a host of ideas for utilizing existing skills and facilities to provide a better, more efficient and cheaper service to the patients. The snag is that in order to use these skills at their most effective, money, albeit in relatively small amounts, is necessary, and I began to wonder how well the promise to trusts of greater financial freedoms was working out.

I went to see St Luke's, which is very different from the Bradford Royal Infirmary. St Luke's, as I mentioned before, was chosen as the site for the development of a brand new hospital. Phase one of the redevelopment plan was to build new wards: this is going ahead and will be completed shortly. The problem is that phase two of the redevelopment plan, which was to build links between the new wards and the operating theatres, has been cancelled. The original plan was to demolish the old St Luke's entirely, but the trust was unable to raise the necessary capital from the NHS Management Executive (NHSME) in London. The NHSME is the body responsible for sanctioning capital released to hospitals trusts. In an attempt to cut costs, a number of savings were made during construction of the new hospital, such as foregoing the double glazing. I thought this a short sighted economy. The new unit at St Luke's will provide 200 beds, but 200 beds which at some stage will need considerable additional capital expenditure because of the original economies. Consistency of direction, and capital injection are the keys for the future, but so far the trust had not managed to persuade the NHSME to provide the necessary funds, despite the fact that this was one of the very advantages promised to trust status hospitals by the government. The trust's External Financing Limit (EFL) – which is set annually by the NHSME and is the maximum amount of borrowing that any trust is allowed in any one year – was £11.6m for the financial year 1991/1992 and £12.5m for

1992/1993. The St Luke's redevelopment programme needs £8.2m to complete the first phase. But an extra £1.5m has had to be found, out of the total capital programme for 1992/1993, to enable the new wards at St Luke's to be linked with the operating theatres and the rest of the hospital.

I started my visit to St Luke's by meeting David Sharpe, senior consultant in plastic surgery. I have met him before, through Bradford university's involvement with St Luke's burns unit, following the Bradford football disaster in May 1985, when 56 people died in a fire caused by rubbish igniting beneath one of the wooden stands. It is difficult to see how anybody could operate in more primitive conditions than David Sharpe and his colleagues. The building which houses the operating theatres at St Luke's is 200 yards from the buildings which house the wards, so that when patients are taken from their hospital beds to the operating theatres they have to travel outside on trolleys, often in cold temperatures, lying under plastic sheeting to protect them from the elements.

David was also very concerned about the inconsistencies of the trust management. He had clashed severely with Mark Baker when Mark gave permission to appoint a third plastic surgeon, and then cancelled the appointment at interview. After Mark Baker left, David was given permission to recruit a further plastic surgeon. Unfortunately he has been unable to recruit anyone since then. News about Mark Baker's behaviour had flashed around plastic surgery units like lightning.

David was very concerned about his chances of attracting good quality people to the unit after this debacle, even though plastic surgery has been one of the stars of St Luke's and indeed St Luke's burns unit is famous throughout the UK. It has established radically improved and innovative forms of treatment. David explained that he was so concerned about his unit's relationship with its chief executive that, had Mark Baker not resigned, David would have seriously considered applying for his whole unit to move to the neighbouring hospitals trust at Leeds. Leading consultants can shift their centres of operation just as university professors can, but until now I had not appreciated how fierce the competition for the best services actually is.

I left David, suitably depressed by the sight of the operating conditions at St Luke's hospital, to meet Philip Bickford Smith, one of Bradford's consultant anaesthetists. Philip was one of the leaders of the opposition to trust status. Philip was so concerned about the application for trust status that he and a number of his colleagues called in management consultants to report on Bradford's trust application prospectus. The management consultants concluded in their report that although the application for trust status was encouraging because of its emphasis on quality and patient satisfaction, it contained no analysis of demand and appeared 'to rest on the assumption that the health authority and/or other purchasers will be willing and able to buy all the services offered . . . [this] . . . is a significant weakness'. The management consultants' report also said that 'the willingness and ability [of the purchasers] to pay the required prices for the services on offer has not been tested'. The management consultants concluded that the trust application was seriously over optimistic. But even though a majority of the trust's medical consultants voted against going for trust status, the application was pushed through by Mark Baker. I was quite relieved, therefore, to find that Philip's attitude, now that trust status was a fact, was very much that what had happened had happened, and they must make the best of it.

Philip was the first to accept that bureaucracy under the trust had been reduced, even though some of it had merely changed and there was still too much paperwork, but he was concerned about the quality of management and administration. The main thing that he talked about, and the point about which I was becoming increasingly concerned, was the availability of capital. The trust concept was sold to the consultants largely on the basis that more capital would be available to enable them to make the changes which they thought necessary in order to operate more efficiently. Indeed Mark Baker believed that hospital costs could be contained, and reduced, by using modern technology, and I had already seen a number of such examples. But the difficulty is that this only works if capital is actually forthcoming. So far in my short visit I had met a number of people who believed that money would be made available for their own particular projects, and even the most cursory glance around the hospitals showed the enormous additional needs which had not, so far, been tackled.

Maureen Woods, one of the nursing sisters and Bradford's representative of the Royal College of Nursing, put yet another perspective on things. She and her colleagues felt that the overall result of trust status was to place ever increasing pressure upon them to do more with less. They were now very short of nurses, but the numbers of directors and business managers had multiplied. The nurses were still, as always, doing their best to keep things going, but Maureen felt that there was not enough willingness to listen to their particular problems and pressures.

I then met David Dawson who replaced Basil Gray as director of the trust's seventeen operating theatres. David felt that there was a lack of strategic direction in the trust: that there were lots of good ideas, but no one to co-ordinate them. He said that because demand for anaesthetic services had increased, but the number of anaesthetists had not, something like 200 potential operating lists were lost in 1991 (approximately 800–900 operations), which meant that people expecting operations went through the trauma of preparing themselves for their operations only to have the operation deferred at the very last minute.

David was yet another individual with plans for easing the load on hospital beds and operating theatres. He had cleared space for a day surgery unit which he thought would cost £300 000 a year and handle 10 000 cases a year, with very low running costs. Compared to the average costs of operating, this represents an enormous saving, as well as a great improvement in the service provided. But David raised a spectre: the poor relationship between the Bradford District Health Authority and the hospitals trust itself. Although the hospitals trust was, in theory, free to seek business wherever they wanted, in practice 90% of the trust's income comes from the Bradford District Health Authority itself (the remaining 10% comes from family doctors), and the health authority wants the trust to cut costs, and at the same time expects them to undertake more and more work. The trust was heading for an over expenditure in 1991/1992, and it was far from clear where the extra money would come from. David felt that the trust's policies and those of the health authority were diametrically opposed, and that

Mark Baker had pushed his way through. Since the district health authority represents the customer, this seems a rather curious way to try to obtain the customer's support, which is obviously essential if the trust is to succeed.

Although the original concept was that money would follow the patient, the Bradford District Health Authority was still insisting on negotiating block contracts for work. From the trust's point of view the problem is that the actual level of work has exceeded the level contracted for by the authority by about 10%. The trust accepted responsibility for something like half the extra costs involved, by increasing productivity and making cost improvements, but the trust wants the authority to reimburse it for the other half. The authority claims that the trust is so badly run that their figures are incorrect and so they will not meet the other half of the trust's claimed shortfall for 1991/1992. The contract between the health authority and the trust for 1992/1993 has still not been signed because the two cannot agree. The health authority want the same volume of work as in 1991/1992 for 2% less money and the trust want to negotiate a cost and volume contract (as set out in the government's original white paper for hospital trusts), ie, to be paid for the work they actually do rather than working a block contract which does not itemize work required.

The health authority does not believe the basis on which the trust's figures are produced. There is, therefore, both a difference on the macro as well as on the micro level, and both sides are constantly squaring up to each other and repeating their arguments with greater and greater force, rather than trying to build bridges. I was gradually beginning to understand, rather more clearly, some of the reasons for Mark Baker's resignation.

It was when I met Peter Fitton, the trust's finance director, that my doubts really began to surface. The first point to emerge during a fair amount of questioning was that, in reality, the management accounts were neither up to date, nor particularly accurate. No one was really clear what the over-run on expenditure would be during 1991/1992. A common misconception of the position of the trusts is that they are expected to make a profit, in fact the reverse is the case. They are merely obliged to ensure that they break even, year on year. Of course the results of an over-run have to be funded from somewhere, and the old system where the district health authority delved into its back pocket to make up the deficit, while administering a corrective slap on the wrist, has long since gone. It is of the greatest possible importance therefore, both from the management point of view and also to help the new trust's relationship with its primary purchaser – the health authority – that an accurate trend of costs is available to the management.

The capital investment position was even more difficult. Despite the evidence to the House of Commons by the Department of Health that 'NHS Trusts are free to acquire, own and dispose of assets, make their own case for capital development direct to the NHSME, and borrow money within agreed limits, primarily for new building and equipment and for up-grading existing buildings', the reality of these freedoms has proved largely non-existent. Bradford's External Financing Limit (EFL) set by the NHSME for 1992/1993 exceeds the EFL set for 1991/1992 by a mere 8%, or £900 000, and St Luke's alone needs £15m a year to bring its buildings and equipment back up to scratch. It seemed to me that the money spent on the new hospital at St Luke's would have produced far greater results if it had been spent on updating the older hospitals, including the old St Luke's. Although the housekeeping at the hospitals is excellent and the standards of cleanliness and general appearance are high, no amount of love and attention can disguise the fact that the buildings themselves are old fashioned, and that there is a shortage of modern equipment.

In fairness, access to capital has always been extraordinarily difficult within the NHS and, despite the fact that most capital programmes require consistency of application over a long period of time, those in the NHS have been done largely on a year by year basis, but everybody concerned knows the rules, and ways can be found of indicating agreement to longer term investment strategies. However, with the advent of the hospital trusts, the NHSME was applying the Treasury rules rigidly. It is now extremely difficult to convince the NHSME that you have a case for long term capital development, and agreements to borrow money have been withheld because of the NHSME's fear of breaching the public sector borrowing limits. The trust's very means of salvation has disappeared into the sand.

It seems to me that financially my friends in the Bradford Hospitals Trust are suffering on both counts: they cannot persuade the NHSME to release long term capital and they are involved in a no win argument over revenue with their primary customer – the Bradford District Health Authority – and they have neither the facts nor the support to fight their way through. Their strategy is to try to buy their way out of these restrictions by judicious capital expenditure to improve their services and their productivity, while access to long term capital is denied. But it is far from clear whether, even if they can sell some of the assets at their command, the money realized from the sale of those assets would be available to them to ease the capital restrictions they are suffering in other areas, or whether that money would disappear straight back into the Treasury.

My sympathy for the scale of the trust's management problems was growing, although I found it incredible that the management accounts were still so poor after the trust had been operating for over a year. Trying to run any organization without immediate and relevant accounting information is like trying to play blind man's bluff when drunk. I had some experience of the opacity of NHS accountancy systems from my visit to the Shropshire District Health Authority, but I fully expected that a major difference between health authorities and hospitals trusts would be clear, simple, timely and transparent accounts. The reality of the position which faced the managers of the Bradford Hospitals Trust was that, while they had a hazy idea of the costs of beds, there was virtually no activity cost available to them, and the actual costs achieved against the budget forecast became available so long after the event that it was almost impossible to take remedial action. Peter Fitton was extremely helpful and produced plenty of paper, but the basic data which would enable me to form a simple, but accurate, overview of the activities of the trust's operations was simply not available.

Amongst the documents that I was given was the trust's development plan for the next two years, and I was somewhat alarmed to see that a number of the projects which the various consultants had described to me on my visits to the hospitals, were not included in the development plan. It seemed likely that many of the clinical directors were expecting to obtain the same money as last year, and that disappointment, wasted effort and disillusion was an inevitable consequence. I asked how the development plan and strategy of the trust were co-ordinated with the Bradford District Health Authority, but because the two are in such conflict at the moment they are not planning anything together, which is a disastrous state of affairs.

I asked Peter if he could let me have some information on bed costs at the various hospitals, and received a large amount of information about occupancy but nothing on direct costs. Almost any request for simple financial information produced a substantial amount of data but no real answers. Even with the aid of imagination and ingenuity this information was difficult to boil down into the facts which are necessary in order to make cost comparisons between alternatives. In the absence of firm data to work with I decided to continue the visit, and to look at the various other activities of the trust so that I could formulate some views about what the problems were, and what might be done.

In March 1992, I went to see the other two hospitals in the trust: Woodlands Orthopaedic and Bierley Hall. At Bierley Hall they had just completed renovations to the psycho-geriatric wards, only to be told by the Bradford Health Authority that they hadn't got the contract for psycho-geriatric patients. This contract went to another trust, which has yet to build a psycho-geriatric ward. This to me was yet another example of the total failure of communication between the hospitals trust and its primary customer.

At Woodlands hospital I discovered that operations were being cancelled because the number of senior anaesthetists that the trust can employ is limited, and only senior anaesthetists can work at Woodlands because it is an isolated site. It is too far from Bradford for a junior anaesthetist, who must have instant access to a senior colleague, should the need arise. There was also a huge ward with only two children in it.

I went to talk to the health reporter, Clare Walker, on Bradford's *Telegraph & Argus* to find out how the trust was looked upon by the citizens of Bradford – the majority of whom had originally voted against going for trust status. The *Telegraph & Argus* is an absolutely splendid paper, which is usually constructively helpful to the cause of Bradford as a whole. It was unfailingly helpful to us at the university, although naturally quick to criticize if we did stupid things. It is generous in its acknowledgement of efforts to put things right, has a large circulation in the Bradford area, and vast influence with the population at large. The *Telegraph & Argus* sees itself playing a key and constructive role in the creation of a better future for Bradford and its people. Clare Walker told me that during Mark Baker's period as chief executive little good news from the trust reached the community, and she also told me that the community felt that the trust had not delivered, that nothing had changed since the days before the trust and that everything was at a standstill.

I knew that David Jackson had been appointed chief executive of the trust in March 1992. David was director of hospital services at the United Leeds Hospitals Trust, before he came to the Bradford Hospitals Trust. I waited a couple of weeks for him to settle in, and then I went back to Bradford to visit him. I wanted to hear his views on the problems facing the trust.

I began my meeting with David by saying that I felt that the good news was that all the consultants I had met, most of whom had originally opposed going for trust status, were now highly motivated to make the trust succeed. The bad news, however, was that the trust's capital requirements are enormous and are not being met, and the accountancy situation caused me a great deal of concern, not least because it did not seem to me that there was any sense of urgency about trying to make the accounting system better, quicker and more relevant.

I then told David that I thought communication both inside and outside the trust was appalling and that public relations were extremely sour. I discovered that one of David's top priorities was better public relations for the trust. David knew how bad the trust's public image was and he intended to tackle these problems immediately. David also told me that the waiting lists for ear nose and throat patients, far from being cut, were so long that patients were being bussed sixty miles to Grimsby. David said that none of the consultants whom I met previously had received any of the money they thought they would get, and, worst of all, the trust was still at loggerheads with its prime purchaser, the Bradford District Health Authority. I said that something must be done about this terrible relationship.

I then decided that I would find out for myself how the health authority felt about the trust, so I went to talk to Philip Hewitson, the general manager of the Bradford District Health Authority. Philip told me that he thought that the trust's overspend in 1991/1992 was due to poor management and that the trust, although they claimed the opposite, were not doing more work than the health authority had contracted them for. He said that although there may have been some increase in activity, it was in very low cost areas which the Bradford Health Authority had paid the trust for already. Philip did not think that the authority owed the trust, but the trust, due to poor management, had got their numbers wrong.

I said that the trust and the health authority must pull together if the trust was to have a chance, and Philip said that he was meeting David Jackson every week, whereas meetings with Mark Baker had been rare events. This, at least, was encouraging.

I thought about what Philip Hewitson had said and at the next possible opportunity I went back for my final meeting with David Jackson and Rodney Walker, about ten days later. I needed to know whether Rodney Walker, the chairman of the trust, was as concerned as I was about various areas of the management of the trust and I needed a better idea of the relationship between the trust and the public from Rodney's point of view, and in particular, his view of the trust's relationship with the Bradford Health Authority.

Despite my concerns about the number of things that needed to be done, on balance I still thought that the movement towards trust status and away from direct health authority control was helpful, if only because of the tremendous support and involvement of the doctors and the medical staff I met. I suspected that the problems with the nurses were as much ones of clarity of communication and explanation as anything else, and even the nurses who, as always, bore the brunt of the pressures of change, still supported the overall trust concept. These are precious advantages to start with, but I wondered how long they would endure if the management failed to capitalize on the current goodwill and instead destroyed confidence by failing to deliver what they had apparently promised.

Rodney told me that most of the freedoms promised when hospitals were being encouraged to apply for trust status were illusory. I suggested that someone from the trust should talk to the Department of Health to tell them about the trust's problems. And then I told Rodney and David what I saw as the trust's problems. First of all I said that their accountancy system was hopeless and so they were steering completely blind. If the trust doesn't know where it is – financially – going, and by how much it is overspent, how can it expect the Bradford Health Authority or the NHSME to believe it when it puts in requests for payment for extra work, or more capital. This must be sorted out.

Secondly I said that the management structure of the trust was not good. It appeared that under Mark Baker the structure had been set up in great big vertical tiers with very little sideways communication between the different clinical directors and specialisms. The managers seemed to me to work inside watertight compartments without communicating with each other.

Thirdly I said that the capital situation was terrible, but it would be bound to remain so until the trust itself knew what its financial position really was. And fourthly and finally, I said that they must formulate and agree a strategy between them: the clinical directors must be involved, information must be pooled and a strategy drawn up with some believable numbers in it. Then this strategy must be sold with all possible zeal to the health authority and to the NHSME. The dreadful relationship with the health authority MUST be improved, and could, I felt sure, be improved with proper numbers, management and strategy. I also felt that ultimately they would have to rationalize and close the two smaller hospitals, Woodlands and Bierley Hall.

Then I gave them a chance to tell me their side of the story. They told me that they had £3m capital to spend and I suggested that they use it to establish a new management system to encourage and reward consultants for achieving objectives set in the new strategy: for instance why not reward consultants who come in on budget by giving them extra capital to spend on equipment which, in the long run, will save the trust money: equipment such as Shaun's angiography machine.

David Jackson told me that their finances were now in better shape. The finance director, Peter Fitton, had been replaced by a new finance director, Peter Ward, and for the first time since the trust was set up, decent financial figures were available and they had a much better idea of their financial position. And they were already setting about changing the management structure of the trust. Managers are now talking to each other and co-ordinating activities.

I was impressed and pleased to hear about these improvements, but, above everything, however, I pointed out the absolute necessity for them to agree their forward strategies with their primary customers. The fact that the Bradford District Health Authority was seeking to shift resources into primary health care meant that the trust's strategy must reflect that change. Moreover, it was quite useless to have a strategy which involved improving productivity through use of capital, unless you were certain that such capital would be made available. The starting point of all this must be a better link between the customer and the trust management, and a strategy which was realistically linked to the amounts of money which could be raised.

At the time of my final meeting with Rodney Walker and David Jackson, the general election campaign was under way. Understandably both of them were in some doubt as to whether they would be in a position to carry forward my ideas, or, indeed, their own, after the election. I was left with the feeling that, as always in public sector activities, everything depended on David's ability as a manager to ensure that all the various parties involved pulled in the same direction – something that Mark Baker had singularly failed to achieve. Organizations need people like Mark Baker to shake up their thinking, and to create new ideas, but ultimately management is about clarity of intention, realism and getting people moving in the same direction for the same common aim. I hope, for the sake of the people of Bradford, that the new team are more successful at this than the old one was.

POSTSCRIPT: JUNE 1993

Following the victory of the Conservatives at the General Election the executives of the Trust began to move towards the idea that the Trust should close down not two, but three out of their four hospitals and put all their resources into building and running one large hospital for the people of Bradford. This idea was given a bit of a boost by the discovery in early summer that, owing to new EC health and safety regulations, they were going to have to spend around £50m just bringing their existing stock up to a minimum standard. If you're going to have to spend £50m just to prop up the existing system, why not use that money in a more radical way?

The initial idea was to close down Woodlands, Bierley Hall and St Luke's, and put all their resources into their main hospital, the Royal Infirmary. But they rapidly discovered that it would be difficult to obtain planning permission to make the necessary expansion at the Royal Infirmary site. They therefore decided that the only logical thing to do would be to demolish the ageing buildings at St Luke's and build a new 800 bed hospital on the site at an estimated cost of £100m. They have received permission from the Department of Health to pursue this idea and are currently waiting to hear from the Treasury if they will actually get the money.

CHAPTER FOUR

THE CHARLES LETTS
GROUP

TROUBLE
SHOOTER

Very few family companies survive for 200 years, and even fewer whose names are synonymous with their product. Just as Hoover is the generic term for a carpet sweeper, so Letts is the generic term for a diary. John Letts established a stationery business in the City of London in 1796, and published the world's first printed diary in 1812. John Letts' printed diaries were designed for particular customers: amongst them the merchant traders of the City of London. The information section at the beginning of the diaries invariably included tide tables so that the merchant traders could look up the movement of ships to and from the Port of London. And because the diaries were printed for the first time, future, as well as past, events could be recorded.

There is still a firm called Charles Letts & Co Limited, and they still produce diaries. Indeed, they are now one of the world's largest producers of quality diaries and they still design diaries with particular customers in mind: sports diaries, children's diaries and academic year diaries, to name just three. However Charles Letts hit the bumpers in 1990: the results for the year to 31 January 1991 showed a loss of £4m on a turnover of £29m, and the loss was incurred despite a relatively small drop in turnover accompanied by a much larger decrease in margins – almost 10%. The Letts Annual Report for the year ending 31 January 1991 made pretty sorry reading:

	1988*	1989*	1990*	1991*
	£000	£000	£000	£000
Turnover	25 574	28 006	29 010	28 784
Retained profit or (loss)	286	316	248	(3970)

* year end 31 January

The diary business has characteristics which qualify it for trouble in times of high interest rates. In my capacity as chairman of the board of *The Economist*, I have gained some understanding of the difficulties of running a successful diary business: the prime selling time for diaries is very short but diary manufacturers produce diaries all year round. There have been attempts to print dateless diaries, six-monthly diaries, and diaries that run on something other than an annual basis, but the great majority of diaries are sold just before the end of one year, and quickly discarded at the end of the next. The cost of carrying the necessary stock until the money from this annual splurge materializes has gone up considerably over the years, and so I was not surprised to discover that Charles Letts, for all its proud history dating back to 1796, was in difficulties in the 1990s.

The present generation of the Letts family have, for some time, been trying to find ways of entering other fields of business to offset the inevitably cyclical pattern of the diary business. The overall UK market for diaries is declining and although there could be opportunities overseas, the UK market is changing fast, and is already heavily saturated. Letts current UK market share is around 30%, and even with constant innovation it would be difficult for them to increase their share. So diversification held the key to growth and to balancing the seasonal nature of the diary business. In 1980 Letts had what I consider to be a pretty inspired idea. They asked Lancaster university to help them work out ideas for diversification. The university suggested that they publish educational books, and in particular a series of revision guides. There cannot be a parent or grandparent who has not bought and, in many cases, studied, these revision guides in preparation for their child's GCSE and A level exams. Every student needs help when revising for exams: Letts had discovered a modest gold mine and, with moderate updating, the products would sell for years.

Letts then set about diversifying into other areas of publishing. In 1982 they began distributing the Berlitz travel guides, and in 1987 they acquired the exclusive rights to the Berlitz travel guide UK distribution franchise. In 1990 they recruited the dynamic Carole Saunders to help them start up a general books business. Carole has considerable publishing experience and was very clear about what she wanted to do. Her aim was to produce full colour books with a long selling life which would, in her view, benefit from the Letts brand name. Charles Letts Publishing now produce – among others – books on cookery, craft and design, gardening and health, pocket guides to flora and fauna, and the Ivanhoe guides which demystify an industry or a profession: for instance there is an Ivanhoe guide to management consultants and one which explains the intricacies of the legal profession. Carole has set up a clear house style and targeted her books very carefully.

Quite plainly what contributed to Letts' dive from profit to loss in 1990 was that their attempts to diversify had been caught by the recession and high interest rates, and a number of diversifications had not yet had time to prove their worth. It was a generally difficult year anyway, and as if these problems were not enough, Letts' 1990 diary sales to the Middle East – worth £1m – were severely reduced when Iraq invaded Kuwait in August 1990. Diaries destined for Kuwait and the Gulf – worth £500 000 – were already printed, and printed in Arabic, so the stock could not be diverted to other world markets. This was a serious loss for Letts, particularly as the balance sheet showed every sign that the company was undercapitalized already. Their capital and reserves have almost halved between 1990 and 1991. I was beginning to understand why Letts were keen to take part in the *Troubleshooter* series.

When disaster struck, the family did not stand idly by. They took a number of very sensible actions to address the cost structure of the group, and managed to reduce costs by about 13%. However, reducing costs never has an instant effect. It almost always costs immediate money to reduce staff numbers, and it takes time to realize the savings which new ways of organizing things produce. And Letts, which prides itself both on its longevity and its relationship with its people, was not simply going to fire its employees, so the cost of reducing numbers was high. They also had to find ways of raising capital in the short term.

The trouble with this situation is that the businesses you can most easily sell are almost always the businesses you really want to hold on to. It must have cost the Letts family a tremendous amount of agonizing to face up to the inevitability of selling the jewel in their crown. However, needs must when the devil drives, and to their credit the family bravely faced the facts and sold the revision guides – their educational books business – for a very handy capital injection of £3.75m in July 1991. This enabled them to keep going. The educational books business had grown steadily since 1980 until it had a turnover of £2.6m and was making a substantial contribution to profits. Together with their extremely efficient finance director, Peter Casben, Letts refinanced the company, albeit at some considerable potential future cost. I did not find out until later the full extent of the overhang of debt which they were going to have to trade themselves out of, and it was only when I began to talk to people inside the company that I fully appreciated the problems they were facing.

Publishing books in the UK is a nightmare occupation: Dr Frank Fishwick writes in *The Bookseller* of 21 February 1992 that the UK's market for books is approximately one-fifth the size of the US market, but in 1991 the UK published just over 67700 new titles and new editions against the US's 48000 (approximate figure). The Publishers Association points out that the US figures exclude translations and unchanged reprints, but even bearing that in mind the figures show that the UK publishes more books for a significantly smaller market. And publishers face stiff competition for the attention of the reader from videos, newspapers and magazines, television and radio. As if that's not enough, the cost of producing books has moved sharply downwards in relative terms, and so the break even point for a new book is comparatively low. It is very easy for a publisher to enter the business, and so too many products chase too small a market. However, even in the darkest nights there are always flashes of light, and the really big bestsellers make vast amounts of money, both for their publishers and for their authors. Similarly, books which become standard reference works will always sell.

I decided to see how Letts' products sold in the shops. I went to a bookshop in Ipswich which deals extensively with Letts' products, both diaries and books. Although I went to the bookshop in April 1992, they were almost completely sold out of 1992 diaries. Woe betide the unhappy man or woman who lost a diary, or had not had the forethought to buy one earlier. When I looked at Letts' general books I saw that other well known publishers were producing competing books on practically all the subjects which Letts covered. Letts' books are good quality and competitively priced, but I did not think that they had enough points of difference to distinguish them substantially from their competitors.

I arranged to meet Anthony Letts, the chairman of the Charles Letts group, at Mayfair Trunks Limited in Shepherd's Market, London. Mayfair Trunks Limited is a retail outlet which Letts bought in 1990. Anthony is a sixth generation member of the Letts family, and he is as proud and knowledgeable about the history and background of the Charles Letts group as you would expect. He studied economics at Cambridge, winning the Adam Smith prize in 1958, and he studied industrial administration at Yale university. He is an extremely nice man and was prepared to be very open about the company and look some uncomfortable facts in the face. When the going is tough, cherished dreams and hopes have to be jettisoned, and in order to make the correct decisions it is necessary to be ruthlessly honest in the analysis of what has gone wrong. Since those who are making the analysis are more often than not those who have made the mistakes, it takes a particularly open mind to draw the right conclusions, especially in a family business when the business is as close to your heart as another member of the family. Mistakes are not usually made because of ineptitude, but more frequently because a view is taken of the future which, in practice, never comes to pass. There are plenty of excuses for the many businessmen who have made misjudgments in the late 1980s and early 1990s. It is very difficult indeed to forecast when steady growth will plunge into serious decline. It is all too easy to be caught off balance, with finances weakened by the first stages of an investment which would have been wholly appropriate if things had gone as originally predicted. The Charles Letts group was caught off balance in 1990 and so, I judged, was Mayfair Trunks Limited. The Letts family correctly concluded that one of their strengths lay in the brand name and the history of the company. The marketing of brands is more of an art than a science. It is fortunately an art at which the British have demonstrated considerable skills. Whether it be in the field of quality pipes, such as Dunhill, or natural skin care products, such as The Body Shop, British companies have managed, over the past years, to create superb worldwide businesses on the back of famous brand names. However, brand names do not sell themselves. They must be continuously kept up to date, and there must be constant investment in advertising, design, and renewal of the products, so that the whole concept, while benefiting from the past, remains appropriate to the present and ready for the future. For companies like Letts, investment in branding is the equivalent of investment in research and development for chemical and pharmaceutical companies. Up to date, influential brands are today's fuel for tomorrow's business.

The purchase of Mayfair Trunks Limited was an investment in branding to solidify Charles Letts' up market position, with the Japanese and American markets particularly in mind. The shop is elegant and breathes quality. I was full of admiration for the elegant lettering and design, which I later found permeated all Charles Letts' products. Mayfair Trunks is a small, exclusive business which has developed an enviable reputation for selling and repairing high quality luggage. The company is the possessor of a royal warrant, that most sought after sign of a quality supplier. After all, if it's good enough for the royal household, it should be good enough for anyone else. I know a little of the difficulties of obtaining a royal warrant since, after many years of effort, ICI obtained its first warrant during my period of chairmanship. We were all intensely proud to have achieved the warrant, and it greatly stimulated us to maintain the quality of our products and services.

Mayfair Trunks Limited's sales breakdown is: 40% luggage, 50% gifts and small leather goods, and 10% stationery. The snag with Mayfair Trunks is that it is losing a significant amount of money. When Letts bought it, it really needed a turnover of £250 000 plus per annum to break even, but sales during the tough years of 1990 and 1991 have been closer to £120000. To make matters worse, only about 5% of all the goods sold in Mayfair Trunks originate from Letts, although some of these have now achieved international distribution. The goods that I saw were entirely consistent with the image that Letts want to project, but while I applauded the consistency of approach, I wondered whether the effect generated by the possession of the shop could justify the current losses.

Anthony thought that the shop could break even within two years, if the long heralded economic upturn occurred, but I was uneasy. It is notoriously dangerous to rely on a change in economic circumstances to dig a business out of a hole. Even a really large business can do very little to affect the overall economic situation of a country, so you are relying on something which you cannot control. Invariably the only recipe for salvation is to tackle the things which you can control, and it seemed to me that the future of Mayfair Trunks Limited should be a major area for attention.

However, it was too early to start looking for solutions. I needed to know how Anthony thought they had got themselves into their present position, and what he thought they should do to fight their way clear towards a bright future. We left Mayfair Trunks Limited and continued our discussion in a pleasant French restaurant, L'Artiste Muscle, immediately opposite Charles Letts' shop. Over a glass of wine Anthony told me what he thought had happened to the Charles Letts group. He blamed the situation almost entirely on four external financial events which had occurred simultaneously and which were completely out of Letts' control. First, the recession had reduced the level of sales when Letts had geared themselves up for an increase and second, interest rates had soared, significantly affecting the seasonal diary business which manufactures much of its product well in advance of sales. Third, North American turnover, which in a good year represents 25% of the company's total turnover, was adversely affected by the substantially lower value of the dollar when converted back into sterling and fourth, the Iraqi invasion of Kuwait halved Letts' diary sales to the Middle Eastern market. At the same time as these cruel blows of fate were raining down, their costs had run away, and it seemed fairly obvious that a measure of control had been lost.

When they realized that these disasters were about to hit them they rationalized their structure – in November 1990 – into three main operating activities, each headed by a managing director who joined the board of Charles Letts (Holdings) Limited. The three main operating activities now are: Charles Letts & Co Limited, the book and diary publishing company; Charles Letts (Scotland), responsible for manufacturing and distribution; and Letts of London Limited, responsible for marketing and distribution in North America. Anthony's brother Martin is non-executive chairman of Charles Letts (Scotland) where Letts' manufacturing, printing, binding and distribution businesses are housed in their factory at Dalkeith, near Edinburgh.

Letts are relying on the Dalkeith factory for vital cost reductions to get the business back on an even keel. But offsetting the vast amounts of money which were pouring out of the business was such an urgent requirement that they could not wait for the benefits of cost cutting to seep through gradually, and it was then that they reluctantly decided to sell the educational books business. At the same time they sold the firm's long established, old fashioned London headquarters in Southwark and bought offices in Parkgate Road, near Battersea Bridge, London. Profiting from the excess of commercial property available in London at that time, they managed to negotiate a reverse premium and a rent-free period in Parkgate Road.

Anthony explained that he was still looking for some less seasonal business to counter the intrinsic financial problems of diary manufacturing. But he was anxious to hold on to the other parts of his publishing business and the company had, in his view, attacked their costs pretty ruthlessly, reducing them by something like £2m. When they sold their old fashioned London headquarters they had taken the opportunity to cut the number of employees. Now there are only seventy people employed in London, representing corporate management, the publishing department and the marketing team.

They are undertaking a fundamental reappraisal of their sales and marketing philosophy, and they know that they must close the gap between production and sales of their diaries. They also feel that they have concentrated too much on the UK diary market, and failed adequately to exploit opportunities overseas. They decided to move

David Hall, president of Letts of London Limited, in America, to the UK. David built up a really profitable business for Letts in North America, and part of his new job is to look at other areas of the world where he can emulate his achievement in North America. Anthony was also full of hope for Japan, which was proving to be a very profitable market, and where they enjoyed the quality image which accompanies good margins. Unfortunately Letts' total turnover in Japan is still under £500000. Anthony explained some of the forces governing the UK diary industry: independent booksellers and retailers are moving out of the diary business, and large corporate buyers are pushing their own label products in preference to the branded ones.

The following day I went to Charles Letts's smart new Parkgate Road offices, which are modern, airy and very much in keeping with the image that Letts want to project. Anthony Letts greeted me and speedily handed me over to David Hall. David is a professional marketing man with varied experience, including a period with Guinness, an excellent alma mater for anyone interested in branding and selling. David had just been appointed group sales and marketing director. I asked him how he felt about the prospects for growth. He explained that he was confident that business could be improved internationally and in North America. The sales breakdown for the year ending January 1992 looks like this:

February 1991 – January 1992

	UK	North America	International	TOTAL
DIARIES	£12.5m	£7m	£3m	£22.5m
PUBLISHING				
Berlitz	£2m			£2m
Books	£3m			£3m
PRINTING &				
BINDING	£2m			£2m
			TOTAL SALES:	£29.5m

In North America they had branched out from their basic diary business into other areas of corporate gifts and 'recognition' products. David explained that their real strength was their access to large corporate customers through the diary business, so they had developed various products which could be grafted on to the basic diary business. They were now selling a whole range of record books; awards in glass, marble and wood; manuscript scrolls and timepieces; and a range of leather goods, all of which are increasingly in demand because companies are trying to find non-monetary ways to recognize and reward special employee achievement. Letts of London Limited, in America, were producing beautifully lettered certificates, sometimes on vellum, which were given to top salesmen at sales conferences, and golfing or fishing record books which could be given to valued customers in the same way that diaries are traditionally given. All these products had to be top quality and beautifully designed if they were to achieve one of Letts' prime objectives: to spread the business.

David told me that the company's peak level of borrowing, which lasted a month, had reached nearly £14m. This seemed to me an horrific figure when set against the undercapitalization of the company. David did not think there was much future in trying to increase the UK diary market share. He felt that the cost and effort involved in trying to increase the business beyond their current market share of around 30% was almost certainly better deployed elsewhere. He seemed to have thought quite realistically about the various market options available to Letts, and I was impressed by his positive attitude. However, when I asked who was responsible for profit on individual orders, I was shocked to find that David's sales and marketing team was responsible for maximizing revenue, but not profit on each order. As far as I could see, no one had clear profit responsibility for individual orders.

In an attempt to maximize the money they could make from the assets which the group realized in 1990, they had changed to a system of throughput costing. There was a general view that it was proving helpful in changing their strategic direction. Without doubt the difficulty with throughput as a measurement is that although it maximizes return on a marginal basis, it is not a very good guide from a strategic point of view. I've seen dozens of companies where the sales team are supposed to increase revenues and the manufacturers are supposed to reduce costs, but in my experience profit does not fall out of the middle unless each person is individually responsible for profit on each and every one of his orders. Throughput optimizes cash, but not necessarily profit. But I still had not met Peter Casben, the finance director, so I was not yet clear how vital profit – as opposed to the generation of cash – was for the company.

I went on to meet David Hall's sales and marketing team, which included Charles Letts (a seventh generation member of the family – son of Martin), who was receiving his baptism of fire in the business. I wanted to find out how the sales team saw their competitive position and whether they thought that their factory was as good as the toughest of their overseas competitors. Rather to my surprise I discovered that they were all convinced that the Charles Letts group's real expertise was in small bound diaries and books: they believed that in this area they produced the finest products in the world. They also thought that they were competitively placed in the large desk diaries market and that they could match prices anywhere, although they were not starting from any cost advantage – Letts' products are neither more nor less expensive to produce than their competitors' products – and therefore the money had to be made in the marketing and positioning of their products in the marketplace.

The other area which speedily emerged was the relative inflexibility of the manufacturing system at the Scottish factory. I was told, but found it difficult to believe, that the basic production orders for standard diaries for the large multiple retailers had to be fixed by April, even though they would not be delivered to the retailers until August or September. This policy could be both risky and potentially expensive: some of Letts' large retail customers do not wish to place their orders as early as April and so Letts risk manufacturing and carrying stock which may, in the end, not be sold. Fairly obviously dead stock in diaries is truly dead: it cannot be sold the following year.

The sales team gave me an example of how potential profit had been lost with Woolworths because the factory had to have the orders committed in April, but Woolworths made it plain they would not place their order until July. In July Woolworths took a policy decision not to sell any items over a particular price, which meant that they did not want the diaries that Letts had produced especially for them because they were too expensive. The business was finally retrieved, but with a reduced margin. I began to wonder about the links between the selling and the manufacturing sides of the business. I found it incredible that, when the rest of the world was heading towards just in time manufacturing, where products are made just in time for delivery and no finished stock is held, this sales team was facing a slow, old fashioned way of doing things.

The sales and marketing team told me that it is possible to increase their standard diary orders later in the year, but the additional manpower required at that time and the higher cost of short runs inevitably makes these extra diaries more expensive. The reason that the factory requires production orders for standard diaries by April is to leave room to concentrate on customized corporate gift diaries – with high added value – later in the year. The sales and marketing team said they would prefer much greater flexibility on standard orders from the factory, although they acknowledged that the factory was trying to be more flexible. Apparently, under normal circumstances, it could take anything up to six weeks to produce a diary, a period which I found absolutely mind boggling.

Warming to their theme the sales and marketing team pointed out that they also had to plan the following year's designs for diaries eighteen months in advance. A diary for use from January 1993 has to be designed and planned by mid-1991. This means that the sales and marketing team have to plan and design diaries for their customers when they do not know what the actual sales figures for the current year are. I was beginning to get a less than satisfactory picture of the factory in Scotland and I made a mental note to investigate further when I went to the factory myself.

My next meeting was with Peter Casben, the finance director. Peter joined Letts in February 1989 and he is a first-class professional with a considerable background in finance: he trained at Price Waterhouse and was a management consultant there. Subsequently he became a finance director in the pharmaceutical and electrical engineering industries. He has a firm grasp of the risks that Letts are running which is just as well, because he'd only been with the group for a short time before the finance began to run out.

In November 1991 the Charles Letts group was put onto the Midland Bank's intensive care list, and every penny spent was scrutinized and controlled. Peter refinanced the company after the injection of money from the sale of the educational books business, and the recovery plan, which he showed me, was then implemented. The recovery plan included some rationalization of Letts' products and range of diaries; staff redundancies and a plan to run the business for cash.

The shareholding position of the group is that the family holds 58% of the shares, and the 3i venture capital group holds 21%. The remaining 21% is held by various individuals and companies. The peak borrowings were covered by factoring their sales with Griffin Factors Limited who provided up to £7m, but the rest of the money, within which Peter was trying to control the company, was produced by Hambros. Hambros offered a £7m overdraft facility, and £3m in a form of redeemable preference share. The preference share had to be rewarded by dividends, as well as interest payments, and had to be repaid over three years. Repayments began in 1992 which meant that the business had to turn a profit of over £1m a year from the year ending January 1993. It is a tribute to Peter's abilities that refinancing was possible at all. The company was perilously close to a forced sale and loss of family control, but so far neither of these things have happened.

The more I looked at the profit record, and future needs for profit, the more concerned I became. Letts achieved a £2m turnaround in the year ending January 1992 (see page 112), and they are looking for a further £2m in the year ending January 1993. They must achieve a trading profit of £1m for three years from the year ending January 1993 if they are to repay their bankers with any sort of regularity, and although this is budgeted for the year ending January 1993, the last time Letts achieved £1m profit after tax was in the year ending January 1985. In recent years the profit after tax has been between £600000–£700000 a year at best.

	1988†	1989†	1990†	1991†	1992†
	£000	£000	£000	£000	£000
Turnover	25 574	28 006	29 010	28 784	29 723
Profit or (loss) on ordinary activities after taxation	590	703	632	(3751)	591*

*includes £2m of net exceptional profit from the sale of the educational books business.
†year end 31 January.

Peter was the first Letts' executive I met who shared my sense of urgency and alarm at the task that the company was facing. When a company is in financial trouble it is always difficult to judge the reactions of its management. It is of no use whatsoever if the managers run around like headless chickens, indeed it is one of the tasks of top management in such a situation to manage firmly and clearly and to demonstrate complete confidence in their recovery plan. However, at the same time, the managers should be operating under a pretty hefty head of steam because they are acutely aware of the deadly breath of potential financial failure breathing down their necks. The people I had talked to so far did not show the urgency which I would have expected in a company facing the tremendous difficulties that the Charles Letts group was facing.

Letts commitment to 3i and the need to continue payments to both the family and the group pension funds mean that Letts must maintain its dividend flow. The 3i and pension fund commitments together total £250 000 a year. I began to worry about the viability of keeping the group in family hands. I cannot pretend that family control is essential, but it would be terribly sad if, after nearly seven generations, the family lost control of their business. The family are all so committed to the business and the seventh generation is being trained up. I wondered how the prospect of the family losing control was viewed by the managers who had been brought in. I discovered that, without exception, the managers were dedicated to trying to ensure that the business remained a family one if possible. That is a real tribute to Anthony, Martin and their family. I admired the managers for their loyalty and determination, but I particularly admired the family's ability to inspire such commitment and loyalty amongst their employees, many of whom had joined the company relatively recently.

My next call was to visit Chris Nott and Carole Saunders: the books publishing people. Carole has considerable publishing experience and, at one time, she put together a management buy-out at Merehurst Limited. Carole breathes commitment, drive and enthusiasm, and her team are equally dynamic and determined. Carole recruited her team from scratch, and was particularly proud of having built up a business with a £5m turnover, and sixty titles in two years. She was full of the international opportunities for her books. She and her team have set up a house style and they were driving at one hell of a pace. In fact the pace here was much more what I had expected, but failed, to find in the rest of the business. Despite the fact that they had done so well, however, the books business had consumed £1.5m in cash, which the group could ill afford. They were hoping to make a small profit during the year ending January 1993. When I analyzed the accounts for the publishing division I realized that most of the profit came from the Berlitz franchise and the Ivanhoe guides. These were well handled and, between them, contributed to nearly half the total books business turnover. The cash was being used for new publications. Originally Charles Letts' entry into book publishing was intended to provide counter-cyclical work for the diary factory. However, the fact that Carole's business required complex four-colour printing meant that they barely utilized the Letts factory machinery.

I had expected to find Carole and her team demotivated, and concerned that they were being restrained by the financial position of the parent company. To my absolute amazement this was far from the truth. They felt totally confident that they could double their turnover in five years, to £10m, while working within the existing cash flow. They felt that they could manage the rate of introduction of new products and ideas in line with the money that they could generate themselves. They pooh-poohed any suggestion that their products were not sufficiently differentiated, and might not sell well. They were thrilled with the success they were having overseas and were convinced that, provided the Charles Letts group was patient with them, they could fulfil their agreed role.

The books publishing team's impression of the diary business was that it was very old fashioned and slow moving, and they were scornful about the slow rate of adjustment in the rest of the company. Managers in other parts of the company readily admitted to me that Carole and her team were a breath of fresh air, and their constant questions about the way things were done had had a very good effect thoughout the company.

It was beginning to dawn on me that the factory might be the tail that wagged the dog. I wondered whether it would be possible to do without the factory altogether. After all the diary business began as a publishing house, and very few publishing houses control their own printing. It seemed to me that if the family was prepared to cut back to that degree then it would be able to retain a business, but whether it would be a viable business was another question. I needed more information before I could make a sensible judgment, but I realized that the idea of selling the factory would not be enthusiastically received by the Letts brothers. They were extremely proud that they had, in their own words, 'done a Wapping'. They had left London in 1964 and set up an entirely new printing and binding factory near Edinburgh. They had moved miles away from the restrictive practices of the Fleet Street dominated printing unions and they had opened new warehouse and distribution facilities in Scotland in 1980. They were proud of the flexible ways of working in their Scottish factory, and I knew that the general view was that the Scottish factory could produce small bound books at competitive cost. I also knew that costs had been substantially reduced, and that they were planning further reductions. So I went to Scotland to see for myself.

I met Martin Letts at the Dalhousie Castle Hotel, where I had spent the night. We met in the library which seemed a somewhat incongruous setting for our first encounter, because Martin appears to be the quintessential English squire who, by his own admission, is never happier than when he is out with his horses and his beloved foxhounds, and who professes not to read or be intellectual. Martin dressed in tweeds and the sort of flat cap so beloved of hunting, shooting and fishing people and he seemed the antithesis of his brother Anthony, the intellectual, who is very much at home in London and in the world of international business.

But it only took me a few minutes to realize that, despite all appearances to the contrary, Martin is highly realistic and has a natural feel for his business. I began to suspect that he used his bluff country squire appearance as a means of deflecting attention from his clear thinking mind. Martin was responsible for setting up the printing and binding plant at Dalkeith in 1964, and he had obviously thought deeply about the position of the business. While he wished to retain family control if possible, he felt that the continuation of the business was the most important thing, and – this is particularly interesting – he felt that if continuation of the business could only be done without the family at the helm, then he was quite prepared to discuss the possibility. Martin was prepared to consider almost anything, no matter how radical, in order to preserve the business.

Martin is a non-executive chairman, who believes in giving his employees considerable discretion and room to manoeuvre, even when they are doing things which do not have his wholehearted approval. At the same time it is quite clear that he is only too ready to proffer advice when asked, and that he sees himself as the coach and developer of his people. He was extremely proud, but realistic, about Norman Cuthbertson the managing director of Charles Letts (Scotland), whom he personally selected at interview. He knew Norman's strengths, but was also aware of his limitations. He described Norman as the reliable chief engineer of a wartime ship who, when the ship is torpedoed, continually reassures the captain that he will get him back to harbour somehow.

In Martin's view the factory is fully competitive as far as binding and finishing is concerned, but it may have difficulty remaining competitive in printing. Martin has great confidence in Letts' binding facility but was prepared to consider an alternative arrangement for printing if that made sense. It was when we were discussing the way forward for the whole company that Martin rang most bells with me. He thought that their overheads were too high, and that it was essential to rationalize further and reduce the number of products. However, he also thought that the company's great strength was its brand, and that their future lay in selling more products under the Letts of London brand name: an idea with which David Hall agreed. Martin thought that the company could develop in the business gifts field. I mentioned the sales team's frustration at the long diary production lead times which forced the sales team to confirm their basic standard diary orders before some of their large retail customers were willing to commit, and Martin agreed that production was nothing like as close to sales as it should be. Later on in the day he confided that he felt that this was a serious problem. He also said that he felt that members of the family should occupy non-executive positions in the firm – as he did. He was clear about the reasons why Letts were in the situation they were in, but was less confident than Anthony about their ability to trade out of their present position.

The more I talked to Martin the more I liked him. He is realistically clear thinking and open minded. When I asked him what could be done on the printing side he pointed out that many other firms were forming alliances with printers. Martin also felt they had been slow to recognize the problems that the business faced, and he shared my sense of urgency about grappling with these difficult problems. He took me to the factory, which was much bigger than I had imagined, and introduced me to Norman Cuthbertson. Norman is an Edinburgh-educated Scot who has been in manufacturing with large companies practically all his life. He is an absolutely splendid manufacturing man. He worked with Reyrolle Belmos as chief designer and works manager from 1968–1973, and with the General Electric Company as works manager and engineering director from 1973–1978. He was director of manufacturing with Veeder Root from 1978–1986, and then he came to Letts. Norman is a very large man and the sort of individual who protects his own patch with single-minded intensity. As far as he was concerned the task in hand was to run the existing equipment and get more out of it, and he was very proud of the achievements of the factory. He had much to be proud about.

Charles Letts (Scotland) was the first firm in the printing and book binding sector to achieve BS (British Standard) 5750 on 11 June 1986. BS5750 was established in 1979 as part of the government's national quality campaign. To achieve BS5750, a company has to be able to show that it manages its businesses with quality uppermost in its mind in all aspects of its activities. BS5750 is a comprehensive system of procedures which guarantee quality: raw materials, production systems, finished goods and customer services are all checked. More and more British companies are now applying for this accreditation. I have seen the effect that going for BS5750 has on the management of a company, and I believe very strongly that it is only a matter of time before it will not be possible to operate or to sell to other businesses unless you can demonstrate that you function in the way that qualifies you for BS5750. Once you have qualified for BS5750, inspectors arrive, unannounced, twice a year, to make sure that you continue to qualify. It is one of the very best moves that the British Standards Institution has made, and it is of immense importance for the future of British business.

Norman took me through the printing house and instantly two of the problems that the company is facing became apparent. Much of the plant is more than twenty years old, and I was amazed at the number of individual pieces being printed: diaries are produced in a number of formats and assembled in an extremely complicated way: over 400 diary components are printed annually and then put together to create the end products. And there are myriad specialized runs, ranging from a special print run of 500, all the way up to runs of 20 000, or more. The technology of printing, as I know from my chairmanship of *The Economist*, is moving at an absolutely terrifying rate: new and expensive machinery is coming on line the whole time. The factory is making strenuous efforts to reduce the number of pieces printed, and has managed a 20% reduction in the last year, but the business is still overloaded by the range and diversity of its products.

The more I walked around the factory, the more apparent it was that the process of rationalizing both the number and the range of products needed to go very much further: enormous savings could be made. I asked Norman how long it took for a diary to move through the works from start to finish, and he told me that the average time is between three to four weeks. Practically all businesses now recognize that there is real money to be saved by producing things more quickly. Rationalizing the production process, and continually reducing the number and variety of products made, can substantially shorten the time that any single item is worked on. One of the reasons why the Dalkeith factory has been slow to move in this direction is that they manufacture many of their standard stock products ahead of time and store them in the warehouse, to await the selling season at the end of the year. I questioned Norman about the sales team's claim that the factory was inflexible about its lead times, and he seemed defensive. He told me that it was absolutely essential to have a production plan for the year, but, in emergencies, they could produce items very quickly. Their aim was to clear the lines of standard stock in order to have the capacity, at peak times, to manufacture special – customized – diaries. They could fulfil special orders within a week by clearing all the lines the whole way through, but this – to me – was clearly uneconomic. Norman claimed that they had tested their printing costs against buying in, and that it was still cheaper to print for themselves. I suspected that he was comparing his marginal costs with the full costs, plus profit, of an external supplier.

The problem in the printing section is quite clear. The machine stock stands at about £350000 net book value, but its total replacement cost – to bring it up to scratch – could be as high as £2.5m. The printing side requires large amounts of money invested if it is to be competitive with the best. Nevertheless, starting from where they were starting, it is difficult to argue that they should not make the best of the machinery and equipment that they have, and this is what the whole of the management felt. I asked Norman about the competition and, in common with everyone I had met at Letts, he thought that they had real advantages in the binding and finishing of the products: nobody, including overseas firms, could compete. Norman's view of the way ahead was to form a partnership to exploit the excess capacity of the plant, and to reequip with new machinery. Letts' base load would be the production of diaries and they would fill up with other products which a partner might wish to produce. In an effort to load the plant Norman had taken on £1.75m worth of external printing and binding contracts, which he claimed made a contribution. But he was limited in what he could do, both by the antiquity of some of the equipment and the limited range of colour printing machinery he had available. This was why the factory could not print the books business products.

I was then handed over to David Watts, the factory production manager, and one of seven managers who reported directly to Norman. David took me around the binding and finishing departments and I began to understand why they were so confident that they could compete. They had installed a number of modern machines in order to automate activities, many of which were developed by their own development engineer, Bob Arkell. However, much of the work was still done by hand: I saw an automatic sewing machine standing beside a hand-fed machine. A few quick sums showed that the automatic machine paid for itself within a couple of years and, since the machine cost about £80 000, it was obvious that the hand-fed machines should be phased out fast. I was shown an automatic gilding machine, which gilded the edges of the paper, and I saw gilding being done by hand which was mind bogglingly time-consuming. The gilding machine cost about £175 000 and provides the best gilding facility in the UK industry. Letts have two of these machines and they have authorized the purchase of a third. I mentally gave the management very high marks for their willingness to invest in essential machinery in their present parlous financial condition: the modern machinery would maintain their competitive advantage in binding and finishing.

I saw a number of other examples of specialist machines which Letts had developed as I continued my tour of the factory. Ribbons were inserted mechanically, gilt corners were put on semi-automatically, and there was a marvellous machine which produced the outer covers for the diaries which David showed me with great pride. The contrast with the remnants of the leather binding department, which I saw next, could not have been more marked. Leather covers were stamped out of a sheet by hand, using a small press. There was substantial wastage, although I was told that the wastage was used for other purposes, such as bookmarks. Throughout the factory, the same functions were performed both by automated machinery and slower, old fashioned methods. And despite the automation of many of the binding processes, this process was still too slow and too expensive because of the countless number of small lots. I questioned David about the links with the sales team and the flexibility of the factory, and he readily agreed that they left something to be desired.

Later I met the other middle managers, including the customer services and distribution manager, Keith Taylor, and the production control manager, Derek Bennett. They were pretty critical of the problems induced by the distance between themselves and London, and the difficulties of developing new products and new business. They all readily agreed that, since the arrival of David Hall, things were improving, but nevertheless they thought that the distance between the commercial departments in London and the factory in Scotland was a major problem. These views were more than confirmed when I met James Moore, the group financial controller, who took over responsibility for the accounts for the group in March 1992. James almost exploded as he described Letts' slowness in tackling problems, his concerns about the inability of trading out of their current situation, and who was managing the way forward. He had very clear feelings about what needed to be done, and he thought that Letts were still merely tinkering with the financial aspects of the whole problem. As the day wore on I became clearer about ways to tackle the pressing problems of this beleaguered company.

I ended my visit to the factory by giving my preliminary conclusions to the two brothers, Anthony and Martin, Peter Casben, the finance director, and Norman Cuthbertson. I said that I thought a sense of urgency was desperately lacking and was essential if they were to deal effectively with their problems. I was extremely dubious about their ability to trade out of their current position, unless they took much harsher action to cut back to their core business. The absolute minimum core business would be a business which just published and commissioned diaries, and which sold branded bought in goods in the UK and overseas. Staff would have to be reduced sharply, to between thirty and fifty in total. The core business I was recommending was drastically small and I hoped they could do better, but at least my recommended minimum core would ensure that a long established firm remained an entity with the family able to retain control. If they were successful, they could move ahead again later. As far as I was concerned every additional activity beyond my stated minimum core business had to justify itself, not only by its ability to pay its own way, but also by its strategic contribution, and in particular the demands that it would, or would not, make on future capital.

I was less sure of the viability of manufacturing when compared with the costs of an established book publisher who is able, at minimum, to do the printing on an almost marginal basis, and who could cope with the loading on his plant very much more easily than Letts could, enabling him to phase the diary printing more easily into his annual plan. I was convinced that at present they had a narrow advantage on the binding and finishing side of the business, and I suspected, although I needed to do some more work on this, that that side would be able to contribute to the basic core. Even though they had already taken pretty draconian steps to reduce their running costs, I was concerned about whether it was possible to maintain a two-site operation, with a substantial part of the company in London and the main production unit in Scotland. I needed to look at that problem more closely.

I had a number of smaller concerns which I also raised. I was worried about the time that it took to produce a diary, and astonished at the relative luxury of seeking an annual production plan. In my view the factory should become very much more flexible and responsive to the sales team if it was to justify its existence, and I thought that this problem was exacerbated both by the distance between the production and the sales people, and the range and complexity of the products they produced. A much more flexible production system was essential so that standard diary orders could be taken late in the year and delivered very quickly, even if this meant buying in.

I thought they should only remain in businesses where they were sure that they could continue to invest, so that those businesses remained competitive with the best in the world. The product range must be substantially rationalized, again, and this should be done in conjunction with the sales people. And I was concerned at the absence of integrating mechanisms, below board level, between sales and production, particularly regarding new product development. I was also concerned about the lack of clear responsibility for profit, between sales and production. I understood the reasons for changing to throughput measurement, but I was not sure that it was the best way to cope with the very heavy financial pressures that the business faced.

Some of these points appeared to be accepted, although my worries about the lack of urgency were hotly disputed by all of them. Martin said that the fact that they did not look as though they were panicking did not mean that they were not discussing drastic ideas. They were looking at the idea of a printing partner as well as a publishing partner. I explained that I was worried that they were clutching at straws. I did not think it would be easy to find partners in either of those fields, and so then the question was: what would they do if partnerships were not possible? I thought it necessary to home in much more harshly on the actual business objectives at this stage, and I thought that they would find this easier if they faced the worst that could happen and looked upon anything else as happy chance. Again I was struck by the open mindedness and willingness of the whole management team to listen, and to try to face up to the very difficult position in which the Charles Letts group found itself.

I was still worried that I did not know enough about the buyers' attitudes to the bulk buying of diaries and so I decided to make some enquiries. I went to see Al Ward, who is currently the president of the British Office Systems and Stationery Federation. Al is a true specialist in the area of office stationery. He spent thirty-seven years in the trade, both buying and selling, working for various organizations which now belong to the W.H. Smith group. I asked him what key elements diary buyers looked for when choosing their diary suppliers, to make sure that I was not advising Anthony and Martin to take an approach which might subsequently prove disastrous.

Somewhat to my surprise, and despite cheaper diaries produced by foreign printers who heavily undercut costs, it appears that the vital thing to most buyers is confidence in the collation of the diary itself. Although it does not seem a terribly difficult task to get the pages in the right order and to ensure that the British edition does not contain the high days and holidays of, say, Mozambique, the buyer never takes this skill for granted. Firms like Letts start with a major advantage in this respect because they have been collating diaries for 180 years and are considered to be absolutely reliable.

The next thing that most buyers look for is a strong, good quality binding and Al's view is that control of binding is a real advantage. He made it clear that diary publishing is a highly competitive business and that, while buyers particularly look for these points, they are unlikely to pay a substantial overprice for them. He also said that many of the buyers were still keen to handle the branded diaries produced by firms like Letts and that this was a matter which they took into consideration when making bulk purchases for own label purposes.

There is little doubt that if Letts decided to subcontract their printing they might gain advantage by printing overseas, rather than in the UK where there could be a danger of the subcontractors dealing direct with the customers. The chances of this would also be lessened if their subcontracting was handled by more than one supplier.

All in all, it did not look as though my idea that Letts' absolute core business as a 'publisher' of diaries – commissioning and guaranteeing the product – was a realistic one, and anyway I already knew that the Letts family were unlikely to be enthusiastic about such a radical approach. I therefore decided that in my final discussions with Letts I would push for a core business which included origination, collation and binding.

But it was with a heavy heart that I met Anthony and Martin for my final session because Norman Cuthbertson, the managing director of Charles Letts (Scotland), had died suddenly from a heart attack. At the same time that Letts suffered this tragic loss, Chris Nott, the managing director of Charles Letts & Co Limited in London, had left the company. I asked Anthony and Martin how they intended to replace these two managers, and whether they saw this as an opportunity – albeit a sad one – to bring London and Scotland together. It emerged at this stage that they were unwilling to unite the two, but they had taken on board the urgent necessity to work on closer collaboration between the selling and production arms of the business.

On the financial side I was pleased to hear that things were already improving: their current financial situation was better than I had expected. Although the time of year was a difficult one from which to take a precise view of the way that the diary business was going, their order intake was very close to budget, and they had been able to take more out of their costs. These were good signs, particularly in a recession, but I still felt that it was going to be very difficult for them to trade out of the position they were in.

The increase in profits was very largely achieved by 'purifying the business'. This meant rigorously going through all the accounts where they made profit and ensuring that their available effort was redirected to service those accounts, rather than others which were less profitable. They had followed this approach with all their customers, and particularly with export markets, and it was already showing results.

But despite these encouraging signs, I felt strongly that the Charles Letts group of the future would have to be a smaller operation. The company was, and would continue to be, seriously undercapitalized for a considerable period of time. Anthony and Martin were adamant that, if at all possible, they wanted to retain family control of the company, and all their thinking was done on that basis. I said that I had believed from the beginning that the company could survive as a family company, but only if they made some radical changes to their business, and soon. I said that I had modified my view about the size of their absolute core business to include retaining control of the collating and binding of the diaries.

I then suggested four ways in which they could raise the necessary capital. First they could try to trade themselves out of their current position, but to repeat myself, I was much less sanguine than they were about their ability to do so. Secondly they could sell the printing plant – I was not keen on reequipping because of the capital required. Thirdly, they could sell the publishing business – under present circumstances if they retain the publishing business they will have to hold it back – and fourthly the family could sell out of all, or part, of the company.

I told Martin and Anthony, bluntly, that I suspected that they were not facing up to the inevitability of having to make one or more of these difficult decisions which might reduce the size of the group but realize the much needed capital. I said that I thought they were deferring the agony. I understood their strong desire to keep the company under family control, but to ensure that outcome they must face up to the other difficult choices that I had just put to them. The most difficult thing for a family business to do is to face up to the inevitability of situations. A family business naturally wants to maintain its heritage, and it must have seemed to Anthony and Martin that I was asking them to sell their heritage, their birthright.

However, Anthony and Martin won my admiration for their common sense approach. They agreed that they had little choice but to plan on the basis of capital limitations for some considerable time to come. We discussed the printing options and they told me that since my last visit they been working on figures for a modern flexible plant and calculated that it might pay for itself on the basis of the savings it would achieve against the existing set up. We discussed how large the printing plant should be. I said that if they bought something it should only be capable of producing less than they needed. This would then necessitate at least some buying in of printed material, and I had already checked with Al Ward and others that this was not likely to put them at a commercial disadvantage. I still felt that the alternative of contracting all the printing out would save them more money in the long haul, but we agreed that collation and binding were Letts' key points of difference and should remain under Letts' control.

We were then joined by David Hall, Carole Saunders and Peter Casben. I reiterated the view that they would have to produce fewer types of diaries in a smaller, more specialized, factory. The heart of the problem was to find ways to make the company sufficiently profitable and so build up the capital reserves. I supported David Hall's idea of diversifying into business gifts, because this would be using the same sales force and selling to the same customer base. I said that if the growth of Carole's publishing business and its new titles was restricted then the publishing arm need not be a drain on the group. But I could not for the life of me see how the publishing business could achieve its potential if it was kept in the group and held back. Nor did I think that the group's resources were sufficient to sustain the capability of the publishing business.

Poor Carole was rather upset at this blunt assessment, and with some justification, since she had succeeded in reducing cash calls on the business. The difficulty is that she has achieved a certain momentum in the business which would be artificially held back if her growth prospects were continuously restricted. Only a few of her publications can use the printing facilities that are available to Letts, and the business is therefore one which could readily be sold at an appropriate stage. It is a totally different line of business from the educational books business which had also provided additional load into the Scottish printing plant. Carole's niche publications, where she has already managed to establish an outstanding position in the craft market, were a different commercial proposition. Most publishers do not make a great deal of money – even when things go well – and they can lose enormous sums when things go badly. So both from the risk point of view, and because of the difficulties of the parent company holding Carole's business back, I felt that the publishing business should be sold. I chided them for hanging on to Mayfair Trunks Limited, which really did not seem to me to add anything significant to the Letts brand name, even though they still believed that this business was about to break even.

The trouble with both the publishing and the Mayfair Trunks businesses is that breaking even is not good enough. In a group which is so very short of money, difficult comparisons have to be made and tough decisions have to be taken about where best to invest the limited funds. Letts have to decide whether to spend the money renewing the diary manufacturing plant with a potentially high rate of return against existing plant, or to carry on with the publishing and the Mayfair Trunks businesses which are not directly related to what we all agreed was the core business for the future.

We had a good discussion and yet again I was impressed by their common sense approach and attempt to look at the business from a detached point of view. It is particularly difficult for families to stand back and view their businesses objectively, and I was full of admiration for their determination to do so. However I didn't feel that in their hearts they were prepared to make really big changes. The danger in companies like this is not that they do too much, but that they do too little. So the art is to be vicious at this stage, before it is too late.

The real questions are: how big a group should they be, and are they prepared to take the sort of radical measures that will ensure their long term future? Considering the intrinsic difficulties of the diary business I thought that the turnaround they had achieved so far was a near miracle. Nevertheless, if I was asked to guess what the Charles Letts group would be doing in five years' time, I would hope for this: the company will be concentrated in Dalkeith in Scotland with a small London presence. The salesmen will be selling from their homes, and the company will be a diary and business gift firm, positioned firmly at the luxury end of the market.

POSTSCRIPT: JUNE 1993

In autumn 1992 David Hall and Peter Casben were made joint managing directors of the company. This February they moved, along with the sales and marketing departments, to Dalkeith. The London-based publishing division has not been sold, but it has been reduced in size and scope, and Carole Saunders has left the company. Now, as I had hoped, the bulk of the company is concentrated in Scotland and just fifteen staff are left in Letts' London offices, including Anthony Letts who remains Chairman, dividing his time between London and Dalkeith.

In Dalkeith, factory volume has been reduced by 25% at the lower end of the market, as Letts aim to go for lower-volume and higher-margain work. They are introducing synchronized manufacturing which means that diaries should get through the factory more quickly from order to completion, enabling the company to become much more responsive to the market. They have also been able to install a modern high-speed Web press, by leasing from an American bible printer, in exchange for printing their European bibles. All of this has meant that total staff numbers are down by one hundred.

As a result of these measures, costs have been reduced by £3m, and Anthony Letts believes the business should be on line for a healthy profit this year. I shall be delighted to see it happen.

CHAPTER FIVE

NORTON MOTORS LIMITED

J ames Lansdowne Norton, who founded the Norton Manufacturing Company Limited in 1898, made his first complete motor cycle in 1902. He had a strong preference for lightweight machines and whenever the technical press suggested that heavier machines were a better choice, Norton would buy advertising space in the same journal to contest the point. Part of one of Norton's advertisements in *The Motor Cycle* of 8 August 1904, reads: 'We build light and heavy motors and ride both, but prefer the Norton light ones . . . efficiency is in the design and build, not [in] a big engine and weight.' Unfortunately James Norton paid more attention to his products than to his profits, with the inevitable result that in 1913 the Norton Manufacturing Company went into liquidation. And it is reported that, on his deathbed, James Norton was working on a design for an aeroplane.

Today Norton Motors Limited, many incarnations later, still trades under the name of its founder and still, like him, believes in lightweight motors (Norton motorbikes are driven by Norton lightweight rotary engines); Norton still pays more attention to its products than to its profits (it is in serious financial trouble); and Norton has a strong connection with aircraft (Norton designs and manufactures rotary engines for light aircraft). So the spirit of James Norton lives on but his company is in trouble, and unless the current Norton management finds a fast road back to profit there won't be any products left.

All my attempts to help Norton find this road were bedeviled by the absence of reliable figures, and later, when I visited Norton Motors' factory at Shenstone, Staffordshire, the horrendous financial limitations under which they are working became abundantly clear. Money is so short, and Norton Motors' credit is so poor, that much of the time is spent chasing up bills so that money can be rushed to a parts supplier before he will deliver the parts necessary for assembly. And all the time the assembly line waits idle.

Earlier *Troubleshooter* visits have been criticized by business schools and the accountancy profession for their apparently light use of numbers and financial figures. This criticism is probably justified, if only because balance sheets, management accounts and profit and loss figures do not transfer easily to television – however no one should imagine that a *Troubleshooter* visit is not supported by the relevant fiscal and management accounts. The starting point of every visit is a lengthy perusal of the published accounts. In most cases a close reading of these accounts will reveal the areas which raise the question marks from which everything else stems. However, every now and then there are no accounts, or the ones that exist are so misleading as to be positively unhelpful. Navigation through business problems depends on the charts, soundings and fixes that can be taken from the accounts. Norton Motors' lack of reliable accounts made it very difficult for me to find landmarks or to gauge the depth of the water above which they were struggling to keep their heads. If a company cannot provide an outsider with these essential navigational tools, it is highly unlikely to be able to provide them for itself, and without them, sooner or later, it will end up on the rocks.

The sad irony of this is that the Norton name makes the blood course faster in the veins of almost any Englishman over the age of thirty. *Esquire* in its July/August 1992 issue said: 'Norton is to bikes what Aston Martin is to cars.' The distinctive Norton logo and general aura of excellence, together with the power of the Norton engines which consistently won Norton many races, created a legend. Norton won the very first Isle of Man TT in 1907. A Norton bike was the best motorbike in the world, and it was British to boot. The legend spread to America and across the Channel. Mention Norton to Americans,

Germans or Italians and you get the same rapturous reaction. Norton Motors even managed to keep its head (just) above water in the 1970s when fierce Japanese competition devastated the British motorbike industry, so when I was given the chance to visit Norton in my *Troubleshooter* guise I didn't hesitate.

In 1969 Norton acquired the rights for the revolutionary Wankel engine. You probably have to be my age to remember that it was the Wankel engine that was going to change internal combustion engineering in every field, forever. The Wankel engine had all the attraction and glamour which appeals to a non-engineer like myself. Its advantages are obvious: for a start there is only one moving part (pistons are replaced by a rotor), and only two parts in all, and it promised, and indeed delivered, a fantastic power to weight ratio. The rights to the Wankel engine were purchased in Japan, Britain, and, of course, in Germany. Norton Motors designs and manufactures Wankel-type rotary engines under its own patents and a licensing agreement from Wankel GmbH. But there was a long and ominous period of quiet before products – from Norton or anyone else – started to emerge. However, Mazda appear to be winning the battle to produce commercially successful rotary engines: total cumulative production of Mazda rotary-powered vehicles exceeds 1.5m, and they have sold roughly 743 000 Mazda RX-7 Turbo cars – the world's only rotary engine sports car. In June 1991 a Mazda with a rotary engine won at Le Mans.

Norton, Mazda and one Dr Paul Moller (whose brainchild, the M400 'flying car', is powered by eight rotary engines) are the only people in the world who make rotary engines, but they're very expensive compared to a conventional engine, which makes the machines they're put into also very expensive, although the price is often mitigated by the additional potential speed: in August 1991 a motorcycle streamliner with a Norton F1 rotary engine, turbocharged by Alex Macfadzean of Engine and Dynamometer Services, broke the British motorcycle land speed record by over eight miles per hour: the streamliner's speed was 200.9 miles per hour.

I was honoured to think I might be able to play some small part in maintaining the existence of such a proud British name as Norton. It was only once I had accepted, with such alacrity and enthusiasm, that I found that there were no charts. Norton had fallen prey to a phenomenon of the 1980s: the belief that the more acquisitions you make, the quicker the profits will flow. Businessman and former merchant banker Philippe Le Roux, recognizing the potency of the Norton brand name and its instant effect on people's hearts and wallets, took the business on.

In February 1987 Philippe Le Roux headed a group of investors who bought Norton's motorcycle and engineering interests and the rights to the Norton and the BSA names. I wondered whether Philippe Le Roux's experience as a merchant banker was appropriate for running a demanding company which rested, above everything else, on engineering and managerial excellence, and he knew nothing about motorbikes or the technology involved: he did not even have a licence to drive a motorbike, but that did not deter him.

Le Roux wanted to do two things: he wanted to finance the development of a new Norton race bike – the rotary-engined F1 – so that Norton race bikes could once again conquer the world, and he wanted Norton to develop its rotary engine business and bring it to successful commercial fruition. Le Roux believed that this was possible, but when you look at the amounts of effort and money that are available to Norton's competitors, it would seem unlikely that a relatively small number of undercapitalized and underfunded people should be able to take on, and beat, the rest of the world. Nevertheless that is what Philippe Le Roux believed he could do.

Le Roux decided that the way to finance his plans for Norton was to build up an industrial mini-conglomerate by acquisition. The concept appeared to be that the newly acquired parts of the company would raise sufficient finance to revivify Norton and take it into the profitable uplands of success. None of these aims have so far been achieved. The three deals that Le Roux engineered have not benefitted the company to such a degree that Le Roux himself left Norton Motors in January 1991, and in March 1991 Norton Motors became the subject of a Department of Trade and Industry (DTI) investigation. The DTI report has not been published yet (August 1992), probably because the DTI inspectors have so far been as unsuccessful as I have in unravelling reality from myth, and capability from hope. I think it is fair to say that Norton has gone the way of many other companies: it appears to have been brought down by people who saw the opportunity of surfing to success on the back of a distinctive brand name.

Le Roux's three deals were: the acquisition of an American pipe-fitting producer, Pro-Fit Pipes Inc., in 1988; a complicated London property deal in 1989, which collapsed when the bottom fell out of the London commercial property market in the autumn of 1989; and the acquisition of a German fastening company, FUS Fasteners, in 1990. Now – the summer of 1992 – Norton's new management are attempting to sell Pro-Fit and FUS. There are something like 13 000 Norton shareholders, all of whom backed their memories of Norton's once pre-eminent position in the British motorcycle industry with their money, and all of whom appear to have lost their money.

After the departure of Philippe Le Roux and his associates, an engineer named David Macdonald was brought in to rescue the company. David Macdonald's career has been one of somewhat mixed success. He is a former aeronautical engineer and was chief executive of a Yeovil-based company called Advanced Material Systems, a company which develops plastics and composite materials. He had some racing experience in the 1970s, and was involved with a number of other companies which have gone into receivership.

One of the more fascinating aspects of trying to unravel Norton's problems and to help them, has been to resolve in my own mind whether David Macdonald is a saint or a sinner. He has certainly been the subject of the sort of press comment which I would not wish on my worst enemy. Each time I discussed the future of the company with David, the ground appeared to shift. Although this is hardly the basis for building up trust between us, it is consistent with the perplexity of a man who has inherited one hell of a mess and is trying to find a way ahead which would at least save something for the shareholders. David is, apparently, knowledgeable and he is never stumped for an answer. Every answer he gives is plausible and may well be correct, but I was concerned by a lack of consistency in his answers. Under normal circumstances a speedy recourse to the accounts would have enabled me to nail some of David's statements as fact or fiction, but in Norton's case, as I have said more than once already, these charts, soundings and fixes simply did not exist. I was also pretty unimpressed with Macdonald's business plan for Norton. It seemed to me hopelessly unrealistic.

Another problem of following the Norton story was that I could not reach the major institutional shareholders, or Norton's bankers, the Midland, until the very last minute. It was upon their generosity and optimism which the future survival of Norton totally depended, and it was they who appointed David Macdonald to attempt another rescue operation for the confused company which Norton had become.

My first contact with Norton was in August 1991 and, even as I write this a year later in August 1992, I have still not seen enough figures to provide a clear understanding of the reality of the company. However, some things are factual and plain. Norton has actually manufactured a number of rotary engines and a small number of Norton motorbikes. And through the generous sponsorship of Imperial Tobacco – specifically John Player Special – Norton has succeeded in fielding a successful race team which, although run on a shoestring, has achieved near miracles in challenging, and in some cases vanquishing, the formidable teams put up against them by the Japanese manufacturers.

Initially I made the assumption that Norton Motors was a motorcycle manufacturing company and that its future lay in that area. That is why I began my *Troubleshooter* visit to Norton by going to the Grand Prix at Castle Donington in August 1991. For me this was a new and eye-opening experience in more ways than one. Because I grew up during the war, my total period of motorbike ownership amounted to about six weeks. Motorbikes were not easily transportable in a submarine (although I did try this for a short period) and after the war I was able to scrape together enough money to move straight on to a small car. Although I was modestly interested in the sport I never watched motorcycle racing at all. I had not followed it on the sports pages and indeed, apart from a period in the early 1930s when I had been mildly interested in dirt track racing, I had about as much knowledge of motorbikes and motorbike racing as you would expect a Papuan of average education to have.

My introduction to motorcycle racing was an absolutely delightful experience, apart from the noise. It seems to me that anybody who wishes to race cannot resist continuously revving up his engine, whether on the track or not. However, I have seldom been anywhere where there was a better behaved crowd or where the atmosphere of interest, knowledge and enthusiasm was so strong. Moreover, unlike some other areas of competitive racing, where the competition becomes bitter, it seemed to me that in this area at least there was an extremely sporting amount of give and take between both the riders, the race managers and the mechanics. However, when I went to the pits to visit Norton's team of people working on Norton's F1 motorbike (also known as the 'Black Bomber' and developed by Norton when Le Roux was chief executive), I was considerably shaken. Barry Symmons, Norton's race team manager, has a ten-strong team and two riders, but they take on rivals who can call on thousands of technicians and hundreds of riders.

I have never believed that sheer numbers guarantee wins, but it is a fact that the odds are stacked against a small team, however capable, when that team is so obviously outnumbered. A typical Japanese team would be fielding a whole stable of bikes, whereas Barry and his boys were working on a maximum of two, indeed when I met them it was rather under one and a half: the second F1 was being dismantled at the time! But although the Norton team are low in numbers, their profile is extremely high. Everyone I spoke to in the vast crowd at Castle Donington was interested in Norton, and two pages of the programme were devoted to welcoming Norton back. The bike itself looked stunning, jet black and sleek, and its rider, 'Rocket' Ron Haslam is an exceptionally good rider, and even better on a wet surface.

Ron is a surprisingly slender and gentle man whose young son was already beginning to ride around on a tiny replica Norton. Somehow you do not expect to find a professional racing man with a soft emotional side to him, and yet Ron's wish to ride for Norton was based on the fact that he wanted to be back on the British scene, on a British bike, and that his very first motorbike had been a Norton Commando. Nobody could have accused Ron Haslam of working for Norton for financial reasons.

It was at this stage that I began to understand the implications of the lack of funding in Norton Motors. The race team are trying to race every weekend and resolve any problems during the week. This put their two bikes, two riders and race team of ten under extremely heavy pressure. Sleep and relaxation do not feature strongly for Barry Symmons and his team. Moreover, I soon found out that there weren't many people back at the factory to provide support for them.

It was absolutely essential that Norton qualified over this weekend in its first Grand Prix race since the early 1960s. Motor racing success is essential if Norton are to break back into the small niche market which they are aiming at, because the scale of production will always ensure that a Norton bike will be an expensive bike. If Ron Haslam and the 'Black Bomber' qualified, it would mean that a British race team was involved in the Grand Prix for the first time for almost thirty years.

On that same day at Castle Donington I met David Macdonald and his finance director, Lindsay Smith, for the first time. I heard their version of how they had been lured into the business, and the problems that they were facing in trying to unravel the complications that Philippe Le Roux and his team had left to Norton Motors. Far from producing a good cashflow for the group, the diversifications into America and Germany had merely added to the company's problems. The first acquisition had opened up a whole area of problems, which the second acquisition was supposed to resolve, and so on. It is perfectly possible to roll the future ahead in this way but unless the company is soundly based, it catches up with you eventually. This is, of course, what happened to Norton. But somewhere buried inside the company there is still a real business, although getting at it and saving it is going to be extraordinarily difficult without any cashflow. Predictably I found David and Lindsay totally concerned about the problems of cash generation, which was obviously essential for them to continue in business at all. I gathered that their plan was to try to refinance the company and to develop other uses for the rotary engine as well as for the motorbikes, although at this stage they still believed that the future lay in manufacturing motorbikes.

I ended my day more impressed than I can say with the qualities and dedication of the race manager, Barry Symmons, Ron Haslam and Norton's race team. Not only did all of them believe in their product, but the public were really rooting for them. However, sadly, whichever way you look at it, it really is a matter of David and Goliath. Norton's team are up against teams with enormous resources at their disposal. Apart from the question of whether Norton can survive financially to fight another day, the real question is whether a small, but highly motivated, team has a cat in hell's chance against the sheer power of the Japanese. I asked a few spectators what they thought of Norton's chances. There was no question that everyone was keen to see them succeed, but not too many people gave them more than the slimmest of chances of doing so. However, that particular weekend in August was a good one for Norton motorcycles: 'Rocket' Ron finished a creditable twelfth in the British Grand Prix on Norton's F1 motorbike, and he won a round of the *Motor Cycle News* TT Superbike race. Perhaps these successes heralded a new dawn for Norton. They could certainly do with one.

My next call was to the factory in Staffordshire, to see what was left of Norton Motors. Here the harsh reality behind the noise, emotion and enthusiasm of the racetrack became apparent. Although the factory was trying to show its best face, there were only a handful of men, and an even smaller handful of bikes in various stages of assembly. They were really struggling and they had had to reduce their prices even though the volume of sales was non-existent. Norton currently has two bikes in production – the F1 sport, son of the F1, and the Commander – and they are developing a replacement for the F1 sport. A Norton F1 originally cost between £12 000 – £13 000 but David Macdonald realized that Norton couldn't sell anything like enough bikes at that price, so they developed the F1 sport, and priced it at about £8500. This bike sells to the 35+ age bracket with high disposable incomes: it is a single-seater sports bike. The Norton Commander is a two-seater touring bike which costs about £6600 and sells to the 45+ age bracket. It also sells to the Police, the RAC, and the BBC for their couriers.

The factory had three computer-controlled flexible machining centres. These machines had replaced something like ninety others, and enabled Norton to manufacture most of the basic parts that they needed in-house. The machines were fully automatic and could operate around the clock but sadly, at present, they were only operating on a single shift basis. I asked whether they could not be operated as a separate machining centre, but it appeared that cash shortages precluded this approach. Norton were hoping to sell some 200 motorcycles a year, but it was quite apparent from the small number of men and the even smaller number of motorbikes in production, that they did not have the finance to support such a level of sales. Graham Williams, the managing director at the factory, wanted to concentrate their major effort in the mid-range of race based bikes, where he believed they could produce better value for money than Honda and Yamaha, while still commanding a fairly rarefied price. Top of the range race based bikes sell from £9000 to as high as £40000; Norton's F1 sport, at £8500, fits into the mid-range price bracket which is between £7000–£9000. Graham had come from Rolls Royce and, in addition to running the factory, was also head of the development department. Talking to Graham I began to realize that Norton Motors saw itself as a motorbike company which also happened to make rotary engines, and that if it was to have a future it might have to be a rotary engine manufacturer that also happened to make motorbikes.

I had spent much of my time at the track trying to find out what the intrinsic superiority of the rotary engine in a motorbike frame was, compared with a normal reciprocating engine. Everybody had explained the benefits of the power to weight ratio and had told me that the machine rode quite differently from a normal motorbike. However, there were significant disadvantages: the engine runs extremely hot, and the oil system is a total loss lubrication system (other bikes use a recirculating system). But Norton are looking at ways of reclaiming and re-using some of the oil, and are planning to include special design characteristics to do this in the new F1 sport replacement. They are also paying special attention to aerodynamic difficulties and air flow ducting to ensure low engine operating temperatures, and they have patents on their air cooling system which is absolutely critical to the success of the engine. The fact that the engine is small and powerful means that the problem of getting the waste heat away is key, and it is in this area that Norton have significant advantages over the competition. But I became more and more uncertain that the motorbike was the best outlet for the rotary engine: even the most optimistic protagonist seemed unable to think in terms of more than a few hundred motorbikes per year. At this low level it becomes extremely difficult to support a dealer network, particularly for a totally different sort of engine. Every dealer has to be trained, and has to carry stocks of spares for the Wankel engine, even though it is meant to be a low-maintenance operation. The dealers themselves have to make a living, and it is quite apparent that there simply is not enough money in the system.

It was also apparent that even £100 000 of working capital would release enormous amounts of engineering effort to reduce the actual cost of the operation. The factory were keen to achieve cost savings by reverse value engineering and I am sure they could have achieved significant savings, but almost everyone concerned was fully involved in trying to get enough product out just to pay the bills. Moreover, it is going to be extraordinarily difficult to get out of this bind because such things as operating the flexible machining centres as a business are hampered by the lack of cash. Time and time again, I came across parts of the factory where operations were being carried out by hand at high cost because lack of volume and money meant that products could not be bought in, or were uneconomical to manufacture in the factory. This is, of course, the very situation that afflicts companies who have lost control of their cashflow. It was immensely depressing to see it happening in reality.

I then went to the engine assembly shop where I actually saw a rotary engine for the first time. Even though I had seen one of these engines mounted on a bike, when I saw one on a bench I could not believe how simple and light it was. I could easily lift the lightest engine in one hand – it weighed 22lb (10kg) – and at 38 horsepower it delivers something like twice as much power for its weight as a comparable conventional engine. Their power to weight ratio really is incredible: it is the highest ratio ever achieved by a production rotary engine. Norton's rotary engines are designed specifically for RPVs (remotely piloted vehicles) and military target drones (unmanned aircraft). With modification they can be developed as the power units for small man-carrying aircraft such as microlights and powered gliders.

Although Norton have competition in this field, they are technically ahead of anybody else and the drone aircraft for military training purposes is a secure market – if only because real bullets are occasionally shot at them and replacements are needed. However, the problem with defence contracts is that, although the business is secure when you get it, there is either nothing at all or an absolute wealth of potential business which completely swamps you. It tends to be feast or famine and is just the sort of business that an undercapitalized company like Norton can do without. However, in Norton's situation they really have to take any business, no matter what problems it presents. Not only do they not have any cash, but there is no part of their business which could represent a cash cow – or even a cash calf.

I then met David Garside, the director of engineering. In many ways he was the father of the aircraft applications for the rotary engines. He joined BSA in 1969 in order to work on the rotary engines, and so has been working on them for over twenty years. He was as pessimistic as I was becoming about the outcome for the motorbike but, on the other hand, was full of confidence for the rotary engine applications in light aircraft. He explained to me that the Wankel really could compete against a large, complex, Japanese four cylinder, twin overhead cam, four valve engine. It was smoother, lighter and smaller than a four cylinder engine. If the volume could be obtained the Wankel could be cheaper, but the difficulty is that it has never managed to find its way into the market in sufficient numbers to realize its full economic potential. It is a chicken and egg situation. You cannot get the quantity unless the cost goes down, and you cannot get the cost down unless you get the quantity. Either of these would require more money in the system. And the motorbikes need to keep pace with changes in legislation on noise regulations and exhaust emissions, particularly since Germany has opted for even tighter requirements than the Europe-wide legislation which comes into force in January 1993.

David was absolutely clear that he felt that the only future for the company lay in dividing the military and civil aircraft businesses from the motorcycle business. He could not see any way in which the motorcycle business could generate enough money to do the development work that was still required. The military side would be able to raise sufficient funds to assist the civil aviation area and, in any event, the Americans were prepared to pay for the development of the manufacturing technology for their drone programme. The US government has been funding research, with an American company called AAI, to try to develop a diesel version of the Wankel so that US military aircraft can be diesel-powered. The first one flew in April 1992.

David Garside felt so strongly about the separation of Norton's two businesses that he had put suggestions forward for a management buy-out of the rotary engine businesses, possibly supplying the motorbikes and other applications. The problem with such a management buy-out is that it would remove the heart of the business. David was also quite critical about applications for their rotary engines where they could not command the premium price, and he felt that, at least at present, the engine business represented nearly 80% of the total business, but was carrying the overheads associated with the motorbike and other activities. By the end of the day I was convinced that the rotary engine business represented a better financial and volume opportunity than the motorbikes. There was simply no way in which the company could continue in its present format. David Garside was highly critical of the number of options that were being simultaneously pursued by David Macdonald, and was as amazed as I was that the institutional shareholders had kept the company afloat as long as they had.

By the time I met David Morris, the marketing director, it was becoming increasingly clear to me that the only future for Norton lay in becoming an engine company, exploiting its engine technology and supplying to others who made bikes, drones and so on. At this stage David Macdonald was talking about selling something like 5000 engines, which was in marked contrast both to the capability of funding and the actual sales that had been made. I had very great difficulty lining up David Macdonald's ideas about what could be done with the financial capability of the company.

David Morris told me that tentative discussions with Cagiva, a major Italian motorbike company, to buy Norton engines and to allow Norton access to Cagiva components for Norton motorbikes, had eventually come to nothing; but that a deal to provide rotary engines to a jet ski company was being discussed (jet skis are those machines that look like a motorbike on a single waterski); and so was a deal to develop a high speed portable fire pump – based on Norton rotary engines – with a leading UK fire pump company. The last phase of trials on the engines for the fire pumps has been successfully completed and the prospects look good for a sale of between 2000–3000 Norton engines. Portable fire-fighting pumps have to be carried and manhandled, and the very low weight and high power of Norton's engines have a natural advantage for such an application: with Norton's engines powering the pumps a four-man-lift fire pump becomes a two-man-lift fire pump.

When I left the factory I was sure that the core Norton business was not the motorbike business, but the rotary engine business. The rotary engine is clearly ideal for light aircraft, and the military will pay for any further development costs. I can't see why anyone would want a rotary engine in a motorbike and I haven't yet found anyone who can convince me that they have any real advantages for a motorbike, but I thought that the fire pump application was just the sort of area Norton should be investigating.

I now made yet another desperate attempt to try to get some numbers, but yet again none were forthcoming. I kept on being told that the institutional investors were still supportive, but for the life of me I could not see why they should continue to support a company which appeared to have no clear focus or business plan. I decided to make some independent checks, both on the manned aircraft business and particularly on the motorbike business.

My next meeting was therefore with Malcolm Faires, who had negotiated an arrangement with David Macdonald to purchase and develop the Norton engine for use in civilian light aircraft. Malcolm is a light aircraft enthusiast whose knowledge of the business seemed to me to be encyclopaedic. I met him on a rather windy private airfield where he was test flying one of the light aircraft that his company produced. He runs a company called Mid West Aero Engines Limited, and he has been quick to see the real advantages that the Norton engine could offer light manned aircraft. This is an area where the power to weight ratio of the engine, combined with its smooth running, offers very significant advantages which even a layman like myself could see. The Norton engine is about half the weight of its competitors for the same power and Malcolm was full of confidence that he would be able to build up the business to a significant level. He was contracted to buy 150 units for the first year and believed that, with proper marketing, it should be possible to increase to a minimum of 500 units a year, with the potential to rise to 1500. Malcolm also saw the possibility of developing the Norton engine for power gliders and microlight aircraft, which would all add to the future potential demand. From his own point of view the deal he had struck with Norton was an extremely sensible one. He was committed to a relatively small number of units and wasn't exposed to much risk. At the same time he had exclusivity for manned aircraft applications. This all looked like good news for Malcolm and his aircraft company, but didn't seem to me to do very much for Norton.

Next I went to meet Frank Westworth and Julian Ryder. Frank is the editor of *Used Bike Guide* and *Classic Bike Guide*, and Julian is a journalist with *Motorcycle International*. A more unlikely couple of motorbike experts is difficult to imagine. Julian looked like everyone's mental picture of a biker, but Frank looked more like a journalist. But there is no question that they really know their stuff about motorbikes and Frank is a great Norton enthusiast: he owns a Norton Commando (a bike which went out of production in the late 1970s), a Norton Classic (a limited edition of 100 Classics – Norton's first rotary engine motorbike – were manufactured and sold between 1987 and 1988, Frank's is number 63), and a Norton Commander.

Both Frank and Julian were extremely doubtful about whether Norton really could build up a demand for motorbikes that would exceed 1000 units a year. They felt that the attraction of the Norton bikes was that they had an impressive torque delivery, a wonderfully simple, light engine and an unequalled smooth ride. But in their view Norton bikes were unlikely ever to develop into more than a niche business. They thought that the Norton Commander could fill a niche somewhere between BMW and Honda, as a grand touring bike, and, if it was positioned in that market, their view was that Norton might manage to sell 750 a year, and at a better margin. They certainly did not believe that any significant number of motorbikes could be sold during the current year, and in the event this proved to be more than correct.

Both of them were extremely cynical and doubtful about David Macdonald's chances of success. Ryder had written some pretty damning articles about his business track record: they obviously had him firmly in the sinner slot.

I increasingly felt that, since there was no way that I could make the numbers add up, the company simply had to be operating at an overall loss. Once a company gets into this situation things tend to get rapidly worse. The nub of the problem lay in the sustainable demand for the engines, and it seemed increasingly unlikely that this would be forthcoming as far as the production of motorbikes was concerned, despite the company's continuing efforts and success on the race track.

I asked to meet David Macdonald again, both to try and check some of these impressions with him, and also to ask him why he did not allow the company to go bankrupt. The process of bankruptcy would at least ensure that the engine business could be bought as a separate entity, by somebody who was interested in it in its own right, rather than trying to make it work amongst all the various other unrelated activities which Philippe Le Roux had bought into the company in his attempts at diversification. Moreover, bankruptcy seemed to me to be the only way to deal with the substantial debts that I suspected Norton must have. It would also help to reduce the company's commitments to support a shareholder base which, on present form, could not possibly be rewarded.

When I saw him again, David Macdonald seemed to be shifting his ground once more. He agreed that the correct solution might well be for the company to go bankrupt, but insisted that the institutional investors were still not keen for this to happen. I found this curious since, as a generalization, institutions are usually quick to cut their losses, and I had not seen any business plan which suggested that there was a future for the company. I repeated my belief that the only future I could see for the company would be as an engine producer. However a few sums on the back of an envelope showed that for an engine producer to be successful on the scale that was needed, a very large volume of engines would be required. At least 10 000 units a year would have to be sold consistently if the business was even to service a new capital base. For the life of me I could not see where such numbers would come from.

David Macdonald pointed out that the potential deal with the UK fire pump company could bring in fairly substantial orders, however experience shows that developments of this type take much longer than people expect. It is never a simple matter of putting an engine into a motorbike, a car, a fire pump or an aeroplane and just letting the thing work. There are invariably problems of adjustment and other practical, albeit quite small, problems to be resolved before you can be confident you have a reliable and smooth running operation. Again I simply could not see how the order book could grow to a stage where the present haemorrhage of money stopped. The more I looked at things the more dubious I became about the whole operation. I could not make out whether David Macdonald was an honest man who was trying to feel his way through a morass of opposing possibilities and having difficulty deciding which was the most likely, or whether he was in the business for some unfathomable personal ambition. None of this was helped by his continual changes of tack, and the fact that any numbers that I obtained never seemed to be the same on more than one occasion. In addition, David said that the main reason he was interested in Norton was that, as an engineer, he believed that the Norton engine would be an ideal outlet for new material technology such as carbon fibre reinforced plastics. Here again I was not convinced. Changing an engine into new materials is a job which takes years rather than months, and would cost a commensurate amount of money. Somebody had to be found to foot the bill, both for all the development work in the meantime, as well as the outgoings on the business such as it was.

The more we talked the more doubtful I became. The only solution was to try and get behind Macdonald, to meet the institutional investors, or at least some of them. Here I hit the inevitable problems that the *Troubleshooter* programmes are continuously skirting around: not everybody is willing to expose their motives or thinking before a substantial television audience. I had to wait a long time before the institutional investors felt in a position to meet me but eventually, in early August 1992, I met one of their representatives, Neil Osborn, the investment manager of the Aberdeen Trust. At the same time I met Sir Tommy Macpherson. This meeting took place exactly a year to the day after I had first seen the Norton F1 motorbike at Castle Donington.

Sir Tommy had tentatively agreed, at the behest of the Midland Bank (Norton's primary creditor), to head up a new Norton company which would essentially buy out the old Norton, so that it started with no accumulated debts. This new company would, it was hoped, take over the Norton engine business. And, at long last, they had got hold of a forward business plan from Macdonald which, to my surprise, the bank and the investors were prepared to support. I also received a *bonne bouche* in the shape of the first set of accounts of any kind that I'd seen: they showed accumulated losses in Norton Motors of £7m, and an annual operating loss of approximately £200 000. Neil Osborn explained that his company had written off the money that they had advanced to Norton in the past, but of course they still had a substantial equity holding. They were prepared to risk a small amount of new money, in the hope that by doing so they would get something back. However, at the time of writing, the institutional investors have not yet committed themselves. The Midland Bank's position as the primary creditor had been absolutely crucial and the bank had behaved most honourably throughout.

Norton are just about to publish a set of audited accounts for the first time for at least two years, and then they intend to raise something like £2.5m by floating the new Norton company on the stockmarket. Only about £480 000 of this £2.5m will actually end up with Norton Motors. The Midland Bank have agreed to convert a substantial amount of their debt into an equity stake in the new company, as well as obtaining a royalty on engine sales. In addition they have given Norton Motors an interest holiday, which meant, in effect, that they would be paying interest on £1m only in the first year, and that interest on further monies which the Midland had already extended to the company would only become payable after three to five years. This would give them the necessary breathing space in which to try to make a success of the new company. I asked Sir Tommy how he saw the future of the business, pointing out that he would need a very substantial sale of engines if the business was to be successful. Apparently he and the institutional investors were expecting sales of 20 000 units or more within a relatively short period of time. I certainly have no wish to detract from the possibilities of Norton's continued success, but I do find it difficult to see how that number of units can be achieved in any reasonable period of time. Moreover, even with £480 000, the company would still be grossly undercapitalized for such a level of production.

Sir Tommy told me that the unmanned flight business was going to be sold to a management buy-out set up by David Garside, and the buy-out deal should be signed by the end of September. This would put some money into Norton, as well as hopefully giving an outlet for sales of engines for the future. Sir Tommy was appointing Lindsay Smith, who had been Norton's deputy chief executive and finance director, as the new managing director and, while I wished Lindsay every success, I did point out that he may not have had sufficient previous management experience of such a complex operation as he was about to take on. David Macdonald would be reappointed as chief engineer of the new company. The German company – FUS Fasteners – had been sold for what was in effect a walkaway price, but that was hardly surprising. It would be difficult to command any price at all for a company whose ownership is in as much doubt as theirs. I quote part of the sale contract between Norton and FUS Fasteners' new owners to illustrate: 'If either the Vendor or Norton Group Holdings Plc does not have title . . . or unencumbered title to any or all of the Assets, the Shares, the German Quotas or the English Shares, the Purchaser shall not be entitled to terminate or to rescind this Agreement.' I must say I chuckled when I read this contract. Philippe Le Roux's other acquisition, the American company called Pro-Fit, was being restructured and with any luck would not be a problem to sell.

Malcolm Faires was still reckoning to buy between 100 and 150 engines a year, but actual motorbike sales, despite the very optimistic views that had been expressed by David Macdonald, had been less than 150 during the year. However Norton had just signed a joint venture deal with the Carnell Motor Group to distribute Norton motorcycles in the UK and overseas. The target figure for the first year's sales is 500 motorcycles, and this should rise to a minimum of 1000 motorcycles by year three. Norton are also in discussion with a major Japanese engine company – and other engine companies – with a view to forming strategic alliances to export Norton's engine technology. The joint venture with Carnell is a major breakthrough for Norton, but the fact still remains that the total engine unit offtake in the first year would be 500 into motorbikes, 150 into unmanned flight and 150 into manned flight. Norton would have to cut their costs very severely if they were to be able to operate even at breakeven with such a small offtake. Everything still really depended on getting the deal with the UK fire pump company and they have not yet committed.

I expressed the view to Sir Tommy and Neil Osborn that the policies that Norton were following were very high risk. I could not see how they could build the business to the sort of size that the Midland Bank and the other shareholders would need if the business were to be worthwhile. Even if I took the most optimistic view it seemed to me that they were likely to face a very uphill battle. They were expecting to make the overwhelming bulk of their sales from an outlet into which the engines had never been sold before, and as a broad generalization, it was likely to take two or three times as long as they expected (because the timing of these things is always slower than one expects) and to cost two or three times as much money, and the company was still going to be inadequately funded.

Nevertheless I hoped, as I had from the very beginning, that the Norton business could succeed. There is nothing worse than having a business which has an intrinsic life of its own which is submerged inside a mess of other conflicting problems. There is no doubt that there is a highly desirable business there, albeit a small one, making rotary engines for a variety of outlets. There is also no doubt that the rotary engine would benefit from a good deal of further development, despite the fact that it has already been in existence for over twenty years. This development will undoubtedly be expensive. When Mazda, so much better funded and with access to so many more engineers, have taken so long to succeed, one cannot but admire the willingness of the Midland Bank and their colleagues in the City of London to have another go at trying to maintain the Norton engine business. At a time when financial institutions in the UK are continuously under attack for their short term views and lack of commitment to UK manufacturing, one can only hope that Norton succeeds, yet again, in rising from the ashes of its past.

The achievements of the race team also give me hope. Largely through the enthusiasm and dedication of its tiny team of engineers and riders, Norton has enjoyed considerable TT success during the past year, despite being operated on a shoestring: on June 5 1992 Steve Hislop came second on a Norton race bike in a formula one race on the Isle of Man, and on 12 June 1992 he came first and Robert Dunlop came third on Norton race bikes in the Isle of Man Senior TT. Steve Hislop also set a new fastest average race record.

But I told Sir Tommy that I felt that the new Norton company should focus its effort on its rotary engines and not on its motorbikes. Norton is an engine company that happens to make motorbikes – albeit beautifully engineered, highly distinctive motorbikes – not the other way round as I thought when I went to Castle Donington. Sir Tommy pointed out that Norton must continue to manufacture motorbikes, because it is the motorbikes that keep the Norton name alive. I agreed, but said that Norton should cut the number of bike parts manufactured at their Shenstone factory – at the moment they manufacture 50% of their parts – and that the factory should become a bike assembly shop. We discussed the possibility that Norton should not manufacture any bike parts at all and maybe even get someone else to assemble the bikes, but we agreed that it was essential that Norton continued to assemble the engines for their bikes.

The Norton name is a great British brand name and, even though Norton have made more comebacks than Frank Sinatra, I feel that if they get it right this time, it needn't be their swansong. It is as true in business as anywhere else that while there's life there's hope, but it depends on the commitment and dedication of the business people. Despite my endless difficulties in trying to resolve my personal doubts about David Macdonald, one thing is clear: Norton Motors would not have survived at all if it had not been for him and Lindsay Smith. I still do not see what personal gain David has derived from the entire operation, except the satisfaction of knowing that a great British brand name, which would have disappeared altogether, has another chance of survival which is almost entirely due to his, and Lindsay's, persistence and faith. I guess for a lot of us that in itself would be ample reward.

POSTSCRIPT   As of the beginning of December 1992, Norton is trying to raise £3 million on the stock market to ensure the Group's continuing survival. Michael Noakes, an experienced industrialist and for the past five years Chief Executive of Boustead plc, is intended to be Chief Executive of the refinanced group. Sir Thomas Macpherson will become Chairman and David Macdonald will have a technical role. Everything depends upon the Midland Bank's preparedness to accept the new financial plan. Only then can the City be approached for equity capital.

POSTSCRIPT: JUNE 1993

Norton are still in business and still making and selling bikes and engines. A new F2 road model, based on the bike that won the Isle of Man TT in 1992, is almost ready for production. They have, however, not yet received any new money and still owe the bank £7m.

There has been a considerable change of people at Norton. The chairman, Sir Tommy Macpherson, and Michael Noakes are no longer associated with the company. Lindsay Smith is no longer group finance director. In fact the group itself no longer exists – the American pipe-making subsidiary, having been sold off. In December 1992 the unmanned aero engine business was sold to Alvis, and the director of engineering David Garside went with it.

The latest hope for Norton comes in the form of a United States investment company called Wildrose Ventures, who have expressed an interest in putting £2m into the company. If this happens, the jobs of fifty workers will be ensured, the Midland Bank will do a debt-for-equity swap on the £7m they're owed, and Norton's 12,000 shareholders will receive a small share in the new company.

David Macdonald, who is still chief executive, believes that this deal will happen and that it will soon enable Norton to begin selling petrol engines at a rate of 5000 a year. He is optimistic about the future and believes that better products and the development of industrial engines will help once more make Norton into a name to be reckoned with.

The report of the Inspectors appointed by the Secretary of State for Trade and Industry was published early in 1993. As a result, the Serious Fraud Office is investigating the previous management and the events up to 1990.

CHAPTER SIX

THE SOUTH YORKSHIRE POLICE FORCE

TROUBLE SHOOTER

The management problems of the police are unique. Unlike any other organization I have come across, most decisions are taken at the very bottom of the hierarchy. This means that those at the top find themselves managing constables on the beat or in the car, at the command centre or investigating a case, who have already taken vital decisions from which everything else follows. It is a total inversion of the normal management problem. Moreover because the police are concerned with administration of the law, the decisions taken by the constables initiate a series of events which cannot easily be stopped. This, obviously, protects the citizen, but it also places responsibility firmly on the younger and, in some cases, least experienced of the police. There is, after all, no one to tell the constables whether they should make an arrest or press a charge. There is no one to tell them whether or not to enter a building from which the sounds of a scuffle are coming. And there are so many laws in the UK that it is difficult to apply them all with vigour and impartiality.

Policing is, therefore, selective and variable, and because of the limited amount of money available there are not enough police on the beat. The average ratio of police to public, in England and Wales, is 1:404 – that is one member of the whole police force, including administrative and clerical staff, for every 404 citizens. In the South Yorkshire area the average ratio of police to public is even lower, 1:433.

This means that the concept of policing with the consent of the public is a very real one. Laws which are totally rejected by the public are unlikely to be successfully forced through by a single individual against over 400 reluctant or antipathetic citizens.

I was surprised, but also very intrigued, when the South Yorkshire Police invited me to visit them and offer some management advice. I was surprised because the police in the UK are not generally known to be an open organization. They have a reputation for secrecy and for rejecting criticism, and they have been consistently criticized over the past few years by the media and by the public. I was intrigued because of my long standing interest in the problems of police management. I took over from Lord Sieff as chairman of the Police Foundation in 1984. The Police Foundation is a charity, supported by businesses and charitable trusts, which conducts independent research to help the police forces in the UK carry out their responsibilities more effectively and efficiently.

The South Yorkshire Police have had major problems. They, the Nottinghamshire Constabulary and the Derbyshire Constabulary bore the brunt of the pressure during the year of the miners' strike from March 1984 to March 1985, and Orgreave, where there was considerble strike action, and Cortonwood pit where the strike began, are both in the South Yorkshire Police area. I, and many other people in the UK, was extremely unhappy about the deterioration in the relationship between the police and the public as a result of the violent confrontations on the picket lines during that strike. Confidence in the police is a fragile thing and has been hard won over a long period of time. I have never thought that the UK police force should become a paramilitary force. Indeed since 1981, the police throughout the UK have taken great trouble to return to a way of working which historically always existed and which emphasizes the communal nature of their work: they are trying to ensure that as many areas as possible are covered by a community constable who is responsible for policing that area and whose name is available to all the residents in that area, whether that area is a small village or part of a large metropolis.

But the images that appeared every night on our television screens during the miners' strike – of police in full riot gear confronting miners on the picket lines – flatly contradicted the image of a police force that was trying to build up good relationships with the residents in each community and the irony is that until then, the South Yorkshire Police had been proud of their good relationship with the miners. It was an extremely difficult situation for the police constables who, in many cases, came from mining families themselves. I was a friend and admirer of the man who was then the Chief Constable of Nottinghamshire, Charles McLachlan, and I know what a toll the strike took on him and I can easily imagine the pain that the strike inflicted upon the police constables who had to police their neighbours, friends and sometimes their own families.

The South Yorkshire Police also carried the burden of responsibility for the horrific disaster at the Hillsborough football ground in April 1989, when ninety-five people died. I am bound to say I felt that Hillsborough was a disaster waiting to happen, and although Lord Justice Taylor, in his official report, pointed out that many factors led to the tragedy, he laid the blame squarely on the police for opening the gates and allowing a surge of people onto the already overcrowded terraces (standing room only). The Taylor report recommended that all stadiums with a capacity of 10000 or more must be all-seater – no standing room – by 1999.

It is not surprising, therefore, that by the time the Chief Constable, Peter Wright, retired in May 1990, the South Yorkshire Police Force was feeling pretty sorry for itself. Richard Wells, the Chief Constable who took over from Peter Wright, was promoted from Deputy Assistant Commissioner in charge of the North West of London, to Chief Constable of South Yorkshire on 1 June 1990. He is a prototype of the new generation of senior police officers. The past few years have seen some very big changes in the police force as one generation of chief constables retire and a new, younger, group take their place. For a start Richard's father was a Royal Marine and Richard graduated in modern languages and literature from Oxford university. The previous generation of chief constables usually followed their fathers into the force and often held no academic qualifications. Richard joined the police for personal and idealistic reasons: he wanted to make the country a better place. He began his service in London, with the

Metropolitan Police Force in August 1962. The Metropolitan Police is one of the toughest initiations to police work imaginable, but it is an invaluable school because it covers every possible community, crime and problem that a police officer is ever likely to have to deal with. Richard started in the ranks, as every police officer does. Although there are those who feel that an officer class should be recruited directly into the police forces, I do not agree. I think it is absolutely essential for the police to start their careers in the ranks and to take those vital decisions on the ground, so that they have direct experience of the unique management problem that all police forces face. I have always blessed my own entry into industry as a work-study officer, even though I disliked the job, because it gave me first-hand experience of how things actually happened rather than what managers liked to think happened.

Richard Wells served twenty-eight years with the Metropolitan Police Force, covering areas as diverse as the affluent West End of London to some of the most deprived areas of the East End. He undertook a wide range of command and management courses at the Police Staff College and has practical experience in operational command, training, community relations and, perhaps most significant, media relations. I met him many years ago when he was in charge of media relations for the Metropolitan Police and I was doing some work with Sir Kenneth Newman, the then Chief Commissioner of the Metropolitan Police. As well as comfortable familiarity with the media and a very considerable regard for the necessity of police involvement within the community, Richard is also extremely interested in the subject of management and he is a companion of the British Institute of Management. He is both an operational and a thinking policeman with very high ideals about the kind of police force that he wants to lead. Nevertheless, when I was invited to have a look at the South Yorkshire Police and their current management programme, I was not immediately sure whether Richard's aim was genuinely to ask for my help, or to provide his police force with some useful public relations. It would certainly not be the first time that an organization has asked me, in my *Troubleshooter* guise, to advise them on strategy and management, when their prime interest was free advertising. In fact, one of the results of calling in the *Troubleshooter* – I have been told by those who invited me – is the positive impact of public exposure. So I wondered about Richard's motives.

We had not really set out to deal with public sector organizations in the *Troubleshooter* series because it is much easier to understand business problems, and certainly easier to measure business success, by profit and loss. Even though the effects of bad business decisions may be masked by profitability for many years, ultimately a badly-run business pays the price and so do all within it. Unless a business makes a consistent profit, it folds up completely and those within it lose their livelihood.

However, the problems of bad management in the public sector do not exact the same form of retribution. Bad management in the public sector can lead to a depressing downward spiral of low morale, poor recruitment and even worse performance. In many ways managing in organizations without clear financial parameters is much more difficult than managing in the business world. A public sector organization is very often confused about who its customers are, and there is often an equal amount of confusion in the customers' minds about what constitutes a good product or a good service. All too often non-profit making (public sector) organizations see the continuation of their own existence as an end in itself and they are notoriously subject to the growth of bureaucracy. Such organizations often lack a clear focus, something which they desperately need because they usually employ very large numbers of people and the range and complexity of their tasks is considerable. And today in the UK, public sector businesses are under tremendous pressure to change, to save money and to become more efficient. So management in a public sector organization faces a different set of problems, but the principles of management are the same whatever the type of business or organization.

The problem with a public sector organization is to know where to begin. Fortunately the South Yorkshire Police publish an annual report (as do all the forty-three police forces in England and Wales). The report gave me a snapshot of the force and of its primary players and their areas of responsibility. However, although the report contained detailed statistics about the number of crimes committed and the value

THE SOUTH YORKSHIRE POLICE FORCE | 159

of stolen property etc., it did not contain accounts. There was no description of the South Yorkshire Police Force's activities in terms of profit and loss. I was also given the South Yorkshire Police Force's strategic plan, as well as the budgets and the capital plan, and Richard Wells's 1991 Statement of Purpose and Values, his 10 Point Plan and his Six-Hill Horizon. These last three documents are reproduced on pages 156 and 157.

As an ordinary citizen I have no argument with the Statement of Purpose and Values or the 10 Point Plan. They outline very clearly the sort of police force I would wish to pay for and the ways in which I would expect such a force to behave. But when I imagined myself as a policeman reading the documents, I found myself wondering what the documents told me about where my priorities lay and how the apportionment of money and effort would be made. The documents are a description of how things should be done rather than a clear definition of what needs to be done.

I decided to start by meeting some community representatives in order to test the degree to which the South Yorkshire Police Force's approach was supported by them, and to find out what the problems were. A meeting was set up with a small number of South Yorkshire's community representatives in a public house called The Queen's Ground. Of course a handful of people cannot speak for everyone, but they gave me a broad picture. This group all had some knowledge of or contact with the police. A number sat on the community police forums set up in each sub-division so that the police and representatives of the community could meet to discuss strategy, problems and concerns. Some represented minority interests and some were concerned with crime prevention. Many of the reactions to the police were predictable, although some were not. Without exception the people with whom I spoke felt that more resources, both in terms of money and menpower, were needed by the police, and all of them were appreciative of the efforts being made to develop community policing and put the police back on the beat. They wanted to see still more effort put into crime prevention and control.

On the negative side there were concerns about the police attitude to minorities, particularly to black people, and concerns about internal

The South Yorkshire Police Service

Statement of Purpose and Values

Our Purpose   on behalf of the general public is:

- to uphold the Rule of Law
- to keep the Queen's Peace
- to prevent and detect crime
- to protect life and to help and reassure people in need

Our Values   In achieving our purpose, we must at all times strive to:

- act within the law, serving with integrity the ends of justice
- act fairly and reasonably, without fear or favour and without prejudice of any kind
- ensure that the rights of all citizens – especially the vulnerable – are safeguarded, regardless of status, race, colour, religion, sex or social background
- be courageous in facing physical danger or moral challenge
- be honest, courteous and tactful in all that we do and say
- use persuasion, common sense and good humour wherever possible as an alternative to the exercise of force and, if force is finally necessary, to use only that which is necessary to accomplish our lawful duty

Our Way of Working   In upholding these fundamental values, it will help us to be more effective in working together and with our communities if we:

- maintain the dignity of our office yet display humanity and compassion
- constantly practise high standards of personal and professional conduct
- remember that, although the office of constable carries power and authority, respect must be earned
- listen and try to understand the other person's point of view
- confront those who bully or exploit on behalf of those less than able to protect themselves
- act with a willingness to try new ways of working
- speak moderately, yet firmly and proudly of what we do well
- admit our failings promptly and apologise for our mistakes
- show determination and resourcefulness in helping others

Justice with Courage

South Yorkshire Police

Chief Constable's '10 Point Plan'

1 Emphasis on public service

2 Staff care for customer care

3 Human face

4 Reasonableness of action

5 Communication of doubt upwards

6 Catching people doing right

7 Regular meetings to establish common ground

8 Do not waste any energy fighting each other

9 Honesty with courtesy

10 Allow individuality

The South Yorkshire Police Service

Our Six-Hill Horizon

Within five years, or as soon as practicable, to have a South Yorkshire Police Service which:

a is more open, relaxed and honest with ourselves and the public;

b is more aware of our environment, sensitive to change and positioning ourselves to respond to change;

c is more clear about our role and our identity and is obviously and justifiably proud of itself;

d is more closely in touch with our customers, puts them first and delivers what they want quickly, effectively and courteously;

e makes its decisions at the appropriate levels;

f is the envy of all other forces.

police attitudes: there was a strong feeling that justice was not always meted out to police who failed in their responsibilities. The community representatives were concerned that when the police investigated complaints against themselves they did not do so thoroughly enough, and they thought that more police training should be given to develop police sensitivity to public feelings. They believed that the police force was top heavy: too many people at headquarters and not enough out on the streets, at the sharp end. They were worried about the lack of clear police accountability and they felt that recognition and reward for community policing was not high enough. (There is a prevailing attitude in UK police forces that gives kudos to plain clothes police – those trying to solve crimes – but not to uniformed community police officers on the streets.) There was a fairly strong feeling amongst the people I met that the police were more likely to take action against crime, than to develop successful community policing and help resolve local problems. Again and again, they referred to the contemporary fear that people have of crime and the way that this fear is alleviated just by the sight of police on the beat. The police themselves have made comments about too many chiefs, lack of accountability and the lack of reporting back on objectives, which gave me an inkling of some of the management problems I might meet later. I began to get a feel for the sheer size of the problems that the police had been tackling.

I left my meeting with the community representatives considerably cheered. They were well informed, both about the problems of policing and the aims and ambitions of their local force, and they liked Richard Wells's new policy of openness and honesty towards the media and the public. Bearing in mind the recent history of the South Yorkshire Police Force, it was already apparent that considerable strides had been made to rebuild the bridges between the police and the public that had been so damaged by the miners' strike and the Hillsborough disaster in the 1980s. I was looking forward to my meeting with the Chief Constable, Richard Wells, in the morning.

I went off to my hotel for the night which was a magnificent country house called Hassop Hall, run almost as a family home by a charming couple, Mr and Mrs Chapman. There was a stark contrast between the pub I had just left and the luxury, peace and seclusion of Hassop Hall. The area covered by the South Yorkshire Police is full of stark contrasts too. It stretches for 600 square miles from the limestone beauty of the hills of the Peak District National Park on its western edge, to flat fens on its eastern edge, and from Barnsley – population 227000 – in the north, to Sheffield – population 505000 – in the south. The problems in the urban districts contrast with the problems in the rural districts and the scenery varies as much as the communities.

I met Richard Wells at 8.30a.m. and when I arrived it was apparent that he had already been at work for some time. The headquarters of the South Yorkshire Police Force is a relatively modern building in the heart of Sheffield. It seemed enormous and indeed was crowded with people. The five members of the senior command team – the Chief Constable, his Deputy and three Assistant Chief Constables – all have their offices grouped together on the fourth floor. None of their offices could be described as palatial, but the whole set up gave a feeling of unostentatious efficiency. Richard Wells was immaculately turned out, as indeed are virtually all the police officers I have ever met. It seems a sense of neatness and tidiness comes with the job. I had been told that he liked to work informally but, perhaps because of the television cameras, he was in full uniform, although he immediately showed his familiarity with television as a medium. After thanking him for the invitation I asked him what he felt his problems were and was stunned by the number that came pouring out. Quite plainly this was not a man seeking a public relations boost as I had originally suspected.

Richard Wells is faced with the massive problems of changing entrenched attitudes and ways of organization and operation, which is inevitably a slow process, and yet he is a man in a hurry, a man who is impatient for faster results. It must be lonely to come in as a solitary new man and try to change a business of this size, while still keeping the show on the road. It soon became clear that Richard's priorities were to rebuild bridges with the community, and with the Police Authority, and to give the police a greater belief in themselves. He saw an increase in community policing and a more open style of working – which he was forcing in – as key to these activities. The feedback from

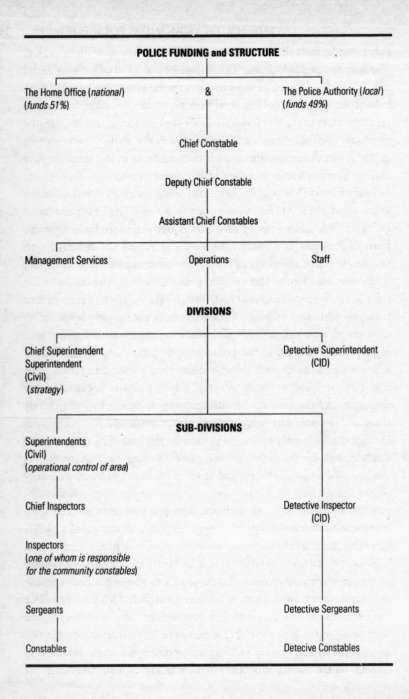

POLICE FUNDING and STRUCTURE

The Home Office (*national*)   &   The Police Authority (*local*)
(*funds 51%*)   (*funds 49%*)

Chief Constable

Deputy Chief Constable

Assistant Chief Constables

Management Services   Operations   Staff

DIVISIONS

Chief Superintendent   Detective Superintendent
Superintendent   (CID)
(Civil)
(*strategy*)

SUB-DIVISIONS

Superintendents
(Civil)
(*operational control of area*)

Chief Inspectors   Detective Inspector
                                    (CID)

Inspectors
(*one of whom is responsible
for the community constables*)

Sergeants   Detective Sergeants

Constables   Detecive Constables

my meeting with the community representatives the night before showed that he had already had some success. I asked him who he thought his customers were, and I was impressed when he replied that, besides the people of South Yorkshire who were the ultimate judge of the performance of the police and his own custodianship, he looked upon the 4300 members of the South Yorkshire Police Force, as well as the Police Authority and the Home Office, as customers who had legitimate expectations which had to be met. Richard made it clear that I could go anywhere and see or ask anything. He asked me to let him know if I had any difficulties anywhere.

The South Yorkshire Police area is divided into five divisions: Sheffield North and Sheffield South, Barnsley, Rotherham and Doncaster. Each division is responsible for three sub-divisions, with the exception of Barnsley, which is responsible for two sub-divisions. The South Yorkshire Police Authority is made up of twelve elected members and six magistrates from the four divisional towns. The chart on page 160 illustrates police reporting structure.

The South Yorkshire Police are woefully underfunded and have had no significant development money for quite a long period. One of Richard's very real achievements has been to obtain a development allocation of £7m from the Home Office to be spent on furthering his ideas for the modernization of his force. His ideas include staff recruitment, a customer survey, an occupational health unit and the acquisition of equipment and vehicles. Although police funding is divided between the Home Office (51%) and the local Police Authority (49%), the Police Authority funding comes largely from community charges which are themselves subject to limits set annually by national government. And the government divides police funding under capital (anything with a three-year-plus shelf life, for instance vehicles, buildings, computerization) and revenue (anything with less than three years' shelf life, for instance wages and small projects). This capital/ revenue funding split is the crude mechanism by which the Home Office seeks to control spending and which, in my opinion, could do with some rethinking. In 1992 the South Yorkshire Police Force's revenue budget was £122m, 84% of which (£102m) is paid out in salaries. Their capital budget for 1992 was cut by half to £3.5m.

I asked Richard what headroom he had to carry out his ideas for modernization of the force, and he explained that it had taken him two years to get permission to devolve budgetary responsibility to the divisions. Even now the amount of headroom for the Chief Superintendents concerned was absolutely minimal, but Richard was very proud of the fact that he had achieved agreement for them to spend up to £750 without reference to headquarters. This may not sound like very much, but it used to be £5! At the same time, his own discretion was limited to £10 000, double what it used to be, but only to be used in emergencies, and between Police Authority meetings. For anything above £10 000 Richard had to obtain clearance from the Police Authority who, while supportive, inevitably imposed further delays on the decision-making process. Richard plainly felt that trying to break out of the tangle of control, habit and precedent was rather like cleaning the Augean stables. It had taken two years to begin to devolve a small amount of authority.

Moreover, while Richard is beginning to devolve responsibility down the organization to divisions and sub-divisions, there are doubts about the financial and management database they have to work from, and therefore in real terms their scope is limited. Richard is also worried about the level of bureaucracy and paperwork which tends to be used as a means of protection against criticism and enquiry rather than to move things along. He is concerned also that, despite his desire to decentralize, many of the changes that he is trying to make seem to force things back to the centre. He cited the problems of measuring police effectiveness as an example. He had recently begun regular public opinion surveys so that he could track changes in the public's perception of police effectiveness, and was immediately faced with a dilemma. More police manpower is needed on the streets, at the sharp end, to make the South Yorkshire Police Force more effective, and yet in order to measure the public's perception of police effectiveness, Richard had had to create a centralized squad of seventeen officers who, it could easily be argued, would be better deployed away from the centre, out on the streets.

Richard explained that he was trying to run the top management of the police with his senior command team who met regularly to discuss the future direction of the force.

The previous night I was sent South Yorkshire's background papers on environmental change against which police strategy is drawn up. The papers were prepared by South Yorkshire's Policy Analysis Unit. The Policy Analysis Unit was set up in October 1991 by Richard Wells and is responsible for recommending strategy and advising on policy issues in consultation with people both inside and outside the police organization. I read the papers with interest, and growing perplexity, because they covered the national situation in some detail, rather more than the local one. It dawned on me that each of the forty-three police forces in England and Wales must be making their own precis of national events: a tremendous duplication. I also felt that the papers were too long and insufficiently selective in the points they made. Very long documents are easy to produce but tend to give people excuses for lack of sharpness in their decision-making. Very frequently they are not read properly, and people take different views about which key points they should be reacting to.

Chief Inspector Davis, the head of the force's Policy Analysis Unit was allocated as my guide during my time with the South Yorkshire Police Force. Unfortunately I only had a limited time with Richard, so I decided to investigate, with Chief Inspector Davis, the answers to all the other questions I would have liked to ask Richard. Personal investigation would give me a better feel for things anyway. I took to Chief Inspector Davis immediately. He is a really practical policeman with both feet firmly on the ground and no illusions about the changes that are necessary if South Yorkshire is to prosper. This is one policeman for whom the Chief Constable's instructions on openness are totally superfluous. He was really keen to see the *Troubleshooter* visit succeed, and he looked upon it as a key point of leverage to promote faster change. Although he is strongly in support of the Chief Constable's aims to make the force more open, he is concerned that there is a lack of clarity about the strategy. In particular he is deeply concerned about the continual centralization of people and responsibilities at headquarters, and the steady reduction of the already inadequate numbers of police on the beat. There were more and more initiatives, but they all seemed to pull people back to the centre. He felt that there was insufficient prioritization of what should be done for the future.

Chief Inspector Davis introduced me to his colleagues in the Policy Analysis Unit. I discussed the strategy document with them. I rather rudely pointed out that it wasn't really a strategy document at all, but just a wish list of what everybody would want in an ideal world, even down to the provision of extra desks and chairs. It did not outline broad police priority areas and, far from being a mechanism for devolving responsibility, it represented a restriction on responsibility and a formidable removal of flexibility. Chief Inspector Davis agreed that so far no proper strategy had been produced and he said that he and his team were now trying to build one up. I asked him how they were going about it. Chief Inspector Davis explained that they were discussing their individual plans with the nineteen other divisions and departments in South Yorkshire and then they would assemble everything into a single document to present to the senior command team. From my own experience I smelled trouble.

To assemble nineteen bottom-up strategies into a single overall strategy would inevitably produce a patchwork quilt of a strategy, with no real focus at all. The end result would be a strategy which would only be owned by the Policy Analysis Unit, and would not have the commitment of anyone. More than likely it would leave almost every contributor dissatisfied. The difficulty with producing strategies is that you have to work from both ends at once. You need a top-down strategy produced by the top team, but this must mesh with the strategic plans being drawn up on the ground. It is only possible to produce strategies which are owned by everybody by endlessly checking what the top leadership would like to achieve against what the people on the ground believe is possible. Moreover, the strategy must be a strategy, not a directive. It must leave plenty of room for individual initiative and action on the part of the units responsible for making it happen.

In the organizations for which I have been responsible I have tried to avoid having a planning department which produced strategies, and I felt that this was the situation in the Policy Analysis Unit. It is absolutely essential that they do not produce a pre-digested strategy for the senior command team, but that the senior command team should work out for themselves their own priorities for the force. The Policy

Analysis Unit's task is then to work out a strategy which makes it possible to achieve those priorities, and to give practical examples of what the strategy would mean for the individual divisions on the ground. I also suggested that the background papers would be best assembled on a single sheet of paper, grouping no more than three or four points under three key headings, and these should be the major points affecting South Yorkshire Police operations over the next few years. The great advantage of this approach is that everyone can find time to read a single page and so there is no excuse not to think about what is written.

I was really impressed with the team at the Policy Analysis Unit. They were all highly intelligent and saw themselves as key to the changes which they, and indeed every other policeman and woman I was to meet in South Yorkshire, were convinced were essential for the future of the force. Chief Inspector Davis was even more impressive. He believed that the growth in private security firms had happened largely because the police had left a gap in the market which the private firms filled. He believed that unless the police were able to demonstrate that they could do a better job, large areas of their responsibilities in crime prevention and research would be taken away and privatized. It was the first time I had ever met a policeman who viewed his business in a competitive sense, a policeman who did not automatically assume that life without a police force was unthinkable.

By now I was itching to meet some of the people on the ground so I went to Woodseats police station, south of Sheffield. Woodseats is a sub-division which polices both urban areas and countryside on the edges of the Peak District. The contrast between Woodseats sub-division and police headquarters in Sheffield could hardly have been sharper. Woodseats was not originally built as a police station. It was inherited by the police after it had been used for various other activities, including a doctor's surgery. Access to the enquiry desk was appalling – it was at the side of the building and down a flight of stairs – and potentially impossible for a handicapped person. The building itself was externally shabby and did nothing to enhance the reputation of the police force. However, pretty surroundings do not necessarily accompany an efficient organization. Inside the station I found very high morale, despite the poor conditions. Just as some of the best teachers triumph over their poor infrastructure, so the Woodseats sub-division of the South Yorkshire Police triumphed over theirs.

John Clark, the Superintendent in charge, quickly brought the realities of local policing problems into focus, when compared with the Chief Constable's plans and hopes. As far as John was concerned he had experienced no devolution of financial resonsibility whatsoever. He had no financial information to tell him what cost what and no management information. John had been told that he would be responsible for his own budgets, but he had just received his annual budget some four or five weeks after the beginning of the financial year, and he had not been invited to take part in setting it. His discretionary overtime budget, which has been devolved to the sub-divisions, had been reduced without reference to him. John was not given the chance to make a bid for money based on actions he would like to take during the next financial year, and this is just the sort of muddle which demotivates people and does nothing to make them want to take responsibility for their own destinies. But John Clark was wryly understanding of the situation and prepared to give the benefit of the doubt to the Chief Constable and his team.

I also met Detective Sergeant Trevor Hoyland, one of four CID sergeants at Woodseats sub-division. The Woodseats sub-division is responsible for policing an area where reported crimes have doubled between 1984 and 1992, but the actual number of policemen available has remained the same: 130. Both John and Trevor reckoned that at least a third of all their time was wasted, and they gave example after example of irritating ways in which more could have been achieved from the same number of people. John pointed out that there was very little collaboration across the divisions and indeed, to use his own words, the next division might as well be in Albania as far as he was concerned. Since the divisional frontiers were purely arbitary, and in some cases straight down the middle of the same road, it is hardly surprising that the public find policing behaviour so radically different from – literally – one side of the street to the other.

The further I looked into the circumstances at the police stations, the more horrified I became. To begin with their communications equipment is extremely antiquated. There are no personal computers at Woodseats and the only typewriters I saw were manual ones. When I saw detectives attempting to transcribe taped interviews on a manual typewriter for the benefit of the Crown Prosecution Service – the public prosecution service for England and Wales – I began to wonder whether it was me who was in Albania. Not a single member of the Woodseats police force had any training in touch-typing, and there were highly paid, highly skilled detectives typing out taped transcripts with two fingers. I asked why these matters could not be handled by typists, and I was told that there was only one typist for the 130 officers. I asked why the typing work could not be given to an external typing agency and I was told that it was police policy not to do this, because of security problems. Trevor and John had already told me that they thought about a third of their time was wasted, and it only took me a couple of minutes, doing sums on the back of an envelope, to work out that £10 000 spent on portable dictating machines, and a proper transcribing service, could increase the productivity of the detective force by getting on for 30%.

I asked John and Trevor how they would spend money on their station, if money was made available, and whether they would spend it on the building? Despite the unprepossessing accommodation at Woodseats, they agreed that their priority would be to spend money on equipment rather than on the building, with the sole exception of the enquiry desk, which they felt had to be made more welcoming and user friendly. They badly needed better communications equipment, and a more modern control room. (The South Yorkshire Police Force is in the process of modernizing its control rooms: the process should be completed within the next eighteen months.) I had been told that superintendents had relatively little flexibility in the way in which they used their staff because police regulations require them to notify their staff of their shift pattern twelve months in advance. It is true that this is a requirement but, as in most organizations, the superintendents and their staff manage to negotiate their way around these inflexibilities to make them work as well as possible in practice, although John pointed out that if he had real power to alter the shift pattern, he could use his manpower more effectively.

Despite the lack of visible effect of the new Chief Constable's plans for better communications and devolved responsibilities to the divisions and sub-divisions, all the policemen I spoke to at Woodseats were very supportive of the direction in which the South Yorkshire Police were moving, but they were anxious to see things speeded up. There was a gulf between headquarters and divisions and sub-divisions and, although they had seen the Chief Constable himself, communication with the rest of headquarters was mostly by memorandum.

My next visit was to Bradfield police station. This served, yet again, to underline the amazing diversity of the area covered by the South Yorkshire Police and the different types of policing that they undertake. Bradfield is a storybook picture of an English country police station. A modern stone building with superb views across the Bradfield moors, it is the home of Constable Mick Hague. When I arrived he and his wife, Shelley, were working in their garden. Shelley is a former policewoman whom Chief Inspector Davis – who was with me – knew when they worked together in Sheffield. Shelley was medically retired as a result of back injuries sustained while apprehending a shoplifter. Despite this unpleasant experience her support for and involvement with the police remained strong.

Mick explained how he allocated his time around his patch, about which he was very proprietorial. Yet again I was struck by the lack of facilities. By now I was used to post-war manual typewriters, but I still expected modern communications equipment, particularly for a police constable on his own. Apart from the telephone, there was really no way of contacting Mick except via his personal issue radio, or when he was in his vehicle. Although constables with personal issue radios keep their radios with them even whey they are officially off-duty, radios can be switched off. When I asked whether there were any bleepers, Mick explained that they were in such short supply that they were only issued to superintendents. The idea of the superintendents of the South Yorkshire Police being the only people who could be raised immediately in the event of a public disturbance struck me as somewhat ludicrous, and another example of how scarce resources were allocated on a hierarchical basis rather than on one of need. There was no word processor, no message system of any sort, and twenty-eight days notice had to be given to change the shift system under which Mick worked. Like all country police he did not shut up shop at the end of his shift, but nevertheless there was a degree of inflexibility built in to the way of working which is a far cry from the relaxed image that most people have of a country policeman's life.

Mick, like all the South Yorkshire Police, thought that a major part of his work was community policing and flying the police flag. Without question one of Richard Wells's successes has been to force the realization down the line that the public need the reassurance of seeing police on the streets. They need to feel that the police are involved in their communities. Mick and his wife were going to a function that evening as guests, but plainly they both saw their involvement in all social and local activities as part of the job.

I ended the day at the opposite end of the South Yorkshire Police Force area, at Doncaster police station which combines the division, under the command of Chief Superintendent Michael Thompson, and the sub-division which was responsible for Doncaster itself, under the same roof. Doncaster is an area I know better than Sheffield because ICI had a factory there which I visited over the years. The area is another very varied one, covering both the Thorne sub-division, a vast rural area including some mining communities, and urban Doncaster itself. Doncaster's prosperity was built on the coal and railway industries.

Chief Superintendent Thompson was one of the old school: he had real doubts about the pace at which the Chief Constable's aims could be achieved. In fact he thought his task was to protect his own people from a rate of change that he did not think they could cope with. Despite this view he had reinforced his community constables by expanding the number of special constables who assist with community policing. This seemed to me to be a realistic way to overcome some of the financial and manpower limitations with which the force was struggling.

The more I looked at the divisional structure, the more I began to wonder why it was necessary to have divisions as well as sub-divisions. Old fashioned management theory is strongly tied to the concept of span of control which teaches that more than six or seven people reporting to a single individual is too many. The world has changed since then and modern communications and technology, as well as new ideas about the role of the centre, have made much broader reporting areas a workable possibility.

So far I had spent most of my time with the police organization rather than with the people actually taking those vital decisions on the ground: the people doing the job. It was time to go out on the beat with the community policemen and women. The first community policeman I met was Mark Webster. He is a massive man: between us we could easily have squashed any miscreants into extinction just by sitting on them. Mark served in nuclear submarines before leaving the navy to join the police, so we had plenty in common, besides an interest in the task in hand. I did not really expect much to happen while I was plodding along beside Mark in Sheffield's Broomhill suburb, but it gave me another view of policing. Mark had the lovely wry sense of humour which seems to be a police speciality. He told me that one of the tasks that he was given, early on in his community policing time, was to build up relationships with Sheffield university. That was the only guidance he was given: to build up relationships with the university. The way he set about building up this relationship was left entirely to him.

But I was impressed with the success that he had achieved in a relatively short time, and interested in the mixed feelings that he had about his university customers. It was Mark who made me realize, for the first time, how much the public rely on the police for the prevention of what might be termed nuisance rather than crime. He pointed out that there was much more work for him to do when the students were in residence than when they were away, largely because of high-spirited activities such as removing traffic bollards. While, from the students' point of view, such things were a bit of fun, from Mark's point of view they were a damned nuisance.

The briefing sessions before Mark's shift invariably list people and things to look out for, but Mark can allocate his time in his area as he considers sensible. His area includes one of the tougher drug dealing parts of Sheffield and, since I knew this was a problem that the Assistant Chief Constable in charge of operations was particularly concerned with, I was interested to see how Mark went about it.

Needless to say as we were walking the beat in the morning there was absolutely nothing to be seen of any kind of activity, but I was assured that things would look very different in the evening if I passed through. I asked Mark how the Chief Constable's initiatives affected his life on the beat, and he said really very little. Plainly he had no fear of speaking up: he had the intrinsic openness of the South Yorkshire people. He was pretty cynical about the Chief Constable's Six Hills initiative. He considered it patronizing, mostly because the paper listing the six aims of the Six Hills initiative had descended upon them without any prior verbal briefing. Mark felt that those at the bottom of the organization, those actually doing the job and taking the vital decisions, like himself, had no access to top management at all, and, as a result, those at the top had very little contemporary understanding of the problems that those at the bottom were coping with. Mark looked on community policing as a long term operation, and he did not overestimate the limited deterrent effect that he could have.

Communications were better in one area: Mark had a better quality radio. Now there were only a limited number of areas on his beat where radio blackspots meant that he was out of touch with the control centre. And because of the nature of Mark's beat, his radio was personal issue which meant that, like Mich Hague, he kept his radio with him even when he was officially off-duty.

However the problems of dictating and typing were absolutely overwhelming and, like every other member of the South Yorkshire Police Force I met, Mark despaired of ever catching up with the paperwork, particularly because he could not type and had never had any typing training. There was a fax machine at the station now, but otherwise there was not much in the way of communications equipment, and practically everything was done by reporting into the station. While I was with Mark he was approached by a number of members of the public on a whole variety of minor problems. I was struck by the ease with which the public dealt with him and the confidence with which he reacted to them.

Next I joined Jane Pearson in her Panda patrol vehicle for part of her shift. Jane also showed great confidence in discussing things absolutely openly, but she did say that a number of her colleagues thought that she was mad to do so! She was particularly critical of the lack of interaction between the people in charge at the top of the police organization, and the people on the beat, like herself, at the bottom. And she was fairly scornful about the impracticality of the uniform she had to wear. Although I thought it looked very attractive, Jane said that it was both old fashioned and hopeless for the job. In fact Jane said that much about the South Yorkshire Police Force was old fashioned. Jane felt that they should be dragged forcibly into the 1990s: she didn't think that the pace of change was anything like fast enough, and they badly needed new equipment for such things as fingerprinting. And Jane, like the rest of her colleagues, had never been trained to touch type, so the transcription of urgent reports took much too long.

But Jane loved the job. Her father had been a policeman and she was really interested in the variety of tasks which came her way. Sadly we were only called to one minor incident while I was with her, which she dealt with with great tact and speed, but I reflected yet again on how lucky we are to attract men and women like Mark and Jane to carry out our policing for us.

I went on to meet John Nesbit, the Chief Superintendent at Sheffield North, which includes Hillsborough. John is a police legend in his own time and he is one of the South Yorkshire Police Force's most charismatic leaders: his men love him. Everyone I met mentioned John's name in terms of awe and affection. He believes in leading from the front and is very much an action man. Sadly he is within a few months of retirement. John was responsible, during the Hillsborough tragedy, for organizing the rescue and emergency services, and his division also covers Sheffield university and most of Sheffield city polytechnic, so that a very large proportion of the responsibilities of the South Yorkshire Police fall on his ground. John is a keen sportsman and he took me to see the force's recreation club at Niagara in Sheffield. He is extremely proud of the club. One of John's claims to fame is that he was the man who arrested Arthur Scargill, the leader of the National Union of Mineworkers, and charged him with obstructing the highway, during the 1984–1985 miners' strike. A minor miners' riot ensued.

John Nesbit's division covers some of the largest council estates in Europe and he, like Mark Webster, drew my attention to the role of the police in preventing the nuisance element which is such a disruption to the peace of mind of ordinary citizens. Like others I met, John was concerned about the lateness of budgeting, and he was very concerned about the lack of human resources in the South Yorkshire Police. When the current force was set up in 1974 – it was an amalgamation of the old West Riding Constabulary, the Sheffield and Rotherham Constabularies, and the Doncaster and Barnsley Borough Constabularies – the ratio of police per head of population was far worse than it is now. But even though the ratio has improved, John said that it was still not good enough. John was particularly concerned that the role of headquarters was increasing, not decreasing, and he thought that communications up the line, both within divisions, and between divisions and headquarters, were poor. He was desparately anxious to see more resources diverted to the front line, and he was worried about the delays between the development of ideas and the actions taken. He felt that time was not on the side of Richard Wells's current initiatives and that there should be more practical action if the Chief Constable was to maintain the undoubted goodwill with which his initiatives were first greeted. John felt that the Chief Constable really needed to put his own stamp on the force, otherwise the philosophies would remain philosophies and nothing practical would change.

While I was at the police recreation club, I looked in on a training session for the Chief Constable's 10 Point Plan. I was interested in the comments of the class, who almost immediately identified lack of trust as a major obstacle in terms of putting the 10 Point Plan into action. Trust is one of those things which it is easier to talk about than to achieve. Very few large organizations have much trust within them, particularly if they have very long lines of communication like the police. But I was surprised to find that lack of trust was a problem within the police. I have always seen considerable mutual respect inside the police, which I put down to the shared experiences of the officers and the constables. But if there are difficulties building up trust, it is invariably because there is a disparity between words and actions: people listen to the words but they believe the actions. No amount of good intention or carefully thought out communication can survive actions which contradict the views expressed. The chief superintendents' and superintendents' belief in devolved responsibility was severely dented by headquarters' tactless handling of the discretionary overtime budgets. If the actions of senior management contradict their professed aims, it is always an uphill struggle to recover the confidence – the trust – of the staff.

On the last stages of my enquiry I went to meet two of the Assistant Chief Constables. I started with Martin Davies, the Assistant Chief Constable in charge of operations and, as luck would have it, I met him just as his people were dealing with a bomb scare – which turned out to be a hoax. Martin is a well travelled policeman. He started with the Cardiff City Police, and then he spent some time with Dorset Police. He attended Police Staff College at Bramshill, and ended up as Divisional Commander at Bournemouth, before arriving in South Yorkshire in 1990. Martin holds two degrees – in law and in social and political history – and he goes about his work with a great deal of thought and deliberation. He is extremely clear about his operational priorities. The number one task is to control the drugs problem. Although South Yorkshire, compared to many other areas in the UK, has a relatively small drugs problem, Martin knows that controlling the drugs problem before it snowballs further also controls drugs-related crime. Martin is clear that successfully fighting the drugs problem is a specialist task. He believes, like many other police officers, that the police force is desperately short of technological backup, certainly by comparison with the individuals they are endeavouring to take on. For instance the South Yorkshire Police do not have encrypted radios which would guarantee the privacy of their conversations, and most of the individuals the police take on have radio scanners and so they can easily listen in to police conversations. Martin has a very carefully thought out set of operations policy priorities, and he too wanted more manpower on the ground, rather than in support services.

I then met Walter Jackson, the Assistant Chief Constable in charge of management services. Here my doubts about Richard Wells's policy of devolved responsibility began to surface in a big way. The real problem was the lack of meaningful accounts and statistics. I said that not enough information was available, either to the centre or to the divisions, about the true cost of current (or past) policing operations, and Walter readily agreed. There was no true cost structure to enable cost comparisions between one activity and another, even though one of their prime aims is to give value for money.

Walter thought something in the way of a ready reckoner could be worked out within six months. But I was surprised that a devolved system of accounts and statistics did not already exist, after all the Chief Constable had been trying for the last two years to get agreement to devolve responsibility to the divisions. I also mentioned the delays in the budget preparation and the lack of involvement with those down the line who had been told that they would be responsible for their own budgets. I made a mental note that what they really needed was a well qualified civilian finance director.

I then turned my attention to utilization of the £7m development money. Walter supported the purchase, or lease, of a force helicopter which, I am bound to say, seemed an enormous single expenditure (£622 000 a year on a leasing arrangement) when much smaller amounts of money would have a tremendous effect on productivity in the divisions. I was still not clear about the basis for the allocation of the precious £7m, nor about the systems for judging the comparative value of various sorts of expenditure on the force's objectives.

Policemen are not trained accountants so I was not terribly surprised by what I found; however, if management responsibility is to be delegated, then a good management accountancy system is an absolute prerequisite so that managers can make informed decisions. I felt that overall financial prioritization and clarity about the amounts of effort and money that should be put into the various fields of activity, was severely lacking. This is plainly not an easy task for a police force which has to cope with a wide number of differing requirements all of which must be met all the time, but this is an area which must be addressed.

I was pretty clear that the members of the senior command team spent quite a lot of time together and were strongly in support of the Chief Constable's overall aims. Five is an ideal number of people to work together effectively and well. I had heard that the Chief Constable intended to enlarge the senior command team to include the chief superintendents. It is certainly essential to involve the chief superintendents in the decision-making process, but I do not think that the senior command team should be enlarged. It would impair its cohesiveness and single-mindedness.

By now I was beginning to develop some feelings and ideas about the management problems and priorities of the South Yorkshire Police Force, but at the moment there were too many thoughts which needed disentangling before I could present a working plan to the senior command team. Moreover, I felt strongly that I needed to know more about the way that the Police Authority looked upon the activities of the force, and also to find out what other police forces were doing within the existing constraints. One of the problems that the UK police forces suffer from is that rewards and recognition are only possible through promotion. A more senior job carries a higher salary level, but good performance in the same job does not, therefore a sprawling hierarchy develops. I had a strong suspicion that the divisional structure was originally set up in order to provide jobs and opportunities for chief superintendents, thus promoting and motivating down the line. I have seen this happen in a great many organizations and, as well as the deleterious effects of long chains of command and slowness of response, more and more work is created internally and less and less effort applied externally.

When I looked at the total of 4300 people in the South Yorkshire Police Force, it seemed that the proportion of administration and supervision staff was far too high. There were far too few police on the streets doing the job. In managerial terms the only way out of this is to reduce the number of levels, and to make a conscious and continuous effort to devolve right out to the sub-divisions. This is particularly apposite in the case of the South Yorkshire Police, because of the differences between the various areas which the sub-divisions cover. Despite Richard Wells's beliefs and determination, the South Yorkshire Police Force appeared to be moving in exactly the opposite direction: closer and closer towards the centre. The difficulty then is to know which button to hit because no organization can respond to too many initiatives at once.

It was already apparent to me that the South Yorkshire Police were not short of initiatives and expectations. But introducing too many initiatives inevitably leads to diffusion of effort, and nothing actually gets done. I suspect that this is what has happened inside the South Yorkshire Police Force.

However before getting to the heart of my advice I wanted to sum up both the encouraging points and the areas which I felt could be improved upon. So I ended this first visit to the South Yorkshire Police by telling the senior command team that I thought that the £7m development money from the Home Office was a significant improvement and the attempts to open up the force had been welcomed, although I was concerned that expectations had been raised within the force which were in danger of being frustrated. I was also impressed by the fact that the police see their relationship with the public as absolutely pivotal to their success, and that Richard Wells's efforts have initiated a transformation in the relationship with his external customers.

These achievements are considerable in a relatively short time, particularly when you bear in mind that it is people's attitudes – and people's attitudes in a 163-year-old organization – which are changing.

The primary area which I felt could be improved upon, from a management point of view, was the lack of strategy. Most of the strategy work that had been done so far related to HOW things were to be done: by being open, honest, caring and trusting, rather than exactly WHAT was to be done. You cannot develop trust unless your actions reinforce your aims, and so unless the actions of the force were illustrative of their professed aims, I thought that that vital quality of trust could not be developed. I saw a gulf between headquarters and the divisions and sub-divisions, and I was particularly worried about the problems of devolution, without an adequate management information system. I urged the senior command team not to increase the quantity of senior management, and I suggested that it should be a priority to shift manpower from the centre to the sharp end.

I thought they also needed to find some way of releasing small amounts of capital to ease the pressures on paperwork. I felt that a minimal amount of equipment, together with some training in touch-typing, would pay off enormously. I questioned the need for divisions within the organization, and wondered whether it might not be possible to remove that layer.

The problem that I had to help Richard Wells and his senior command team with was to decide what the next appropriate actions should be: we were certainly not short of choice. The number of possible initiatives was almost limitless. I said that I needed to go away and think about the alternatives and to do some research into what other forces had managed to achieve, and to talk to one or two other people who knew the police better than I did, before coming back to them with my final recommendations.

My next visit was to the Police Foundation, which I had been involved with for many years. There I met Mollie Weatheritt and Barrie Irving. For over ten years the Police Foundation has been working on all aspects of policing in the UK, and has been accepted throughout the police force as an independent research body. Straight away Barrie pointed out the major problems which police forces are coping with: constraints on capital and delegation, and difficulties in trying to evolve practical strategies. Any police force has a multiplicity of people to satisfy: the Inspectorate of Police, the Home Office, the local Police Authority and the general public.

Barrie pointed out that the Police Authority appoint the Chief Constable and he is accountable to them, so much depends upon the Police Authority's views and how well the Chief Constable deals with them. Barrie thought that there were two basic kinds of chief constable. The first was the chief constable of the old school who saw himself as the producer and director of a big show. The overall result is not the provision of something tangible, but the general feeling that a good production has been staged. The second kind of chief constable took a much more modern management approach: he set objectives which the force worked to achieve.

If you combined a modern chief constable with a supportive forward-thinking Police Authority (and there are some), then you could achieve all sorts of things. Barrie gave examples of a number of police forces who, with Police Authority support, had employed civilian finance directors, and had management information systems in place which had been drawn up by firms of accountants. He also gave examples of forces where a whole layer within the police organizational structure – the divisions – had been completely disbanded, and where the resultant savings in manpower had been used to increase the number of constables and officers available for active policing. Barrie thought that, in an ideal world, approximately 50% of police manpower should actually be working on the street. I was surprised, but pleased, to hear that a number of police forces had already, to paraphrase Jane Pearson, moved into the 1990s – at least a little.

The problems in the management of the South Yorkshire Police relate almost entirely to manpower costs, since they represent 84% of all costs. Civilians, as well as being more plentiful, cost – on average – only half as much as trained policemen and women, so a policy of civilianization to the absolute maximum, ie, getting more officers back on the beat by employing civilians to do administrative jobs, must be a good one. One of the problems of police forces is that they have continually increasing demands placed upon them as more and more laws are passed, and so far virtually none of them have felt able to refuse to undertake any of these additional tasks.

Now that I knew that radical change was not only possible, but had actually been achieved in other police forces with the support of the Police Authority, I decided to call on Sir John Layden, the chairman of the South Yorkshire Police Authority. Sir John is leader of Rotherham Council, where he has the support of 63 out of 66 members, a fact of which he is very proud. He is also secretary of the Miners' Welfare Institute in Maltby, where we met. Sir John was born and brought up in Maltby and it would be difficult to find a more patriotic or devoted politician. He seemed to know every man and woman in the town, and it was obvious that he felt fiercely proprietorial and protective about the pit and its community. Sir John had worked his way up through almost every job at the colliery, before taking over as President and delegate of the Maltby branch of the NUM, following in his father's footsteps. Sir John is the finest type of slightly old fashioned local Labour politician. He has a very keen sense of responsibility to his community, for whom he felt he was acting as champion. He believes in the power of public spending to ameliorate the conditions of the community, and has a fierce and justifiable pride in the sports centre, the swimming pool, the library and the Miners'

Welfare Institute itself. Sir John was responsible for the selection of Richard Wells and was obviously proud of his selection.

I started by asking him what he had been looking for when he was replacing Peter Wright, the previous Chief Constable, and he explained the difficulties involved. After the miners' strike and the Hillsborough disaster, the most important thing was to win back public support and to restore public confidence in the police. It was going to be an extremely difficult job and Sir John had set out to find a combination of police experience and political and public relations skills – not a common combination – but he was more than satisfied that he had found them in Richard Wells. Sir John considered that the relationship between the police and the media had been transformed during Richard's period as Chief Constable. It was true that crime in South Yorkshire was on the increase, but Sir John attributed this more to the overall conditions and high unemployment rates, than to any failure of policing. He was extremely proud of the £7m that had been obtained from central government last year, but believed that the expenditure of this money had to be spoken for item by item by Richard Wells.

We spent some time discussing this philosophy, which was clearly based on the view that it was the Authority's bounden duty to control all expenditure in advance, and to go through the various requests for funds – even requests for funds for relatively inexpensive items – with a fine-toothed comb, before granting permission. I pointed out that the business of asking permission up and down the line was enormously expensive both in terms of administrative costs and of time, and that it made it extremely difficult for the Chief Constable to devolve any real power or responsibility. The fact that the Police Authority invariably accepted such requests did not obviate the amount of time and administrative cost involved in obtaining it. I appreciated that the responsibility for public spending was somewhat different to the responsibility that I normally expected to wield on behalf of my shareholders. Nevertheless, I believed that my shareholders were equally entitled to expect rigid controls, but that these controls could be applied after the event, rather than before, with beneficial results to all concerned. What Sir John was actually doing, in my opinion, was hanging on to the purse strings and centralizing responsibility, and I could not believe that the Police Authority genuinely wished to control the minutiae of the police force's activities in these inefficient ways.

A devolved responsibility for expenditure of £750 to divisions meant in effect that, after dividing the money between the sub-divisions, they could barely afford to buy a wastepaper basket without asking permission. The Chief Constable alone had achieved devolved responsibility for expenditure up to £10000, but that was only to be used in emergencies, and between Police Authority meetings. This whole arrangement was a tremendous removal from the concepts of pushing responsibility as far down the line as possible, which I understood both he and Richard Wells were keen to achieve. I suggested that a shift away from controlling expenditure in advance and towards laying down broad guidelines as to the ways in which the Police Authority expected the money to be spent, and holding Richard Wells to account after the event, would benefit everyone: it would short-circuit the system and allow Richard Wells more flexibility and freedom to devolve responsibility, and the force's administrative costs would drop dramatically.

During our discussion Sir John shifted his ground, and said that he would be more than willing to receive a request for consideration of ways to short-circuit the system, from the Chief Constable. He made it quite clear that he was willing to discuss allowing Richard Wells to account for monies spent after the event, and generally to give him more control over his spending and reporting. He said that he was willing to initiate such discussions. I felt that this was a key change and very much hoped that discussions would take place. I also began to wonder whether Sir John and the Chief Constable were in fact deferring to each other – each waiting for the other to take the initial action which would free the whole system up. I made a mental note to raise this issue when I saw Richard again.

I then turned to civilianization and the rank structure, to see how willing Sir John would be to contemplate more radical change. There was no doubt that he wanted to see more policemen and women on the beat, and felt very strongly that the visual presence of the police was necessary, both to reassure the public and as a deterrent to the vandalism and minor lawlessness which was of so much concern to everyone. He was quite proud of what had been achieved in removing one of the Sheffield sub-divisions from the current South Yorkshire structure, and felt that their progress on civilianization had been substantial. I then turned to the idea of getting a firm of accountants to review the accountancy and management control systems of the force, including its relationship with the Police Authority itself. Again he said that he would be happy to see a proposition put forward to this effect, although I do not think he saw it as being the freedom-enhancing move which I believed it could prove to be. We had a thoroughly enjoyable time together, culminating in a visit to the Maltby pit which is one of the largest and most modern pits in South Yorkshire, with reserves of over 60m tons of coal.

I left my meeting with the chairman of the South Yorkshire Police Authority with a clear feeling that, while the Police Authority could hardly be called progressive and radical in their thinking, they were at least likely to be open to argument, discussion and pressure. This seemed to reinforce the advice I had received at the Police Foundation that, while it was possible to achieve greater flexibility in the management of police resources, this could only be done with tremendous effort, and the closest possible working relationship between the Police Authority and the Chief Constable. There could be no doubt of the mutuality of respect and support between Sir John Layden and Richard Wells. Nevertheless, I was not convinced that the two of them were moving as fast as I thought was necessary. The irony was, however, that both individuals believed that they were introducing operating changes in the South Yorkshire Police Force at breakneck speed.

It seemed to me absolutely essential that my final presentations to the senior command team should be in the form of a simple plan, together with a clear prioritization of what should be done. So I drew up an Agenda for Action which I presented to Richard Wells and his senior command team at our final meeting.

I began our final meeting by reporting on my discussions with Barrie Irving and Mollie Weatheritt, and with Sir John Layden. Changes had been achieved in other police forces, with the support of their local Police Authorities, and I thought this might be possible in South

Yorkshire, particularly because Sir John Layden had said that he would welcome suggestions from Richard Wells for ways to short-circuit and devolve the system. Sir John was willing to think in terms of allocating budgets in advance, and in larger quantities of money. I asked the senior command team how many times they had actually put requests to the Police Authority which had been refused. They replied that their requests were measured in tens, rather than in hundreds or thousands, and that it was not so much a question of requests being refused, but more that it took a long time to persuade the Police Authority to agree.

I asked Richard whether he and Sir John Layden were deferring to each other and suggested that perhaps Richard was not pushing Sir John as hard as Sir John was willing to be pushed. Richard didn't think that was true, but he would be alert to the possibility in his future dealings with Sir John.

I turned to my three-point Agenda for Action. The first and most important thing on my Agenda was that they should ask an external accountancy organization to recommend a financial control system, including a control system from the Police Authority, which could be applied to the whole force. I felt that this might well short-circuit the problems of control from Police Authority level, and Sir John Layden was open to such suggestions.

The second item on my Agenda was to devolve the organization – but only when the financial controls were in place. I recommended getting rid of the divisions altogether, because it seemed to me that divisions were an unnecessary extra layer in the organization, and I feel strongly that extra layers should only exist if they add value to the layer below. I recommended devolving budgets to the sub-divisions, to give the individuals in charge proper control over their sub-divisions and these budgets should ultimately be devolved 100% – or as close to 100% as Richard Wells's own devolved power would allow. They should make a determined attack on simplifying and eliminating all the control systems which had grown up over time. Every single thing which could be decentralized should be decentralized and they should rethink all their reporting systems.

The third item on my Agenda for Action was to increase the proportion of uniformed police at stations, and therefore on the beat, through civilianization and the application of technology.

We had a long discussion and I became aware of the constraints, including those currently imposed by the Home Office, on the senior command team's thinking, which made such radical change difficult. We discussed devolved budgeting and devolution of responsibility. The senior command team said that they could only think for the moment in terms of devolving the part of the revenue budget that was not spent on manpower – up to 13%. They were also worried that they would have no control over the individuals in charge of each area if budgets could eventually be devolved 100% to them: they might decide to use the money in ways that had never been discussed. I said I didn't believe that would happen because the budgets would be agreed in advance, but the chief superintendents – or superintendents as I preferred – would have flexibility within the agreed budgets, so that they could decide whether, for instance, they wanted to hire three more typists or one more officer, within the agreed amounts of money. Real control in any business is always expressed primarily by money and not by numbers of people alone; and control of the money by the individuals on the ground who know what they need empowers those individuals to take decisions within an overall strategy set by the senior command team.

In order to begin the process of change, the senior command team, after consultation both inside and outside the force, should set the priorities for the Agenda for Action, and then those priorities should be delivered by the individuals in charge of each area as those individuals saw fit. A plan was necessary, together with pointers stating the deadlines for achieving each part of the action, and I stressed the importance of the senior command team reporting back to their people as each stage of the plan was achieved.

To my surprise the senior command team seemed enthusiastic, although Richard Wells saw major difficulties in implementing my Agenda for Action. He seemed very concerned about the possibility of getting such a plan through the Police Authority. I asked him if he thought it would help if I explained my views to the Police Authority, and he seemed to think that it might. I reiterated the importance of control being on one primary basis, namely money, and that, within that control, the individuals in each area should be free to choose how their available money was spent. Without such devolved financial responsibility I could not see what impetus there was for civilianization or savings on manpower at all. I felt that trying to control both the money and the numbers and types of people employed was bound to be self-defeating.

Richard and the senior command team were kind enough to say that they thought that my interventions had helped to sharpen their focus.

I think that, despite his great strides in improving openness, Richard Wells is more cautious than he seems and I would be quite surprised if he was willing to push the radical sorts of changes that I was recommending, although I felt that his senior command team would be open to looking at them. There is no doubt that this whole process is going to be a slow and developing one, but the South Yorkshire Police Force is full of people with energy and ideas who need the freedom to put those ideas into action.

If radical change is implemented, the South Yorkshire Police Force will – in my opinion – be able to provide a service which is far better value for money than it is at the moment.

Constables on the beat in South Yorkshire will only be convinced that real change is taking place if they see that senior officers are practising what they preach – doing things, as well as saying how things should be done. The constables also need to see that what is done produces results which enable the force to deliver a more effective service to their customers.

I felt relieved to have achieved anything at all because the police are very difficult to shift, but I felt that there had been a shift in the senior command team's thinking. It is rare to get the police to open up, but they have taken the first step, and I shall watch with great interest to see how the South Yorkshire Police progress in their attempts to change both the values and ways of operating inside this well established and absolutely vital public service.

POSTSCRIPT: JUNE 1993

Last November South Yorkshire published a new business plan to prioritize spending and development from 1993 to 1998. The force now have four key strategies: increasing available operational patrol time; a comprehensive policy of staff care; the development of a management information system; making decisions at the appropriate level. All of these are laudable aims.

However, financial devolution down to the sub-divisions is continuing far too slowly for my taste. At Woodseats, John Clark now has £23,100: £8,100 for travel and subsistence, £8,400 for temporary staff, £3,300 for equipment, furniture and materials, and £3,300 for repairs and maintenance. This represents an improvement but it is still a very long way from the sub-divisions having real control of their financial destiny.

The major capital and revenue budgets are still controlled from the centre, and still have to be approved by the local police authority – anything from the purchase of vehicles to new computer systems has to be approved in detail. However, at the national level there are some hopeful signs: the government is now looking at the whole working relationship between the Home Office, the Police Authority, and Chief Constables. It is also looking at revising the make-up of police authorities, and the way funds are allocated through them. Within the force there are high hopes that there will be greater control of budgets for the Chief Constable. Also, the distinction between capital and revenue budgets is to be removed, which will mean the Chief Constable should be able to invest more freely in technology to save manpower.

CHAPTER SEVEN

TROUBLESHOOTER
REVISITED

**TROUBLE
SHOOTER**

It is more than two years since I was first invited to visit six British companies in my *Troubleshooter* guise, and I have remained in touch with most of them, but now I had the opportunity to go back to see everyone in a short space of time, which gave me a panoramic view of their positions. The *Troubleshooter* revisits were interesting and, for me personally, highly rewarding.

I began, as I did in the original series, by visiting Tri-ang and there I had a terrible shock. I drove to Tri-ang's majestic nineteenth century mill which, with its modern extension, was the home of Tri-ang's business, but I couldn't find the mill. I decided I wasn't in the right place because I was staring at a cleared building site. But I soon discovered that the area was scheduled for housing development, and the mill, which I remembered with Sydney Orchant's daughter's name, Sharna, emblazoned upon it, had been demolished. I couldn't believe it.

I picked my way across the site with a heavy heart and I saw pathetic signs of the past. The plastic wheel of a Tri-ang toy lay forgotten in the rubble, vividly illustrating what I think has gone wrong in the UK over the last few years: the people who eventually occupy the houses on this site will need work and income in order to live in the houses, but the mill and the Tri-ang business which provided that work and income, have gone. How can the people who come to live here support themselves if the businesses don't exist? And how can the UK create wealth and healthy export markets when an empty building site is valued more than a business which contributes to that wealth?

With the benefit of hindsight, I think that even when I visited Tri-ang in 1987, this once great British brand name had already lost the race against time. I believed then that they needed new management, new investment and new machinery. All these things have been achieved, but not in the way I would have liked. Tri-ang was eventually sold to a French company, Clairbois, a member of the Superjouet manufacturing group. It's very sad to think that British Tri-ang toys, including the original Noddy car, are now made in Moirans-en-Montagne, a small town in the Jura region of France. The toys are manufactured in a modern robotized factory under the Tri-ang name and exported back to the UK. I wish we could have kept Tri-ang British and I was depressed by the thought that a successful British brand was now a British import rather than a British export.

I was in a pretty depressed state of mind when I went to visit Sydney Orchant, the man who was Tri-ang's chairman during my first *Troubleshooter* visit. Sydney left Tri-ang in 1988, but for Sydney Tri-ang was in the past and he was looking into the future. Sydney looked healthy and prosperous.

Sydney and I clashed on several issues during my first visit to Tri-ang, but there is something about Sydney's irrepressible commitment to the toy business which commands respect. After leaving Tri-ang, Sydney – spurred on by his wife who suggested that 'he'd better buy himself a company' to keep himself occupied during his retirement – bought another toy company. Unfortunately this company did not work out, but in 1990 Sydney bought his existing company, Sunny Smile, from the receiver and now he is busy breathing new life into it. Sunny Smile's products are for the nursery and pre-school market and the company was founded approximately forty years ago.

Sydney has gone from running a manufacturer of some of the largest toys in the UK to running a manufacturer of some of the smallest, and Sunny Smile itself is tiny compared with Tri-ang, but it might have disappeared totally if Sydney had not bought it. It is remarkable that Sunny Smile exists at all because the toy business in the UK has been in steady decline for some years, and Sunny Smile is not just an importer. Sunny Smile contracts out its manufacturing, providing a large percentage of the workload for a small plastics factory in Scotland.

Sydney's working hours are flexible and he employs just six full time staff. Other employees work on a part time basis, and are on low salaries but high incentives. Fixed costs in Sunny Smile are low and Sydney is doing what he likes doing best: he dreams up the products, and he sells like crazy. He is even exporting a little.

Sydney's business is at minimum risk, with very low overheads. However Sydney does not want Sunny Smile to grow too large, and that worries me. He is determined not to be drawn into expanding the company to any significant size.

The whole Tri-ang episode taught Sydney that expansion was risky, and he only wants enough money from Sunny Smile to satisfy his personal needs. If Sunny Smile prospers I don't think that Sydney will let it grow to a level where it exposes him to risk again and in a way I don't blame him, after all he is in his sixties, and why should he go through all that hassle again? And yet we need companies that can grow, and to have anybody in this country restraining the possibilities of growth cannot be a good thing for the UK. The sad truth is that if we go on losing big companies and replacing them with smaller companies, our manufacturing base will continue to decline. Our only hope of remaining competitive is for the people who drive the smaller companies to be ambitious and grow their companies significantly.

The depression I felt when I saw the empty Tri-ang site did not lift after my visit to Sydney. A once glorious British brand name is no longer British, and Sydney has imposed limitations on the growth of Sunny Smile. These things seemed to me to tell an all too familiar British tale, and yet, without Sydney and his like, things would be even worse than they are. I had to tip my hat, metaphorically, to his indomitable spirit and his determination to continue in the toy business, a business that he knows and loves.

Two of the original six companies turned down my offer of a *Troubleshooter* revisit: Apricot Computers and the Morgan Motor Company. I was particularly sad not to go back to Apricot because they have gone from strength to strength since my first visit in 1989. Despite the misgivings they expressed in 1989, they bit the bullet and sold the manufacturing side of the business. It is impossible to compete in manufacturing on a world stage with a mass market product like a personal computer, unless you are world class. At the time, when I recommended selling manufacturing, Roger Foster – Apricot's founder – argued strongly against the idea. He said it was like telling Boeing to stop making aeroplanes. But business is very often about letting your favourite children go and giving new ones a chance to grow.

They sold the manufacturing side of the business to Mitsubishi, and if ever there was a right decision, that was it. Mitsubishi are world class. The factory in Scotland has been saved – even expanded – and the computers themselves are going from strength to strength. Mitsubishi have brought in both the technical and financial back-up which the manufacturing business needed to hold their own in an increasingly tough and competitive world market place.

Since the sale, Roger's policy has been to concentrate on the areas in which they have a sustainable competitive advantage: software and computer maintenance. The company now trades under the name ACT, and Roger's policy has paid off handsomely. ACT's profits have soared and their share price has doubled, and all this has happened in the middle of a recession. Roger Foster has every reason to be proud of what he has achieved.

There were two companies which were very close to my heart by the end of my *Troubleshooter* visits in 1989: Copella Fruit Juices and Churchill Tableware. Copella because how could I fail to fall in love with the Peake family who are so emotionally, and practically, involved in their businesses, and who took the brave and difficult decision to sell their beloved apple juice business? And Churchill because the Roper brothers were outstandingly open and willing to consider anything to improve the prospects for their tableware business, no matter how outlandish it might seem to them. And, as they said themselves, they achieved something of a sea change in their management style.

I remained in touch with Copella and the Peake family after my first visit: they asked me for advice on a number of occasions following my initial recommendation to sell the Copella apple juice business. I originally urged them to sell out completely and advised them to concentrate on developing the farm and the golf club with its two golf courses. I felt that it would be death by a thousand cuts if they sold part of Copella and continued to be employed by the new owners: it would be very difficult for the Peake family to work with other people who did not have the same emotional attachment to the product which they had developed and built up. However the Peake family decided not to sell out completely as I thought would be best. They sold a majority shareholding in Copella to the Taunton Cider Company, just after my first *Troubleshooter* visit. The younger members of the family continued to work with the Taunton Cider Company.

It was, in fact, an extraordinarily good sale for Copella: Taunton Cider reinvested in Copella, repositioning the product in the market place, and modernizing the factory. But the time eventually came when the Peake family were considering exercising their option to sell the rest of Copella, and they contacted me. I advised them to sell out completely to Taunton, which they did. The whole family learned a lot from working with Taunton Cider, as well as gaining substantially financially.

The Peake family businesses then consisted of: the farming business which includes the apple orchards, the golf club with its two eighteen-hole golf courses, Peake's organic apple juice business – which they did not sell to Taunton – and, of course, a bit of money in the bank.

The golf club and its two golf courses are now making a profit without significant additional capital involvement. And in March 1992 the Peakes at last obtained planning permission to develop their hotel which will be attached to the golf club. They were thinking of extending their facilities to accomplish this, but obviously they hoped to develop the hotel from the profits of other parts of the business, rather than by borrowing. In the meantime, of course, the golf business has become one of the most competitive and busiest in the country. The Peakes are recruiting a new professional manager who will run the golf club on their behalf, and they are quite clear that their policy is to try to develop the club within its own cash flow. They have also brought in a specialist farm manager called David Blake, who is making a real impact on the farm itself.

I was curious to see what the Peakes had done with the money from the sale of the rest of Copella, and they were delighted to show me. Predictably they had taken a flyer. Devora Peake – the founder of the Peake family businesses – saw an apple packing and storage business which was in the hands of the receivers. With her characteristically emotional response, she made an impulse buy. It took Devora just two weeks to complete the purchase.

The apple packing and storage business is on a seven acre site on the edge of Chelmsford at Galleywood, and when the Peakes took me to see it I understood why Devora was so attracted to it. The apple packing line itself is superb, but this part of the business only made a tiny profit for the first eight months, before interest had to be paid, and it is neither covering its borrowing nor providing the family with any cash. It did seem ironic that the Peakes, having just sold Copella, were going straight back into another business where the margins, even in the good times, are pretty low. However, as well as the apple packing business itself, there are twelve or thirteen warehousing units and 5000 tons of cold storage facilities which are let out, and there is permission to develop the site for housing.

The Peakes only need about 120 000 units (cases of between 30lb–40lb each) to pack their own apples, and the break even point of the packing operation is around 188 000 cases. The total packing capacity of the operation is about 300 000 cases and the Peakes provide an apple packing service to other growers to fill that capacity, but the apple packing business can only ever make small amounts of money and has the potential to lose a great deal. Historically, it is a high risk, low reward, labour intensive business, and in the Peakes' undercapitalized situation, I felt that the apple packing business itself was in a dangerously exposed position for them.

I thought that they would make a much better return by letting out the packing hall – some 40 000 square foot – for storage. The Peakes said that it might be very difficult to find a lessee in the present financial climate, which was fair comment. However the warehousing and storage businesses involve little in the way of additional costs once the actual property has been paid for, and I felt that these businesses had more potential than the apple packing business.

The family's business was getting complicated again. They had a warehousing and cold storage business, a packing business, an organic apple juice business, the golf club and potential hotel, and the farm itself.

I was worried that the Peakes were heading back towards an imbalance between assets and income, and in the case of the apple packing itself, no income at all at the moment. This was the situation they found themselves in when I first visited them, and it was why I advised them to sell Copella.

However the Peake family have really worked hard at trying to get their management act together. They went on a management course to sort out their individual strengths and weaknesses, and they subsequently reallocated the jobs in their businesses in accordance with what they discovered, or confirmed, about themselves while on the course.

I don't think it is possible to keep the Peake family down, and it was probably foolish of me to think that the more restricted operations that I had in mind for them, with the money from the sale of the rest of Copella, could possibly keep such a dynamic bunch happy and involved. I really like the whole family, they are a tonic to be with and plainly very fond of each other, and they're devoted to the businesses that they have inherited and developed over the years. They are always looking for new ideas and there is a restlessness about them which I find very stimulating.

This *Troubleshooter* revisit turned out to be a mini-*Troubleshooter* in itself. The Peakes invited me back the following week, and I was glad of the opportunity to go away and do a few sums and think about the whole thing, before meeting them once more.

My next call was to revisit the Shropshire District Health Authority, but I decided to touch base with Ken Morris first. Ken was Shropshire's district general manager during my first visit, but he left the authority to work in a small private enterprise organization, running hospitals with approximately fifty beds on a contractual basis for the NHS, or for private patients. There are six hospitals at the moment, and they have plans to expand. Ironically this firm is busy replacing the type of cottage hospital that Ken was instrumental in shutting down when he was Shropshire's district general manager. It is a small business by comparison with the Shropshire District Health Authority with a turnover of just over £4m, as opposed to Shropshire's £100m+, but it is moving into profitability after a period of expansion. Ken was revelling in the freedom he had to get on with the job, and his knowledge of the NHS, which is now his primary customer, is an enormous help.

Ken is much better suited to a smaller business. He was very happy, and relieved that he no longer had to cope with the political in-fighting or the financial battles of a large public sector organization. It was really good to see that the change had been such a beneficial one for him, and that he was involved in creating new opportunities using the skills that he had developed.

When I originally visited Shropshire I made a bet with Ken: I said that if he could get Shropshire's waiting lists down and run the authority within budget by the end of the financial year, I would give him three bottles of champagne. The waiting lists are now much shorter and the books are balanced, but Ken is no longer the district general manager. I reckoned I owed Ken a bottle and a half of champagne, which I gave him.

My next call was to find out what had happened to the cottage hospitals, who were fighting for their lives when I first visited the Shropshire District Health Authority. When Ken was district general manager he struggled to implement a policy to close various cottage hospitals in order to balance the authority's books. The policy was unpopular and caused a public outcry. Ken managed to obtain agreement from the authority to close six cottage hospitals, but that wasn't enough to make ends meet. The health authority became bogged down in internal management and external political arguments about the closures, and I felt then that Ken had lost the will to find new ways of managing in this very difficult political situation. Nevertheless that was the job of the district general manager. He had to find ways to manage within this complicated and sensitive situation.

The whole nature of the job of district general manager of a health authority has now changed. Since the government's white paper was published in January 1989, inviting hospitals to apply for self-managing trust status in order to establish the NHS internal market, there has been pressure from both the public and the private sectors for changes in the management of health care. The management of hospitals is now left with the doctors, nurses and managers in each hospital, while the job of district general manager – or chief executive as he is now called – of the health authority is no longer to be a sort of 'super' hospital manager, but rather the purchaser of services from well-managed hospitals. The new chief executive of the Shropshire District Health Authority, Colin Hayton, is directly responsible for the management of units which are not trusts, ie, directly managed units, but he will not have managerial authority over any hospitals in his district who apply for and are granted trust status. Hospital trusts will become the providers of health care services and Colin Hayton will manage the purchasing of those services.

So hospital management now seemed much clearer, but sadly, by the time I returned in 1992, only two cottage hospitals existed, but they were thriving and had been radically altered. The Lady Forester hospital at Much Wenlock has been converted and modernized with the support of the Shropshire District Health Authority and, despite becoming mainly a nursing home, it has managed to keep four non fee paying beds for use by general practioners for short term care, thus retaining a large element of its original cottage hospital function. I had originally hoped that exactly this sort of mixed economy solution would be possible.

Much Wenlock was saved by the determination of Dr Alan Gainer, who was a member of the Shropshire District Health Authority and therefore knew what the authority was planning, and by Joyce Moore, who is now retired. She, Sister Gill Reynolds and Dr Alan Gainer put in a tremendous amount of work and rallied the local community. Some first class people were found to help on the business side, and the Friends of the Hospital, a local fund raising group, raised money to help with curtains and odd bits of equipment. There is no doubt that a really valuable and important asset has been retained.

Many of the people who work in the nursing home are local, and I couldn't help grieving for the other cottage hospitals which had lost the battle against closure, but it was good to see that Alan Gainer and Gill Reynolds, who had fought so hard against closure, had won. Gill

Reynolds now manages the whole enterprise, and I am in no doubt that it will go from strength to strength. Unfortunately it is very much easier to shut things down than it is to use a bit of imagination, and management creativity, to preserve something for the long haul. Most of the people I spoke to in Shropshire were now clear that the cottage hospitals should have been preserved.

The second of the surviving smaller hospitals, The Beeches, is now called the Lincoln Grange Nursing Home. It is a hospital for the elderly which I also visited first time round. Here the senior nurse, Anne Deaken, and her colleague Jacqui Howse, spurred on by my first visit, were determined to save the hospital if at all possible. Anne Deaken approached Andrew Hillier, who was then the planning manager at the Coventry Churches Housing Association Extra Care (CCHA Extra Care), to explore the possibility of working with the voluntary sector to save The Beeches. Some time later, Colin Hayton, who knew about Anne's approach to the CCHA, resurrected discussions and the CCHA now run the Lincoln Grange Nursing Home, supported by the health authority. The authority put some much needed money into updating Lincoln Grange and the wards have been radically changed from Nightingale wards (huge wards with little or no division or privacy between beds), to a near domestic environment with single rooms. The nursing home has a family atmosphere about it, and it is much brighter and more welcoming. Although it is good that the health authority have supported this hospital, it is sad that the initiative did not come from the health authority management in the first place, and it is very sad that more small hospitals have not managed to remain open. However, I was pleased to see that two of the cottage hospitals had survived with the mixed economy solutions which I advocated. But I have no doubt that similar ways of reopening some of the other smaller hospitals will have to be found.

The two major hospitals in the Shropshire District Health Authority, the Princess Royal hospital and the Royal Shrewsbury hospital, have dramatically different stories to tell. The new Princess Royal hospital at Telford, which was not yet open when I first visited the authority, is now on line, has everything going for it and seems to be working well. The Princess Royal has, obviously, contributed to the reduction of the authority's waiting lists.

The Princess Royal has applied for trust status in what is known as the 'third wave' of applications. If their application is granted (and the majority of applications for trust status have been granted by the Secretary of State for Health since the first wave of applications were put in, in April 1991), the Princess Royal hospital will become independent of health authority control, and will operate as a trust from April 1993. Two-thirds of all NHS facilities will be NHS trusts by April 1993. The Princess Royal hospital has few capital demands because it is a new hospital, and it has a new team of people.

However the situation at the Royal Shrewsbury is rather different. Trust status for them could be a much more difficult proposition, since their basic problems are undercapitalization and the old fashioned nature of much of the hospital itself. But there now seems to be a positive plan for up-grading the Royal Shrewsbury hospital over the next three to four years.

The Shropshire District Health Authority managed to persuade the West Midlands Regional Health Authority to agree to allow the Royal Shrewsbury hospital to knock down their wartime buildings and sell the land for housing development. The regional health authority sanctioned the use of the money from the land sale to develop the Royal Shrewsbury's new buildings, but unfortunately for the Royal Shrewsbury, land values have since collapsed. However they have at least achieved capital approval from the authority and development is going ahead.

I have remained in touch with the consultants I met in Shropshire and have been invited to talk to them since my first visit, so I had already met the new chief executive of the Shropshire District Health Authority, Colin Hayton. Colin has achieved some impressive results. When I first visited Shropshire they had one of the biggest overspends and one of the longest waiting lists in the country. The books are now balanced, the waiting lists have fallen dramatically in a number of areas, and there are less than 200 people waiting more than a year for an operation.

Both the Princess Royal and the Royal Shrewsbury are now run by hospital management boards which include clinicians, nurses and paramedical staff. The major decisions in the management of the hospitals are now taken with the advice of people who are medically and professionally qualified, and the major change is that the hospital management boards now have far more influence over day to day matters: both in hospital trusts and in directly managed units. However one of the doctors at the Royal Shrewsbury hospital rather sadly informed me that although they understand the strategy much better and are now more involved in the decision-making process, they often find themselves in the position of trying to control a potential overspend and therefore many of the decisions that they debate have to do with trying to find ways of reducing that overspend without making cuts. This is a sorry state of affairs for the Royal Shrewsbury hospital.

General practitioners in Shropshire now have the option to apply for fund holding status, but this is relatively new to Shropshire, and it could be particularly difficult for them because there is still no adequate management information system. Out of sixty general practices in the Shropshire district, there are only eight fund holders at the moment, with another seven thinking about becoming general practice fund holders in 1993. So there is a long way to go to achieve the government's ideal of making the provision of health care in Shropshire responsive to market forces.

The Shropshire District Health Authority, like the whole of the NHS, continues to be short of financial and capital resources, and the doctors whose areas of medicine are being deliberately held back in order to fund other activities, predictably do not like what is happening. But all in all I felt pretty cheered by my visit to Shropshire. There is more clarity and a much greater feeling of drive and things moving on, and there is clearer management within a simplified system. People think they know where they are going, but of course the horrendous problems still remain and new ones continually emerge. That is the way of all management situations, but at least now there is a clear mechanism to cope with the problems, and hopefully to move ahead.

The *Troubleshooter* visit first time round where I felt that I had had the least effect was the visit to the Morgan Motor Company. I bump into Peter and Charles Morgan quite frequently because we live not very far from each other, and although there is no personal antipathy between us, they felt that the press had blown up our differences of opinion out of all proportion. However, I believe that the Morgan Motor Company resisted my suggestions for fulfilling what I saw as the true potential for their business, and I was sad when they declined my offer of a second *Troubleshooter* visit.

My original advice to the Morgan Motor Company was to double production and so reduce their long waiting list, and to increase the price of their cars. The Morgan Motor Company have increased their prices a bit over the past three years, by about 10% a year, although the average annual rate of inflation for the same period was 7%.

During my original visit to the Morgan Motor Company I felt that the company was imbued with a fear of change and that there was an inbuilt wish to hang on to the way things were. Although I felt that Charles Morgan was aware of the need for some change, I believed that radical change was necessary to ensure their survival beyond the end of the century. There was a period, a while back, when demand for Morgan cars fell away and I felt that the fear, particularly Peter Morgan's fear, of a repetition of that time, mortgaged them to their own history, making change very difficult to contemplate. Change is very difficult for people and so much about change is emotional. Change is a threat on an emotional level, and I think that that, coupled with the spectre of a repetition of the fall in demand for Morgan cars, is what holds the Morgan Motor Company back.

Because Peter and Charles did not want to see me, I did the next best thing. I went to see my friend John Worrall, chairman of the Morgan Sports Car Club and a Morgan dealer, whom I met first time round, to see what, if anything, had changed. John manufactures stainless steel accessories for Morgan cars, such as radiator grills, luggage racks and door handles. John told me that the immediate impact of my first *Troubleshooter* visit was to send Morgan's UK waiting list straight through the roof. Although I never did get an answer about the true length of the UK waiting lists from the Morgans on my first visit, rumour had it then that it was as long as ten years. The difficulty about trying to measure the waiting lists for Morgan cars has always been the same. It is only when the cars are actually about to be manufactured that a place on the waiting list is, or is not, confirmed when Morgan contact the potential customer.

But even in this recession, there are still waiting lists for Morgan cars. There are approximately twenty UK listed Morgan agents and their waiting lists vary from five to ten years. Meanwhile Morgan have managed to push production up. They manufactured 412 cars in 1990 and 464 in 1991, an increase of some 12%, although the figure for 1992 (year ending 31 May) was 472, a much smaller increase.

However, Peter and Charles Morgan are very happy with their lot. I like them both, and the fact that we have honest differences of opinion does not worry me. But my own personal interest is to see the Morgan Motor Company go from strength to strength.

I understand that the Morgan Motor Company has installed a manufacturing resource planning computer network at the factory, and Charles Morgan is studying for a diploma in modern manufacturing, leading to an MBA, at Coventry University, so maybe the Morgan Motor Company will introduce the changes which it seems to me that the business opportunities certainly warrant.

But I am still saddened because I think that the Morgan Motor Company could be larger and more successful. I am pleased that they have increased production and put their prices up a little, but they haven't really grasped the nettle: the Morgans aren't as ambitious for their company as I would like them to be. It saddens me that they have failed to take advantage of what I see as a golden business opportunity, with all that that means for all the people involved.

Next I went back to Churchill Tableware, the largest family run pottery business in the UK. I had remained in touch with Churchill and visited them on a number of occasions, so I was fairly up to date with what had happened since my first *Troubleshooter* visit. Nevertheless it was fascinating to meet the whole team again.

Of all the companies that I visited, the Roper brothers – Michael, Stephen and Andrew – have probably gone the farthest in accepting my advice and views. Originally I advised the brothers to invest in their tableware factory. I recommended that they spend money on mechanization and on machines that can apply four colour designs, known as four colour total transfer machines. I wanted to see them cutting production costs and moving their tableware products up market. They really needed to move into the middle market in a big way and spend much more on design. But most of all, I wanted to see the three Roper brothers detaching themselves from the day to day management of the business, setting objectives for, and then delegating to, the excellent managers they had. I wanted to see the brothers allowing their managers the freedom to decide how to implement the objectives.

On my return to Churchill I was delighted to discover that the Roper brothers have pulled out of the very strong executive positions which they held when I first met them, and obviously this has been a difficult change for them. And I was also delighted to discover that the brothers had just appointed Bernard Burns, who was Churchill's new marketing director when I first visited, as managing director of Churchill Tableware. Later I found out that Stephen Roper was worried that Bernard was in too much of a hurry to change too many things, but Churchill has grown dramatically since my last visit and as companies grow it is extremely difficult, but necessary, for the owners to allow their managers the freedom to manage in the ways that those managers think are best.

Bernard took me round Churchill's tableware factory. He has a dream of trying to take all the processes, from the biscuit kiln onwards, and link them together into one continuous process. If this could be achieved the quality would improve and the number of rejects would be reduced dramatically. This would be a real revolution for Churchill, and for the pottery business which traditionally mechanizes individual areas of work but has tended not to think in terms of the whole process. Bernard thought that it would take about five years to implement 80% of his dream. The problem with the tableware factory when I first visited it was that it was production led and not marketing led: it was driven by the need to fill the kiln. It is now much more marketing led, but Bernard would like the balance between production and marketing to favour marketing even more, although that will require more sophisticated control systems than Churchill currently has.

Bernard was bursting with ideas for the tableware factory, and although he acknowledged that much had been achieved, he felt that there was an inertia within the business – due mostly to the fact that the pottery business is hugely conservative – which he was busily fighting against. Bernard felt that there was so much more to do. But as Bernard took me round the tableware factory, I saw a number of changes. They have invested in a new dust pressing unit and in three four colour total transfer machines. Dust pressing is a process which uses clay granules rather than wet clay: it reduces the cost of making plates in bone china and porcelain and produces significant energy savings, but dust pressing machines are expensive, costing around £500 000 each. Churchill's attempts to produce earthenware through dust pressing are innovative and original, but they were suffering the inevitable teething problems in trying to get it to work consistently and satisfactorily.

Churchill had found that it was much more economical to buy four-colour machines than two-colour machines, because, by definition, the throughput rate for two-colour products on four-colour machines is twice the rate achieved on two-colour machines, and, obviously, these machines can also turn out four-colour products. Moreover it means that the design department can produce more colourful up market designs for the four-colour machines. However Bernard was anxious to mechanize even more: he felt that there was much more modernization yet to be done.

Churchill Tableware now employs around 700 people in two factories, despite having automated large parts of the process. The success of Churchill's strategy to move their products up market, contrary to my expectations, has led to the employment of more people because the further up market the product, the more manual skills are required. It has also resulted in the purchase of a new factory. The process is still a batch one and, because of the vast increase in the range of products and designs, Churchill was beginning to hit problems in scheduling and production planning.

I also visited the design department where, besides finding immense changes in the number of designs and in the whole spirit of the place, they were all very excited because they were about to produce a bone china product for the first time. I was able to see some of the prototypes and I began to understand why they believed they could produce at highly competitive prices and push their product range even further up market. They were producing five or six new designs a year, with a much wider range of colouring, as well as developing the technology they had used for the production of the Mille Fleurs range – the new range which Churchill launched just after my first visit – to create greater impressions of colour range from their two colour printing machines. They have done this partly by using a split screen process. Because of the increased range, Churchill was having to do much more market research before selecting the products to major on.

I left my visit to the tableware factory full of enthusiasm: Churchill Tableware was really motoring, Bernard was full of ideas, the design department had their tails well up and were producing new and attractive designs at a rate of knots, and the whole thing was flowing through into profit. There aren't that many products left in the world where you will routinely find 'made in Britain' next to the trademark, but it is still true of the pottery business, and Churchill is making a significant contribution to that business.

I was greatly looking forward to meeting the brothers again, not least because, after my first visit, I had spent quite a bit of time trying to get them to get their act together. One of the problems I had diagnosed was that the personal objectives of the three brothers differed and that therefore they were not putting the unified pressures on their management which were necessary if the company was to achieve real speed. As always the brothers were tremendous value. They were delighted with what they had done, although they were all a bit depressed that the climate was so unfavourable for them to go public, something which they had decided to do and had been looking forward to. They had installed a much more sophisticated costing system and were working on further improvements in that area, and they had made some major investments in their factories.

The brothers attributed their success very largely to moving further up market, and also to the export markets. The hotelware division was operating extremely strongly – totally contrary to the trend – largely because they were selling to the European catering trade, but also because they had recently launched a new hotelware product which was selling well into the UK market. They have revolutionized their approach to marketing and design, and they are spending some

£250 000 a year on the development of their own designs. The difference is dramatic.

Churchill's profits have increased fourfold, their turnover has increased by about 50% and the product range has changed substantially. All of this has been accomplished at a time when the UK market conditions for the pottery industry as a whole have not been good. The prudent financing habits of the Roper brothers have certainly paid off: they did not enter the recession with any significant borrowings.

The brothers are absolutely clear that, to succeed in operating from a British base, they must produce more added value products in quality, design and price. The productivity appears to be static even though the margins are increasing, because the further they move up market, the more they find themselves putting in manual skills. I brought up the fact that Bernard wanted to mechanize the factory far more and radically change it, to realize his dream of a single continuous line from the biscuit kiln onwards. I felt that Bernard must be allowed to change things, and that his job is to change things as fast as he can. The more you change, the more you can change, because you set a pace which inevitably accelerates, and the task is to get there before the competition beat you to it.

Stephen was worried that Bernard was trying to change things too fast, and said that he would be surprised to see a revolution on the shop floor like the one Bernard was pushing for. But Bernard is fired up and keen on dramatic change which I feel is possible. The Churchill Tableware factory must move towards more automation, towards a twenty-four hour, seven-day-a-week operation.

Although there is no doubt that the brothers are determined to continue to implement change, and that they even seem to be accustomed to change, I don't believe that they're going to change as fast as I think they could, although I must say that I am thrilled by what they have done, and by what they are now doing.

Churchill gives me hope. They have achieved considerable growth in the middle of a recession, and perhaps their achievements will give other British businessmen and women the encouragement they so badly need in these depressed times.

Finally, I returned to the Peakes. By now I was more than a little intrigued because they'd told me that they had some news for me. Knowing the Peakes as I do, it could be anything. I didn't even try to guess.

I arrived and was greeted, almost immediately, by the news that the Peakes had bought Copella back: lock, stock and barrel! Taunton Cider were going public and had decided that soft drinks no longer fitted in with their strategy, so the Peakes, who could not bear to see Copella sold on, bought it back. They were in the throes of this deal when I saw them the week before, but they had not been at liberty to tell me about it then. The great thing about this family is that they take my advice – for approximately twenty minutes at a time!

However, buying Copella back was, in fact, a commercially attractive proposition for the Peakes. The family have gained three years development work on the Copella brand, substantial new investment in everything except the pressing area, and a valuable training course. Now that the family have reallocated the jobs between them Roger has taken over as managing director of operations and Stephen as managing director of sales and marketing. Susanna remains finance director. But against all this they have to market the product for themselves now and, as a business, they are still so undercapitalized.

I was quite worried about the state of the family's current borrowings, but the Peakes firmly believe that business is not just about money. They believe in, and love, their product, they want to build and grow things, and they want to give themselves opportunities to manage in creative and challenging ways.

The Taunton Cider Company will continue to distribute Copella products in the UK, except in East Anglia and in London, where Copella will distribute Taunton's products as well as their own.

I suggested that the Peake family badly needed a professional chairman who could look at their businesses as a whole, and who could help them to sort out their priorities. I also advised them that I thought the apple-packing business should become a co-operative.

The Peakes invited me to a charity function at the golf club, where many of their friends and supporters joined them. It was tremendous fun and I couldn't help thinking how far this dynamic group of people have moved in the last three years. I suspect that as long as there is a Peake alive they will be linked to the apple growing business in one way or another, and their determination to add value to their basic fruit farm is something which I can only admire.

Inevitably they will have to hold back some businesses if they are to develop others, and this will mean taking some very hard decisions. Decisions are particularly difficult in the Peake family, because of their devotion to the basic business which Devora and her husband set up so many years ago. I think Copella will always be the magnet that holds them all together, but this makes it even more important that it should be a magnet which pays, rather than one which becomes a problem for them. The apple juice market is still a very tough one, and more and more people are coming into it.

Nevertheless, Copella is different. Since my first *Troubleshooter* visit to Copella, my family and I have found that it is the only apple juice that we enjoy, and we tend to keep it in the house the whole time. It is a superior product, and you can almost taste in it the love, affection and devotion that the Peake family put into it. One thing is certain: even when a new chairman is installed to keep an eye on them, I cannot see myself losing touch with the family and their fortunes over the next few years. I just hope they prosper.

And so I come to the end of my *Troubleshooter* revisits, and it remains true that the businesses who have succeeded are those who have been the most willing to change, and I admire what those businesses have done very much. But the irony is that the demands of tomorrow will be even greater and there is never any let up for the professional manager. There is always another hill to climb, competitors are always hot on your heels and the ability to change must become a way of life.

EPILOGUE

Another *Troubleshooter* series is concluded and I have some time to reflect on the similarities and differences between the first efforts that the *Troubleshooter* team and I made back in 1989, and now. The world in which British companies are now operating could hardly be more different. In the 1980s business people believed the world was there for the taking and the only questions were how far and how fast. Now business people worry about survival, and above everything else they worry about money. They no longer believe – if they ever did – that as long as they are good at their jobs the money will inevitably come along.

All the businesses who took part in the second *Troubleshooter* series have had to cope with the effects of the recession, and all are seriously worried about money and the costs of money. However, as I stressed to the South Yorkshire Police, real control in any business is always expressed by money and not by numbers of people, and to make the most efficient use of the available money, that money must be controlled by individuals on the ground, individuals closest to the situation, individuals who know what is necessary for the business to run as efficiently as possible.

One of the products of my own experience and training is that I look at almost every facet of business against a sort of crude financial ready reckoner. The only common factor between stock, selling effort, production technology and management organization, for example, is cost, particularly ongoing costs, and the effect on return. In many cases the correlations are not clear or precise, but, as in most business decisions, an approximation is good enough, as long as it is on the right scale. This, the ability to visualize speed and direction of movement, and a sense of the time that it takes for a business situation to develop, comprise my tool kit.

Businessmen and women must also pay close attention to the art of management if they are to succeed, especially in the current financial climate. Over the past years there has been a steadily growing interest in management in the UK. There has also been a welcome realization that management is not the same as administration – although it encompasses administrative skills. Management is about deliberate change and constantly moving the business forwards, towards a better position. Interest in management is more and more widespread as the realization is forced upon us that no aspect of our society, be it health, education, finance, manufacturing, or the running of charities, will ever have enough money to do everything. The challenge for the UK, never more relevant than today, is to achieve more with less, through the clarity of our management. Pouring money into badly managed enterprises actually makes the management worse. In many areas of the UK there is plenty of evidence that more money is needed, but so is better management, and better management has to come first.

Better management is less management. In the UK, we have a mania for the overmanagement of minutiae and more and more control, when what is needed is more attention to the broader aspects and thrusts of our businesses, and more trust in those further down the lines to allow them control over how they deliver the goods.

And I still haven't met those mythical Brits who are allegedly skiving and uninvolved. Throughout the making of all the *Troubleshooter* programmes I never met one. Everyone at every level wherever I went wanted their business to succeed, even though they often had very different views about how to achieve success. I saw fear, frustration, perplexity, and many other reactions, but nowhere did I see lack of concern or lack of interest. The people in the companies in this second *Troubleshooter* series are concerned, despite the climate of depression, about how they should be growing, and they are thinking about the future rather than the past. They know that standing still is not an option and that unless they are moving forwards they are actually losing the competitive race.

The *Troubleshooter* series is a bit like a growing pyramid: only one company, Tri-ang, has fallen away, and even that is reborn through Sydney's unquenchable determination to run a successful toy company! It is impossible for me to make these *Troubleshooter* programmes without becoming involved and attached to the businesses, the enterprises and the people who have invited me in. I therefore find that I am concerned with an ever increasing family. I follow their fortunes avidly and I am thrilled when they ask me for my views or advice, and I love it when they ring me up to boast a little of their successes.

The more I see of these sorts of businesses the more I realize that, in the final analysis, it is the aspiration, drive and determination of the people at the top that is the winning factor in the success of their businesses. These qualities have to be matched by the involvement and commitment of all the others in the business if things are to work out, but the scale of success for which they aim must be set from the top.

We are too ready in the UK to bemoan our relative lack of economic success, and we still seem to regard business as a sort of optional extra or a sad inevitability, rather than the basis of our economic future. In some curious way, we seem to think that the economy and individual businesses are not related to each other. We do not prize or honour our business heroes and heroines, and despite the well publicized excesses of a few, the majority of the people I met are driven by a desire for achievement rather than financial greed. The financial rewards are a symbol of success rather than an end in themselves. Yet how lucky we are that we have so many people who do not want to settle for the soft option, who would not be satisfied with taking the money and putting their feet up. We have people in the public sector who have a mission to change and improve their service for the benefit of us all. And we have private businessmen and women whose success in turn enables every one of us to live a little bit better.

I have found this year's *Troubleshooting* journey around Britain surprisingly cheering and in sharp contradiction to the image so often portrayed in the press. I grieve for our business casualties and I have seen far too many at first hand to be complacent about them. Many firms have gone to the wall only partly as a result of their own actions. Yet, time and again, these people refuse to accept defeat, despite the horrendous blows they have suffered: they pick themselves up and throw themselves into the fray again. It is not necessarily a sign of shame for a business to go bust, and the people involved in the collapse of a business suffer enough without the additional punishment of the harsh judgments and criticisms of others who weren't brave enough to enter the fray in the first place.

Do we really recognize the quality of those who shun the quiet life in order to stretch themselves to try to achieve greater success against the best that the rest of the world can put up against them? It is very easy and tempting to settle back and be satisfied with fifth or sixth best. It is very easy to blame someone, or somebody, else: the government, the exchange rate, the Japanese. It takes a rare human quality to risk everything that you have achieved, simply in order to become better.

People who take risks, risk making mistakes. But mistakes so often contain the seeds of success. Most people learn more from their mistakes than they learn from their successes: the trick is to learn from both. Risk-takers know that they may fail, but they may also succeed, and the sorts of people we need in business in the UK are those who are willing to take risks: the very sorts of people who were willing to risk having their approaches to their businesses and the results of their mistakes analysed in front of the large audiences that the *Troubleshooter* series attracts.

It is the fact that I have met so many people of this calibre, people who are willing to stretch themselves and who want to achieve success, at every level in the organizations I visited in 1992, that has made this year a more cheerful experience for me than I had expected. I thank them and assure them, if assurance is needed, of my respect, my regard and my support. For all our sakes I hope they succeed.

INDEX

READ MORE IN PENGUIN

In every corner of the world, on every subject under the sun, Penguin represents quality and variety – the very best in publishing today.

For complete information about books available from Penguin – including Puffins, Penguin Classics and Arkana – and how to order them, write to us at the appropriate address below. Please note that for copyright reasons the selection of books varies from country to country.

In the United Kingdom: Please write to *Dept. EP, Penguin Books Ltd, Bath Road, Harmondsworth, West Drayton, Middlesex UB7 ODA*

In the United States: Please write to *Consumer Sales, Penguin USA, P.O. Box 999, Dept. 17109, Bergenfield, New Jersey 07621-0120*. VISA and MasterCard holders call 1-800-253-6476 to order Penguin titles

In Canada: Please write to *Penguin Books Canada Ltd, 10 Alcorn Avenue, Suite 300, Toronto, Ontario M4V 3B2*

In Australia: Please write to *Penguin Books Australia Ltd, P.O. Box 257, Ringwood, Victoria 3134*

In New Zealand: Please write to *Penguin Books (NZ) Ltd, Private Bag 102902, North Shore Mail Centre, Auckland 10*

In India: Please write to *Penguin Books India Pvt Ltd, 706 Eros Apartments, 56 Nehru Place, New Delhi 110 019*

In the Netherlands: Please write to *Penguin Books Netherlands bv, Postbus 3507, NL-1001 AH Amsterdam*

In Germany: Please write to *Penguin Books Deutschland GmbH, Metzlerstrasse 26, 60594 Frankfurt am Main*

In Spain: Please write to *Penguin Books S. A., Bravo Murillo 19, 1° B, 28015 Madrid*

In Italy: Please write to *Penguin Italia s.r.l., Via Felice Casati 20, I–20124 Milano*

In France: Please write to *Penguin France S. A., 17 rue Lejeune, F–31000 Toulouse*

In Japan: Please write to *Penguin Books Japan, Ishikiribashi Building, 2–5–4, Suido, Bunkyo-ku, Tokyo 112*

In South Africa: Please write to *Longman Penguin Southern Africa (Pty) Ltd, Private Bag X08, Bertsham 2013*

READ MORE IN PENGUIN

BUSINESS

Management and Motivation	Victor H. Vroom and Edward L. Deci
The Art of Japanese Management	Richard Tanner Pascale and Anthony Athos
The Penguin Management Handbook	Thomas Kempner (ed.)
Introducing Management	Peter Lawrence and Ken Elliott (ed.)
An Insight into Management Accounting	John Sizer
Understanding Company Financial Statements	R. H. Parker
Successful Interviewing	Jack Gratus
Offensive Marketing	Hugh Davidson
Corporate Recovery	Stuart Slatter
Corporate Strategy	Igor Ansof
The Manager's Casebook	Woods and Thomas
The New Penguin Guide to Personal Finance	Alison Mitchell
Management Mathematics	Peter Sprent
Accidental Empires	Robert Cringely

READ MORE IN PENGUIN

BUSINESS AND ECONOMICS

North and South David Smith

'This authoritative study ... gives a very effective account of the incredible centralization of decision-making in London, not just in government and administration, but in the press, communications and the management of every major company' – *New Statesman & Society*

I am Right – You are Wrong Edward de Bono

Edward de Bono expects his ideas to outrage conventional thinkers, yet time has been on his side, and the ideas that he first put forward twenty years ago are now accepted mainstream thinking. Here, in this brilliantly argued assault on outmoded thought patterns, he calls for nothing less than a New Renaissance.

Lloyds Bank Small Business Guide Sara Williams

This long-running guide to making a success of your small business deals with real issues in a practical way. 'As comprehensive an introduction to setting up a business as anyone could need' – *Daily Telegraph*

The *Economist* Economics Rupert Pennant-Rea and Clive Crook

Based on a series of 'briefs' published in the *Economist* , this is a clear and accessible guide to the key issues of today's economics for the general reader.

The Rise and Fall of Monetarism David Smith

Now that even Conservatives have consigned monetarism to the scrap heap of history, David Smith draws out the unhappy lessons of a fundamentally flawed economic experiment, driven by a doctrine that for years had been regarded as outmoded and irrelevant.

Understanding Organizations Charles B. Handy

Of practical as well as theoretical interest, this book shows how general concepts can help solve specific organizational problems.

READ MORE IN PENGUIN

BUSINESS AND ECONOMICS

The Affluent Society   John Kenneth Galbraith

Classical economics was born in a harsh world of mass poverty, and it has left us with a set of preoccupations hard to adapt to the realities of our own richer age. Our unfamiliar problems need a new approach, and the reception given to this famous book has shown the value of its fresh, lively ideas.

Understanding the British Economy
Peter Donaldson and John Farquhar

A comprehensive and well-signposted tour of the British economy today; a sound introduction to elements of economic theory; and a balanced account of recent policies are provided by this bestselling text.

A Question of Economics   Peter Donaldson

Twenty key issues – the City, trade unions, 'free market forces' and many others – are presented clearly and fully in this major book based on a television series.

The Economics of the Common Market   Dennis Swann

From the CAP to the EMS, this is an internationally recognized book on the Common Market – now substantially revised.

The Money Machine: How the City Works   Philip Coggan

How are the big deals made? Which are the institutions that really matter? What causes the pound to rise or interest rates to fall? This book provides clear and concise answers to these and many other money-related questions.

Parkinson's Law   C. Northcote Parkinson

'Work expands so as to fill the time available for its completion': that law underlies this 'extraordinarily funny and witty book' (Stephen Potter in the *Sunday Times*) which also makes some painfully serious points about those in business or the Civil Service.

READ MORE IN PENGUIN

POLITICS AND SOCIAL SCIENCES

Conservatism Ted Honderich

'It offers a powerful critique of the major beliefs of modern con-
servatism, and shows how much a rigorous philosopher can contribute to
understanding the fashionable but deeply ruinous absurdities of his times'
– *New Statesman & Society*

The Battle for Scotland Andrew Marr

A nation without a parliament of its own, Scotland has been wrestling with
its identity and status for a century. In this excellent and up-to-date account
of the distinctive history of Scottish politics, Andrew Marr uses party and
individual records, pamphlets, learned works, interviews and literature to
tell a colourful and often surprising account.

Bricks of Shame: Britain's Prisons Vivien Stern

'Her well-researched book presents a chillingly realistic picture of the
British sytstem and lucid argument for changes which could and should be
made before a degrading and explosive situation deteriorates still further'
– *Sunday Times*

Inside the Third World Paul Harrison

This comprehensive book brings home a wealth of facts and analysis on
the often tragic realities of life for the poor people and communities of
Asia, Africa and Latin America.

'Just like a Girl' Sue Sharpe
How Girls Learn to be Women

Sue Sharpe's unprecedented research and analysis of the attitudes and
hopes of teenage girls from four London schools has become a classic of
its kind. This new edition focuses on girls in the nineties – some of whom
could even be the daughters of the teenagers she interviewed in the
seventies – and represents their views and ideas on education, work,
marriage, gender roles, feminism and women's rights.

READ MORE IN PENGUIN

POLITICS AND SOCIAL SCIENCES

National Identity   Anthony D. Smith

In this stimulating new book, Anthony D. Smith asks why the first modern nation states developed in the West. He considers how ethnic origins, religion, language and shared symbols can provide a sense of nation and illuminates his argument with a wealth of detailed examples.

The Feminine Mystique   Betty Friedan

'A brilliantly researched, passionately argued book – a time-bomb flung into the Mom-and-Apple-Pie image . . . Out of the debris of that shattered ideal, the Women's Liberation Movement was born' – Ann Leslie

Faith and Credit   Susan George and Fabrizio Sabelli

In its fifty years of existence, the World Bank has influenced more lives in the Third World than any other institution yet remains largely unknown, even enigmatic. This richly illuminating and lively overview examines the policies of the Bank, its internal culture and the interests it serves.

Political Ideas   Edited by David Thomson

From Machiavelli to Marx – a stimulating and informative introduction to the last 500 years of European political thinkers and political thought.

Structural Anthropology   Volumes 1–2   Claude Lévi-Strauss

'That the complex ensemble of Lévi-Strauss's achievement . . . is one of the most original and intellectually exciting of the present age seems undeniable. No one seriously interested in language or literature, in sociology or psychology, can afford to ignore it' – George Steiner

Invitation to Sociology   Peter L. Berger

Sociology is defined as 'the science of the development and nature and laws of human society'. But what is its purpose? Without belittling its scientific procedures Professor Berger stresses the humanistic affinity of sociology with history and philosophy. It is a discipline which encourages a fuller awareness of the human world . . . with the purpose of bettering it.

READ MORE IN PENGUIN

A CHOICE OF NON-FICTION

The Time Out Film Guide Edited by Tom Milne

The definitive, up-to-the minute directory of over 9,500 films – world cinema from classics and silent epics to reissues and the latest releases – assessed by two decades of *Time Out* reviewers. 'In my opinion the best and most comprehensive' – Barry Norman

The Remarkable Expedition Olivia Manning

The events of an extraordinary attempt in 1887 to rescue Emin Pasha, Governor of Equatoria, are recounted here by the author of *The Balkan Trilogy* and *The Levant Trilogy* and vividly reveal unprecedented heights of magnificent folly in the perennial human search for glorious conquest.

Skulduggery Mark Shand

Mark Shand, his friend and business partner Harry Fane and world-famous but war-weary photographer Don McCullin wanted adventure. So, accompanied by a fat Batak guide, armed only with a first-aid kit and with T-shirts, beads and tobacco for trading, they plunged deep into the heart of Indonesian cannibal country ...

Lenin's Tomb David Remnick

'This account by David Remnick, Moscow correspondent for the *Washington Post* from 1988 to 1992, of the last days of the Soviet Empire is one of the most vivid to date' – *Observer*

Roots Schmoots Howard Jacobson

'This is no exercise in sentimental journeys. Jacobson writes with a rare wit and the book sparkles with his gritty humour ... he displays a deliciously caustic edge in his analysis of what is wrong, and right, with modern Jewry' – *Mail on Sunday*

READ MORE IN PENGUIN

A CHOICE OF NON-FICTION

Bernard Shaw Michael Holroyd
Volume 2 1898–1918 The Pursuit of Power

'A man whose art rested so much upon the exercise of intelligence could not have chosen a more intelligent biographer ... The pursuit of Bernard Shaw has grown, and turned into a pursuit of the whole twentieth century' – Peter Ackroyd in *The Times*

Shots from the Hip Charles Shaar Murray

His classic encapsulation of the moment when rock stars turned junkies as the sixties died; his dissection of rock 'n' roll violence as citizens assaulted the Sex Pistols; superstar encounters from the decline of Paul McCartney to Mick Jagger's request that the author should leave – Charles Shaar Murray's *Shots From the Hip* is also rock history in the making.

Managing on the Edge Richard Pascale

The co-author of the bestselling *The Art of Japanese Management* has once again turned conventional thinking upside down. Conflict and contention in organizations are not just unavoidable – they are positively to be welcomed. The successes and failures of large corporations can help us understand the need to maintain a creative tension between fitting companies together and splitting them apart.

Just Looking John Updike

'Mr Updike can be a very good art critic, and some of these essays are marvellous examples of critical explanation ... a deep understanding of the art emerges ... His reviews of some recent and widely attended shows ... quite surpass the modest disclaimer of the title' – *The New York Times Book Review*

Shelley: The Pursuit Richard Holmes

'Surely the best biography of Shelley ever written ... He makes Shelley's character entirely convincing by showing us the poet at every stage of his development acting upon, and reacting to, people and events' – Stephen Spender

READ MORE IN PENGUIN

A CHOICE OF NON-FICTION

Stones of Empire Jan Morris

There is no corner of India that does not contain some relic of the British presence, whether it is as grand as a palace or as modest as a pillar box. Jan Morris's study of the buildings of British India is as entertaining and enlightening on the nature of imperialism as it is on architecture.

Bitter Fame Anne Stevenson

'A sobering and salutary attempt to estimate what Plath was, what she achieved and what it cost her ... This is the only portrait which answers Ted Hughes's image of the poet as Ariel, not the ethereal bright pure roving sprite, but Ariel trapped in Prospero's pine and raging to be free' – *Sunday Telegraph*

Here We Go Harry Ritchie

From Fuengirola to Calahonda, *Here We Go* is an hilarious tour of the Costa del Sol ... with a difference! 'Simmering with self-mocking humour, it offers a glorious celebration of the traditions of the English tourist, reveals a Spain that Pedro Almodovar couldn't have conjured up in his worst nightmare, and character-assassinates every snob and pseud' – *Time Out*

Children First Penelope Leach

Challenging the simplistic nostalgia of the 'family values' lobby, Leach argues that society today leaves little time for children and no easy way for adults – especially women – to be both solvent, self-respecting citizens and caring parents.

Young Men and Fire Norman Maclean

On 5 August 1949, a crew of fifteen airborne firefighters, the Smokejumpers, stepped into the sky above a remote forest fire in the Montana wilderness. Less than an hour after their jump, all but three were dead or fatally burned. From their tragedy, Norman Maclean builds an unforgettable story of courage, hope and redemption.

READ MORE IN PENGUIN

A CHOICE OF NON-FICTION

My Secret Planet Denis Healey

'This is an anthology of the prose and poetry that has provided pleasure and inspiration to Denis Healey throughout his life ... pleasurable on account of the literature selected and also for the insight it provides of Denis Healey outside the world of politics ... a thoroughly good read' – *The Times*

The Sun King Nancy Mitford

Nancy Mitford's magnificent biography of Louis XIV is also an illuminating examination of France in the late seventeenth and early eighteenth centuries. It covers the intrigues of the court and the love affairs of the king, with extensive illustrations, many in full colour.

This Time Next Week Leslie Thomas

'Mr Thomas's book is all humanity, to which is added a Welshman's mastery of words ... Some of his episodes are hilarious, some unbearably touching, but everyone, staff and children, is looked upon with compassion' – *Observer*. 'Admirably written, with clarity, realism, poignancy and humour' – *Daily Telegraph*

Against the Stranger Janine di Giovanni

'In her powerfully written book Janine di Giovanni evokes the atmosphere of the Palestinian refugee camps in the Gaza Strip ... The effect of the Palestinians' sufferings on the next generation of children is powerfully documented' – *Sunday Express*

Native Stranger Eddy L. Harris

Native Stranger is a startling chronicle of the author's search for himself in Africa, the land of his ancestors. 'Since Richard Wright's *Black Power*, there has been a dearth of travel narratives on Africa by black Americans. *Native Stranger* picks up where Wright left off, and does so with both courage and honesty' – Caryl Phillips in the *Washington Post*

READ MORE IN PENGUIN

A CHOICE OF NON-FICTION

Ginsberg: A Biography Barry Miles

The definitive life of one of this century's most colourful poets. 'A life so dramatic, so dangerous, so committed to hard-volume truth, that his survival is a miracle, his kindness, wisdom and modesty a blessing' – *The Times*. 'Read it to the end' – Michael Horovitz

Coleridge: Early Visions Richard Holmes

'Dazzling ... Holmes has not merely reinterpreted Coleridge; he has re-created him, and his biography has the aura of fiction, the shimmer of an authentic portrait ... a biography like few I have ever read' –*Guardian*. 'Coleridge lives, and talks and loves ... in these pages as never before' – *Independent*

The Speeches of Winston Churchill David Cannadine (ed.)

The most eloquent statesman of his time, Winston Churchill used language as his most powerful weapon. These orations, spanning fifty years, show him gradually honing his rhetoric until, with spectacular effect, 'he mobilized the English language, and sent it into battle'.

Higher than Hope Fatima Meer

A dramatic, personal and intimate biography drawing on letters and reminiscences from Nelson Mandela himself and his close family, *Higher Than Hope* is an important tribute to one of the greatest living figures of our time. It is also a perceptive commentary on the situation in South Africa. No one concerned with politics or humanity can afford to miss it.

Among the Russians Colin Thubron

'The Thubron approach to travelling has an integrity that belongs to another age. And this author's way with words gives his books a value far transcending their topical interest; it is safe to predict that they will be read a century hence' – Dervla Murphy in the *Irish Times*